A Son's Reckoning with Personal
and Collective Trauma in America

DADDY

Tim Lewis, Psy.D.

Learn more at DrTimLewis.com

Published by rose + spiral, an imprint of Raab & Co. I roseandspiral.com

Book cover & layout by Andrew Bell

This book is for general information purposes only. It is not intended
to be a substitute for specific medical or mental health advice.
You should obtain relevant professional or specialist advice before
taking any action based on the information in this book. If you have
questions about a medical or mental health matter, or are experiencing
mental health issues, you should consult with a medical doctor or a
professional mental health provider. If you are currently experiencing a
mental health crisis, dial 911 or go to your nearest hospital emergency
room. Please consult the Resources section for more information about
treatment options and ideas about where to find help.

First Hardcover Edition

Printed in the USA

For wholesale inquires, email wholesale@roseandspiral.com

ISBN: 979-8-9860260-2-2

To my mother, Judy,
who helped me to discover the stars in the darkness.

Contents

Contents

Introduction

The story I'm about to share is a murder mystery. What makes it unusual is that unlike most true-crime sagas and television police procedurals, this tale does not involve unraveling the identity of a killer from among a ragtag mob of suspects. Our plotline doesn't involve a high-stakes game of cat and mouse between the perpetrator and investigator. I have little interest in the methods by which murderers ply their trade or in the gaudy spectacle of the desecrated bodies of the victims. You won't even have to read through to the final chapter to discover "who did it." In fact, I'll tell you right now: When I was twenty-eight years old, my father fatally shot my mother. He then turned the gun on himself and committed suicide.

The moments immediately following this atrocity changed my life forever. After several fragmented hours of police questioning, I finally made my way to the ICU where my mother's body lay tethered to life support. I'll never forget the grave, yet expectant looks on the faces of family and friends who gathered in the hospital's waiting room. I could see that they all hoped I could provide some sort of answer to the question on everyone's mind: "why?"

This book is my attempt to answer that question.

If my father had left a note, or if something out of the ordinary had happened in the weeks leading up to this tragedy, I would've had something of substance to share with my loved ones that day. But, like most bystanders caught off-guard by violence of this kind, I possessed little more than the basic facts: the sound of gunshots, the bleeding bodies, and the sense of being swiftly and helplessly enveloped by the tumult that ensued.

For incidents of lethal domestic violence, people often look to crimes of passion—some real or imagined betrayal that causes the perpetrator to snap. While that's all well and good for the climactic moments of *Law & Order: SVU*, my father's motives are not so clear-cut. In real life, they rarely are. Even relatively simple decisions can take on mind-boggling levels of complexity when we attempt to suss out our individual preferences, predispositions, and outside influences. When it comes to human psychology—both on an individual and collective level—clear and succinct answers often elude us. Instead, some paradox, some contradiction, and some level of elusiveness are always present.

When I set out to write this book, my goals were modest: I felt I had something unique to offer readers from my vantage point as a clinical psychologist and as a survivor of multiple traumas. While there are any number of books and reference materials out there offering valuable, detailed information on these subjects, I'd long wished for a single source that would breathe life into these dry, academic tomes with real-world illustrations that truly captured the essence of my own personal history. I naively thought it was possible to accomplish these goals without delving into the puzzle of my father's motivations, but it turns out it's all interrelated.

Throughout the writing process, I've repeatedly had the uncanny sense of being pulled along on an expedition that felt somehow predetermined. As I saw my words take shape on the pages, I began to perceive a newfound structure to my experiences. Even though I'd been in therapy for a number of years and have relayed many of these incidents to others at one time or another, I have found that writing this book has left me experiencing a confounding mix of anxiety and relief.

Rereading what I'd written, I often became distracted by the voices of colleagues in my head, cautioning me that my level of personal disclosure was "ill-advised." It's true: knowing too much about your therapist is an unnecessary distraction and a stepping stone to unhealthy boundary violations. Professional concerns aside, I began to seriously question the long-term implications of publicly sharing many of the most intimate and embarrassing details of my life. What's more, don't my parents deserve to be left in peace?

Understanding the Motives of a Man Who Didn't Know Himself
Though my father never spoke directly about his childhood, it now seems clear that he experienced physical abuse and emotional neglect as a boy. When he was a teen, his father died quite suddenly. A few years later, my father landed at Normandy on D-Day, somehow surviving over a year in combat that left 30% of his unit dead. It should come as no surprise that my research for this book led rather quickly to a confirmation of a diagnosis that I'd long entertained as a possible driving force behind my father's violent actions: decades of living with unacknowledged (and ipso facto, untreated) post-traumatic stress disorder—PTSD. I imagine for some of you that just coming out and naming it like that might feel a little anticlimactic. The routine nature of my conclusion is attributable to the fact that our culture has undergone a radical shift over the past forty years, moving from hostile denial to warm embrace of the astonishingly high incidence of psychological trauma. These days, the familiar acronym rolls knowingly off our tongues, acting as an all-purpose signifier of those oft-mentioned "demons" lurking beneath the surface of otherwise ordinary lives. After eleven months (and counting) of coronavirus quarantine, as I stream away yet another evening on Netflix, Hulu, and Amazon Prime, I find myself virtually drowning in a sea of brooding, self-destructive male anti-heroes suffering from PTSD and its constellation of associated symptoms. Flashback scenes provide a one-stop rationale for the ruthless violence and off-the-wall behavior of these popular protagonists.

At the outset of this project, I imagined that I would simply end up including a short discussion of PTSD to help round out my personal narrative with some helpful background information about the disorder.

9

However, after just a little digging, solid, scientific-seeming principles began to slip through my fingers like sand. Over the course of my research into our culture's familiar—if not cozy—relationship with trauma, I realized that we've come to mistake medical consensus about a diagnosis known as PTSD with a *certainty* that we know what we're talking about. Like a familiar cousin we see only at weddings and funerals, we might think we know trauma, but we don't.

The Muddy Waters of Dissociative States

One of the crucial features that separates a merely terrible day from a truly traumatic one is the experience of dissociation. In a state of dissociation, otherwise rational people vacate their normal flow of consciousness. They often do so in response to an event that threatens their physical integrity or they witness a grievous injury to another person.[1] Statistically, after such an event, about 15% of survivors go on to develop PTSD.[2]

The first true mystery I stumbled upon in writing this book involved the fascinating, but very messy tale of how science has sought to explain this mental revolving door on the boundaries of consciousness. Unpacking the biography of PTSD required not only an understanding of the history of psychology, but also an appreciation of the forces that have sought to define Western culture's idiosyncratic formulation of human suffering. Along the way, I came across pre-Freudian terms like *railway spine*, *soldier's heart*, *hysteria*, and other euphemistic diagnoses for what is now known as PTSD.[3] My exploration became not just an entertaining dive into medical history, but also a piecing together of the puzzle of my father's behavior, and more broadly an examination of the question of personal responsibility in the perpetration of domestic abuse and other forms of violence.

Today, traumatic childhoods are regularly trotted out to rationalize the appalling behavior of everyone from R. Kelly[4] to Tony Soprano. This dual identity—victim *and* perpetrator—resurfaces in the literature again and again,[5] posing a number of intriguing questions: How do we best deal with the actions of these victims-turned-perpetrators, both culturally and in our personal lives, if they continue to commit acts of emotional or physical harm? How do we explain the fact that only a small fraction of trauma survivors go on to perpetrate domestic abuse or societal violence? Where do people like my father go so wrong? And where, exactly, do others go so right?

Systemic Oppression and Trauma Feed Off One Another

In light of these compelling mysteries, I had to account for the fact that my father did not act alone. His accomplices included a culture that manufactured and reinforced a series of broad-based social controls that dictated the course of his life. While trauma can be the result of a terrible one-off event like a fire or car crash, it is most commonly the byproduct of systemic oppression[6]—which might include growing up in poverty or being sent off to a foreign country to murder enemy fighters and civilians. The domestic violence in my home is just one example of the larger forces of oppression that shape each of our lives.

For my mother, a financially dependent female born into the conservative ethos of mid-century middle America, the oppressions associated with gender bias help illustrate the context of her choices, the fact of her abuse, and the likelihood of her eventual murder. How then are we to contextualize the nature of oppression in my father, a White, Christian, heterosexual male? Acknowledging, much less deconstructing the forces of oppression acting upon this segment of the population is admittedly tricky given the Black Lives Matter movement and today's dialogue around race. While I wholeheartedly agree that there needs to be more space for the voices of those who have traditionally held the least amount of power in our culture, I believe a nuanced understanding of the hardships faced by men like my father can help provide insights into the challenges historically associated with a reduction in the incidence of domestic abuse and other forms of violence.

Americans, regardless of race or country of origin, can all trace the underpinnings of our sociopolitical framework back to Mother England. My search for a deeper understanding of why my father did it eventually led to an exploration of how Anglo-derived hierarchies of power set the stage for the gross inequalities that have historically divided our country. Expanding my reach across the centuries, from colonial Virginia up through the Civil War and on to our brush with Wild West outlaws, I discovered that the dual identity of victim and perpetrator courses through the veins of my ancestors.

These dynamics had far-reaching implications not only for the mystery of my father's motivations, but also for many of the most perplexing questions we face as a nation today. While we are experiencing a renewed collective desire to rein in the forces of racism, I have come to understand that simply identifying these malignancies as an issue of race doesn't begin to address the crux of the problem. To understand racism, we must look at systemic oppression across a broader spectrum of biases—gender bias, heterosexism, xenophobia, among others—which all generate psychological trauma en masse. In this context, how are we to understand the epidemic of oppression, both explicit and unexamined, splintering our country at this very moment?

My Family Is Far From Unique
Like many authors who set out to write about their family, I initially believed my story was unique. At first I was self-conscious about the fact that, given this consequential moment in our nation's history and the importance of keeping all eyes focused on the priorities of human rights movements like #MeToo and Black Lives Matter, the views of yet another middle-aged, cisgender gay guy are not exactly top priority. It wasn't until I delved into my family's casually racist past, and the racism that was instilled in me as a White child growing up in the Midwest, that I realized that the violence that festered in my father's heart is representative of a worldview which is spread forcefully and without consent through all aspects of our society, culture, and government. And while we could certainly call this worldview the patriarchy, or White heteronormative chauvinism, or even colonialism, for the purposes of this book, I'll be calling it Daddy. This term works not just on a personal and narrative level, but it also highlights the fact that this violent worldview is passed down like genes

from one generation to the next, and we're often so steeped in it that we don't even see our worldview as violent until it's too late.

How This Book Is Organized

This book is divided into three sections that follow the story of why my father did what he did and the fallout of his actions.

The first part, Where We Come From, refers to my cultural heritage, my parents, and my immediate family as well as early medical concepts in the genesis of psychological trauma and PTSD.

The next part, Where We Went, examines the nature and effects of violence and systemic oppression within the context of my own life as well as a crucial feature in the story of our nation.

Finally, part three, Where We're Going, explores the consequences of my parents' murder-suicide and how I went about rebuilding my life in the aftermath of their deaths.

Who Is This Book For?

Patients regularly ask me some version of the question, "Is it really possible to put my traumatic past behind me?" For our purposes, I have endeavored to write the book I wish I'd been given many years ago. If you are seeking simple answers to complex questions, answers that will magically help you sleep better at night, then this book is probably not for you—and I'm not sure what book would have those kinds of answers.

Throughout the writing process, I have come to recognize that my mother, father, and I each represent three very different but universal adaptations to traumatic experience which inform the overall structure of the book:

→ My father: A victim turned perpetrator who never became a whole person.

→ My mother: A passive victim who was never able to escape her tormentor.

→ Myself: A passive victim of multiple traumas who was finally able to make his life whole.

Most of us can probably point out people in our lives who fit neatly into these categories, whatever the nature of their trauma. My parents' lives spiraled violently out of control because they were unable to get a handle on the fallout associated with my father's traumatic history. In turn, my life spiraled out of control for some time as well. I was nearly brought down by the layers of trauma and oppression that encompassed my life—responding in ways that either didn't help or dangerously exacerbated my problems. Unskilled at managing interpersonal problems, coping with unresolved childhood emotional abuse and sexuality-based bullying, and fearing for my own life as I mourned the loss of many close friends during the AIDS epidemic, I struggled for years with the effects of PTSD, Borderline Personality Disorder, and substance abuse. Though by no means an exhaustive encyclopedia of treatment recommendations for these disorders, I devote the final chapters of this book to exploring the tools that helped me live more productively with my past—including meditation, therapy, radical acceptance, and education, which can help anyone, no matter their trauma, lay the groundwork for a purpose-driven and fulfilling life.

If you are ready to challenge yourself to learn more about the history of trauma and societal oppression, to look for the common threads in our stories, you will come away from this book with some good ideas about how to have a better relationship with your monsters.

If you find yourself living in a tug of war with thoughts and feelings that hold you prisoner, I will provide some clues about how to ease your grip on that rope. If you feel alone and rejected or react in ways that often push others away, you should understand that loneliness and isolation are endemic to trauma survivors,[7] and that it *is* fixable.

If you are in a relationship with a trauma survivor or a person who seems especially difficult and prickly, you may feel like you are constantly walking on eggshells. This person may have tested the limits of your patience to the point where you have distanced yourself or cut them out of your life entirely. It can be draining to be around many trauma survivors because they seem to refuse to play by the rules, constantly pushing your buttons. They might do things that are obviously self-sabotaging or go so far as to make frightening suicidal threats—or actual attempts. If you are someone trying to understand how to best support a trauma survivor, you should know that you, too, are not alone. Some of the most difficult periods I've experienced in my life were compounded by the ineffective, sometimes outright self-destructive ways I went about trying to escape my emotional pain. I've shared many of these personal anecdotes to help give supporters of trauma survivors greater insight into the traumatic mind as well as a useful framework for coping with these challenges.

Unchecked Collective Trauma Is Tearing Our Country Apart

I know this might sound wild, but many people don't necessarily recognize that they are a trauma survivor or a victim of oppression. I make this point, not as a kumbaya moment to allow us all to wallow in self-pity, but to reinforce the fact that the forces of oppression impact each of our lives. While these circumstances hold the potential to unite us in a common understanding, we now stand at a dangerous tipping point ripped from the pages of George Orwell's *1984*. White supremacists and large segments of the dominant majority have co-opted the language and rationales of social justice to make the case for their own experience of oppression. The final mystery I will address concerns how we might harness our greater understanding of the concept of trauma to inform our understanding of phenomena as varied as cults, dogmatic political parties, conspiracy theorists, and the violent storming of the U.S. Capitol in 2021.

During the final stages of this project, my initial embarrassment and professional concerns about my level of personal disclosure began to diminish. A sense of pride began to develop in the place where shame once thrived. I have reached the conclusion that the public benefit to be gained by my level of personal disclosure far outweighs any potential professional cost. However, I continue to question if I have done my best to tell the story of my father, a man who shared few details of his past, existing, by and large, on a superficial level, never expressing his deeper thoughts and sentiments. I worry that like most casualties of abuse and lethal violence, the reality of my mother's victimhood may completely overshadow her larger identity. I don't think my parents, given who they were at the time of their deaths, would feel anything but embarrassment at having details of their lives revealed in print. Nevertheless, I have come to see a decided nobility to their lives, and I am convinced that they would approve of my making something useful out of the tragedy of their deaths.

My memoir has proved to be far more ambitious than I initially planned. It turns out that my family—really all of our families—are microcosms that mirror the larger societal forces we encounter every day. In that sense, I hope this book will illustrate that we each play a pivotal role in addressing the forces that perpetuate human suffering.

Tim Lewis, Psy.D.
San Francisco, 2022

Part I

Where We Come From

Chapter 1

Kansas City

I don't remember the exact year when people started referring to the style of house I was raised in as "mid-century modern," but I do remember my now clearly misguided certainty that efforts to revive this outdated design wouldn't go far. Our version was a single-story, white brick house organized around a sun-lit, gabled roof entryway. Unlike most homes that provide clues about how their interiors are configured by the size and placement of their windows, our residence was comparatively closed off, offering few easily identifiable openings. I've often imagined these walls of windowless white brick might have provided an ideal screen for those passing by on the busy street outside to project their ideas about how our lives were conducted on the inside. While some may have envied our relative prosperity, others likely found our tastes more than a bit over the top. I wonder if those who shared similar lots ever suspected they were not alone in their unhappy predicaments?

My father, Oscar, designed and built our home in the mid-1960s with an intention to impress. Stepping through emerald-green double doors, an enormous sculpture of Guanyin—the Buddhist goddess of mercy and compassion[8]—would greet startled visitors from behind her heavy-lidded stare. From the entry hall, guests would be dispatched to a series of surprisingly modest-sized rooms whose interiors all but quaked from the shockwaves emitted by the explosion of chinoiserie that scattered baroque arrangements of curios like shrapnel from floor to ceiling. While I sometimes experienced a sense of pride in our home, more often than not I felt embarrassed by its unguarded enthusiasms and conspicuous incongruity in a neighborhood dominated by conservative fifties ranch houses and cracker box starter homes.

Pausing now on the shoulder of the road outside my childhood home to assess the dwelling that unified the first half of my life, my eye detects only subtractions from the far more embellished version that now exists only in my mind. The huge pair of concrete fu dogs, well-tended shrubbery, and ornamental trees that once accessorized the house and expressed a sense of our family's individuality are now absent. The inch-thick, wood shake shingles that provided a warm counterbalance to the brick below have long since been replaced by an unsightly asphalt version that hugs the roofline much too tightly. I notice the original concrete circle driveway is cracked and water from a recent rainstorm has collected in the pockets of its many depressions. A trio of pin oaks, already mature when my parents had them transplanted here, are many stories taller than I remember. The oaks tower over the semi-circle of the front lawn that is strewn with tire tracks around its edges.

The house and I have now both surpassed the half-century mark, and neither of us turns heads like we once did. An unmistakable aspect of timeworn weariness has set in and blurred the crisp balance of qualities that once made the two of us uniquely pleasing. While a new owner might one day restore my childhood home to its former luster, no industrious hipster will ever again regard my sagging flesh from across the room and tenderly embrace the untapped potential in my aging frame. Yet a lovely house and fit body have no enduring impact beyond their ability to please the eye and convey information about the status, taste, and DNA of their inhabitants. The pleasures derived from these containers end at the surface and are only truly compelling when you consider the stories of those who dwell within.

My Family's Cultural Legacy

To fully appreciate these stories, it's crucial to understand not just the people that inhabited this mid-century curiosity, but also the lives of those who came before us. The cultural customs of our English forebears—colonialism, capitalism, and the ordering of people into artificial hierarchies of value—in many ways held greater sway over the fates of my ancestors than any of their individual choices. Economic opportunities, education, social relationships—right down to how and where you spent your days—were largely determined by outside influences. Perhaps it's a bit of a stretch to say that location is destiny, but it wouldn't be an overstatement to say that the through lines of ancestral heritage and American culture that converged on the site of my childhood home would set the stage for much of what would come to follow in my lifetime.

To begin, the home sits directly on the path of the old Santa Fe Trail. While growing up it was still possible to catch sight of the occasional oxen-drawn covered wagon passing by, its passengers now on a jaunt to the annual SantaCaliGon Festival in Independence, Missouri—the old eastern starting point of the three "great trail" routes to the far West. This homespun celebration of fried food and carnival rides commemorates the nineteenth-century pioneers who once undertook the six-month, transcontinental odyssey to the Pacific coast and the boomtown that was created in their wake.[9]

Two hundred years before these wagon trains embarked on the type of journey that has become a touchstone of our national identity, my own, less celebrated ancestors had set out on similar treks. The population of England more than doubled during the seventeenth century, and the island of Great Britain—like a great dam holding back a sea of peasants—began to spring leaks, propelling a stream of opportunists, religious zealots, and misfits across the Atlantic fueled by desperation and hope.[10] Tracing the faint outlines of these distant family branches, it is still possible to witness the awakenings of a small handful of my English and Scottish ancestors as they abandon their familial enclaves to undertake the perilous four-month voyage across the Atlantic.

At the time of first European contact, members of the Algonquin tribe had been long settled in the coastal plains bordering the jagged inlets of lower Chesapeake Bay.[11] Unlike the ascetic, self-flagellating

Puritan separatists whose faith inspired the establishment of Plymouth Plantation 600 miles to the north,[12] the first English settlers to what would become known as the Tidewater Region were principally motivated by financial considerations, establishing the settlement of Jamestown in 1607 as employees of the Virginia Company, a joint stock corporation. England was a struggling nation, its prosperous global empire still many years in the future. Accordingly, King James I and his ministers were unwilling to gamble scarce resources on the development of lands that would have to them seemed as remote as the moon. Instead, wealthy businessmen were able to invest in individual shares of the Virginia Company, offsetting the risk of this uncertain enterprise.[13]

Struggling to find a means of turning a profit for their shareholders, the ranks of these first settlers were regularly decimated by malnutrition, harsh winters, and deadly bouts of disease. After casting about for nearly a decade, the employees of the Virginia Company finally stumbled on a winning formula in the production of tobacco. The cultivation of this crop required more land than the Algonquin were willing to relinquish peacefully. In 1622, the Algonquins' leader, Opechancanough—the elderly uncle of Pocahontas[14]—oversaw the massacre of nearly a quarter of the Virginia Company's settlers in retaliation for their persistent incursions onto tribal lands. Because of this succession of calamities, the Virginia Company's charter was revoked in 1624, and the crown stepped in to take control over the colony's fate.[15] The tobacco industry would continue to take an increasingly prominent role in the colonial economy, spurring intermittent wars between the English and the indigenous peoples of Virginia well into the 1650s.[16] Even here we can see how these lands— and therefore this country—were established not in the grandiose language of the Declaration of Independence but in the throes of financial anxiety and White supremacy. In that sense, not all that much has changed in the subsequent 300 years—as is wont to happen when unresolved trauma and anxiety are left untreated for generations.

Follow the Money

Land was not the only commodity necessary to ensure the continued profitability of the tobacco industry—a plentiful source of labor to cultivate and harvest these crops was also essential. At the time of my ancestors' first arrival in the Tidewater Region, 75% of all immigrants to Virginia were indentured servants from England who had inked covenants, typically seven years in length, for the privilege of relocating to the New World.[17] As harsh as these conditions may have been, life in physical or economic bondage and absent meaningful individual rights and liberties was, for the average person throughout history, an unremarkable situation.

Throughout the Middle Ages, feudalism had been the prevailing system of social order in Europe. Feudalism differed from outright slavery in one essential aspect—a serf was bound to a piece of land, not to another person. They were not considered personal property. Instead, they occupied the same legal category as barns, houses, and fences. Upon transfer of ownership, these "furnishings" remained with the land. A serf could not be sold individually and therefore could keep their family intact.[18]

Serfs were afforded some modicum of humanity, whereas Black families were carelessly ripped apart as part of doing business. One can even here begin to see and feel how a collective trauma such as this—by both the aggressors and the victims—could ripple through generations in sad and painful ways.

During the late Middle Ages, many English serfs, emboldened by the labor shortages and social disorganization brought on by successive waves of deadly bubonic plague, began to move freely around the countryside in search of improved working conditions and higher wages. The Statute of Labourers, passed in 1351, was a measure meant to curb these liberties, effectively assuring the forced servitude of serfs with its decree that any serf under sixty years of age who did not practice a craft must serve *anyone* requiring their labor.[19]

In the sixteenth century, a similar set of circumstances arose during the disarray that immediately followed the final great outbreak of bubonic plague. In 1563, hastened by the vast tracts of land lying fallow due to the untimely deaths of 35% of her subjects, Queen Elizabeth I set about reorganizing and expanding her government. The Statute of Artificers was an effort to address the cataclysmic state of English agriculture and functioned as a convenient cover for the English aristocracy to seize power from guilds that had, for centuries, regulated the labor and training of skilled craftsmen. For the first time, the statute categorized farmworkers as *artificers*, enabling the government to place wage controls and training under the aegis of the ownership class, making the state's authority over the labor market absolute.[20] In 1574, Elizabeth formally "freed" the last of the serfs. In a nod to a collective trauma that is only now barely beginning to heal via the mostly Black-led movement to prioritize rest over work,[21] the Statute specifically stated that one of its goals was to "banish idleness."[22]

Of course, those in positions of wealth and power would continue to impose forced servitude on the populace by ordering human beings into hierarchies of value based on circumstances of birth, racial background, gender, and religion, with these entirely fictional orderings of humanity continuing to flourish in the New World. (In case you skipped the introduction, it's important to understand that for the purposes of this book "Daddy" not only refers to my father, but also the societal force behind this ordering of humanity. The significance of the connection between Daddy and trauma will become clearer as you learn more about my family and the genesis of psychological trauma and PTSD.) While colonial authorities would eventually enact laws to regulate and protect indentured servants, by the beginning of the eighteenth century this entire matter was becoming increasingly irrelevant because the slave trade was flooding the market with even cheaper sources of human labor. In 1705, Virginia's decree, An Act Concerning Servants and Slaves, set strict limits on the length of time a person could be kept in indentured servitude and enshrined into law the institution of slavery for Black people in the colony of Virginia.[23]

A Beachhead in the Wilderness

My ancestors first settled in the Tidewater Region of Virginia starting in the latter half of the seventeenth century, with a few aberrant Dutch and German limbs present for the birth of New Amsterdam and Pennsylvania. Then, like some bacterial colony, these clusters multiplied exponentially over the course of two or three generations, overcrowding their petri dish settlements. This overcrowding served to spawn mutant strains of offspring who then severed their ties to the host culture, only to establish themselves in new, faraway locales.

Key to the overall success of this process was the availability of cheap—if not free—land. In a sort of generational hopscotch ever westward, I can trace extended family packs branching out to establish lives in isolated outposts, without any reasonable expectation of setting eyes on their larger network of kin ever again. Intimately involved in the genocide and brutal displacement of indigenous peoples, these ever-expanding settler hordes gobbled up acreage in a ravenous push, first to the western reaches of the coastal British colonies, and later, into the heartland of the continent.

My mother's ancestors were among the early settlers to an area surrounding Fort Osage, a small river landing at the western edge of the Missouri Territory. Founded in 1808 by William Clark—of Lewis and Clark fame—the fort functioned as a statement to the French and Spanish that Americans were serious about maintaining a permanent settlement in the lands recently acquired in the Louisiana Purchase. Clearing land and constructing homesteads in an area dominated by lightly forested, green rolling hills, these first settlers to Western Missouri tended their crops at the edge of a great continental precipice. Before them, a sea of prairie grass extended into the monumental expanse, unbroken, until finally coming to lap at the base of the Rockies, 600 miles to the west.[24]

With the removal of the Osage tribe and other indigenous peoples from the region, Fort Osage ceased operations during the late 1820s[25] and was replaced with a new city named Independence, which featured a superior river landing a few miles to the west. The town's economy flourished via the commercial opportunities afforded by the recently established Santa Fe Trail, near where my childhood home would be built 130 years later.[26]

The boomtown glory of 1840s Independence was first generated by servicing the army's needs as it waged its war against Mexico, and later, by supporting the lucrative trade routes that opened throughout the southwest when the territories of Santa Fe de Nuevo Mexico and Alta California were ceded to the United States.[27] Outfitting the celebrated pioneer families en route to Oregon and California only sweetened the geographical deal, but by the 1850s, an even more reliable river landing was established to cut miles of difficult terrain off the trip west. This new city, then known as the City of Kansas, would leave Independence forever overshadowed by its up-and-coming neighbor.

Piecing Together a Family Lost to Time

My father's ancestors were relatively late arrivals to Missouri. He seldom spoke of his early life or extended family members, so what I've put together myself feels more like one of those ancient, Aramaic scrolls that have been recovered from a dusty, cliffside cave.

Sifting through marriage records, census data, deeds, and other archives, I have done my best to understand the lives of my father's grandparents, all with deep farming roots in the state of Virginia. I try to imagine what life was like for my great-grandparents as I rifle through the hard facts of lives that mirror one another in the uncanniest of ways. As children, three of my great-grandparents lose their mothers to an early death, only to have their fathers remarry and sire yet more children. In the decade following the Civil War, these three, now young adults, all vacate the exhausted, blood-soaked soil of Virginia to reconfigure their lives, along with their parents and siblings, on the cheap, rich, untilled land of Missouri.

As adults, both of my paternal great-grandfathers worked as laborers. One toiled on the hundred-acre farm he purchased and the other made a living in the concrete trade. For the last half of their lives, the two lived not far from one another in Independence. They worked into their seventies—the farmer transforming into a public-school custodian and the concrete tradesman into a "picture show" manager. Between my two great-grandmothers, they bore and raised a total of fifteen children.

My grandparents, Ethel and Oscar Frederick, Sr.—known throughout his life as O.F.—left no enduring impression on the world, and the existing documentation of their lives attests to this fact. Ethel grew up on her parents' farm in Blue Springs, Missouri, and after finishing high school, she relocated, along with her family to Independence, ten miles to the west. She later worked as a clerk at a dry goods store until the age of twenty-six. That same year, she married my grandfather, a twenty-one-year-old primary school dropout. Four years into their marriage, the census taker finds my grandparents living in a rented house, my father is a toddler, and O.F. is working as a streetcar conductor on the thriving network of inner-city rails that once crisscrossed the Kansas City region.

My Father—The Little Rascal

The scant firsthand accounts of childhood my father shared with us have left me with the image of an only child who was a self-possessed, mischievous hell-raiser. I picture some amalgam of whimsical images from the *Little Rascals* series that ran, not uncoincidentally, concurrent to his own boyhood during the 1920s. I can picture my father as a scrappy sprite setting off firecrackers in rain gutters and knocking over mailboxes. Many years later, the two dozen or so snapshots which survive from that time were assembled by my mother into one of those large collage picture frames. The images follow my father from infancy up through his late teens, revealing details in the life of a cute, smiling boy who appears at ease—if not joyful—in his family trio. The manner of dress and style of the rooms he once inhabited look more like something out of a Walker Evans photo essay rather than the life of someone as near to me as my own father—yet I've noticed that the two of us could have easily passed as brothers when we were young men.

Characterized as a troublemaker, my father might today be diagnosed with Attention Deficit/Hyperactivity Disorder (ADHD) or even Conduct Disorder, a witch's brew of maladies common to troubled children—mostly boys—who are forever breaking the rules and acting out in a physically aggressive manner.[28] We've all encountered at least one of these "conduct-challenged" kids when we were growing up. Mine was a boy named Randy. Throughout elementary school, we all dreaded being assigned to Randy's classroom. He was a small, wiry kid who would endlessly threaten and taunt the other kids. Everyone, including the toughest jocks, would avoid Randy because he hit hard and without warning. The kid practically lived in a chair outside the principal's office. I can still picture Randy's red face and convulsed body as he stood alone and in torment on the playground. Even then, I intuitively understood—I think we all did—that Randy was being abused at home.

Death and Taxes

My grandparents experienced a turn of good fortune during the economic boom of the 1920s. O.F. was employed at a bank and the family purchased a new, 900-square-foot bungalow in Sugar Creek, a town just north of Independence. At the time, the small settlement of Sugar Creek was experiencing its own economic boom thanks to a nearby Standard Oil refinery. The town was also home to Fairmount Park, the largest outdoor amusement park in the area. My father grew up only a few blocks from the gleeful hubbub of the park, which featured a large lake for boating, thrill rides, and an open-air amphitheater where Red Skelton—a superstar of the early age of television—got his start emceeing the dance marathons that were the rage of the day. Sadly, by 1930, one year after the stock market crash, both my grandparents list their occupations on that year's census as "none," and Fairmount Park went bankrupt, closing its doors forever.

Just two years later, O.F. died at the age of thirty-seven. My father was fifteen years old at the time. While I have a dim recollection of hearing that the cause of his death was sudden and heart-related, my father never shared the particulars of O.F.'s death, let alone the emotional impact this loss must have made on his life. Sometimes, after he had put back a few drinks at a dinner out on the town, we would tour around the decaying remnants of jazz age Kansas City. With the diesel engine of his orange Mercedes coupe clattering away, I distinctly remember the strange mix of wistfulness and admiration that would fill my father's voice as some random, distant memory of O.F. was unearthed from the far recesses of his brain.

For adolescents, the sudden death of a parent is a highly stressful and often traumatic life event, in part because the illusion of invincibility, common to most teens, is abruptly shattered. Bouts of grief persist for at least a year, even under the best of circumstances. Those without good emotional support or who are already struggling can be thrown into a severe and extended crisis.[29]

In the aftermath of his father's death, Oscar went for an extended visit, along with one of his grandfathers, to Tucson, Arizona. Apparently, Oscar's unruly behavior had become more than Ethel could handle on her own. The only reason I know about this episode in his life—and the glancing suggestion that he had difficulty adjusting to the reality of his father's death—is because the information was shared with me in the context of an anecdote characteristic of my father. A mischievous little smile formed on his lips as he described the memory of having once spotted 1920s film actress and sex symbol Clara Bow riding a horse "bare chested" at her Tucson ranch.

The bungalow my grandparents owned in 1930 never again appears on any of the records associated with the family. O.F.'s death came at the height of the Depression in 1932, and it's plausible that Ethel lost their small house at a time when the national rate of bank foreclosures was running at a clip of 1,000 per day.[30]

After returning to Sugar Creek, it's highly doubtful that my father ever finished high school. As a teenager, he held a string of odd jobs, including one calamitous stint butchering chickens. In two separate incidents involving a misdirected hatchet, Oscar managed to slice open his left eyeball and sever the entire section above the knuckle of his ring finger. Miraculously, the damage to his eye did not take his sight; however, my father would continue to carry the evidence of these injuries throughout his life in the form of a mottling of his ice-blue iris, and one odd, stump-like digit.

Five years after O.F. died, Oscar married his first wife, Josephine, the eighteen-year-old daughter of a taxi driver. A year later, his mother, Ethel, died suddenly of a cerebral hemorrhage. Of my grandmother, my father shared nothing—no anecdotes and no tender memory to shine even a pinprick of illumination in her vicinity. Two years later, a 1940 draft registration record unequivocally cements the end of my father's youth. He was now a twenty-three-year-old roofer anxiously watching the rising tide of global fascism during World War II.

Upward Mobility

If you're of a certain age, you will probably remember the NBC television program *Mutual of Omaha's Wild Kingdom*. Throughout my childhood, strangers would often excitedly approach Oscar, confusing him for the show's host, Marlin Perkins. As I first came to know my father, he had a trim, but not muscular body—also of mid-century design—with a full head of hair that had "turned white almost overnight!" in his late thirties. I never once saw him without a matching pyramid-shaped mustache on his upper lip. The plaid dress shirts he favored were worn with the top two buttons undone, exposing a shock of hair at his sternum that belied his otherwise hairless torso. Oscar favored Seiko watches and wore a platinum signet ring set at the center with an enormous diamond. He spoke with a southern twang, always surprising to visitors from outside Kansas City. He elongated vowels and swallowed the last syllables of words—he pronounced our hometown "Can City" and "generally" sounded more like "journly."

I've no doubt that the mysteries and silences I associate with my father's past were intentional. Charles Darwin said that "under a keen sense of shame, there is a strong desire for concealment."[31] Keeping secrets about his past allowed Oscar to maintain control over the narrative—and over his family. The privileged, upper-middle-class life I enjoyed as a child looked nothing like the financially precarious boyhood Oscar wanted to forget. I imagine that he must have assumed we'd judge him—as others surely had done—as a powerless, easily disregarded "problem boy."

Although it would only become apparent to me many years later, Oscar actually did make one *statement* about his relationship with his parents—but this was a statement via action, not words. In 1973, my father had my grandparents' remains dug up and reinterred in a new location. After careful research, Ethel and O.F. were whisked from the back forty of a weed-choked necropolis featuring jagged tombstones rising out of the ground in a symphony of Victorian shapes and sizes, to settle permanently behind the elegant iron gates of one Mount Moriah Cemetery. My grandparents' bodies were placed in a private area delineated by a box hedge, the plots overlooking a small lake with a fountain spurting water a dozen feet into the air. Geese were in abundance and the air under the well-groomed elms felt cool even in the oppressive heat of our annual Memorial Day visits. There were acres upon acres of lush green grass that looked deceptively unbroken from a distance, but upon closer inspection revealed neat rows of flat, rectangular bronze plaques identifying the dead below.

No more offerings of roses clipped from our backyard, stuffed into empty coffee cans wrapped in aluminum foil. Here, there were coordinating brass flower urns that could be inserted back into the headstones when not in use. The overall effect of my ill-fated grandparents' move was like going from one of Poe's tales of the macabre to gin and tonics at the nearby Blue Hills Country Club. The same could be said for my father's story up to that point, and this shapeshifting of lives, even in death, is not unfamiliar to many of us rootless and ever-self-improving Americans. But is this anecdote an illustration of Oscar's aspirational lifestyle or evidence of an unbroken chain of love and devotion to his parents?

He also went on to purchase several of the adjacent plots at Mount Moriah, one of which he is now buried in. Like George and Weezy Jefferson, it's true, we were "Movin' on Up" during the seventies, but this plan was hatched as Oscar was closing in on sixty, and it seems likely that he just wanted a nice spot for his wife and a few of his children to circle the wagons for eternity. When my grandparents were moved, no service was held, and no words were said to welcome my grandparents to their "dee-luxe apartment in the sky." On balance, the whole affair was anticlimactic, ambiguous, and totally in character for my father.

No Direction Home: The Loneliness of Adult Orphans

We identify children who have lost both parents as orphans, but why doesn't that same term apply to adult children? I have become accustomed to the fog of aimlessness that tends to loom about me without my parents' compass points to fix my true north. The longing for their simple nods of recognition persists in the shadowy corners of my days, requiring my constant care to not feel lost in a world all too ready to look past "quiet" men like myself. Their recognition would be meaningful in direct proportion to the scope of their understanding of me, their only son, that developed over the many years as each stood key witness to my life's early arc.

As I have watched my own daughter, Gemma, now twelve, grow older, I've come to discern a new flavor to my moments of sorrow for my mother's and father's permanent absence from my life. Like my father, I have no parents to revel in the antics, problems, and achievements of my own child. Such a condition robs your life—and that of your child—of its full potential for meaning. And when both of your parents are only children, as were mine, this void is compounded, leaving no aunts, uncles, or cousins to help fill the seats at tables that can feel much too big and silent for holiday and birthday celebrations.

Though the physical form of a child eventually vanishes into the stooped figure of an old codger, the manifestation of our childhood selves—and their most profound wishes—never completely abandons us. Even if a parent was abusive or hurtful, a part of our consciousness, sometimes buried under six feet of anger and pain, still longs for their knowing looks and expressions of approval. Through my own experience, I've come to understand my father's longing for parents who were no longer living and share in his sense of loss for what might have been. My ear has become delicately attuned to the needs he was expressing in his attempts to bring the members of his family together in death at Mount Moriah Cemetery, as fate never afforded him that opportunity in life. If you're not careful, you can end up striving, like he did, without end, for material rewards and the admiration of others, alone, in the silence of your parents' graves.

What Does It All Mean?

In the book of Genesis, God commands Abraham to sacrifice his only son, Isaac, on Mount Moriah, today known as the Temple Mount in Jerusalem.[32] While there are subtly different interpretations of this parable, the three faiths that now collide on this site all agree on the overriding message of Abraham's plight: man has an obligation to maintain a faith in God, regardless of the collateral damage. While my father never spoke directly to me of God or faith, he did serve for many years on the board of the United Methodist Church just down the street from our house. My family attended services in the A-frame sanctuary, mostly on Christmas and Easter holidays, when folding chairs were wedged around the periphery of the pews to accommodate the swelling numbers of inconsistent parishioners like ourselves. Though I don't believe my father ever took his faith too seriously, I do believe the act of moving his parents' bodies to Mount Moriah suggests something of a wish for a heaven—a place where his entire family would, at long last, be united.

The unequivocal finality of death cannot be comprehended in the weeks and months following a loved one's passing—it takes years to fully absorb the reality that they are gone forever. Decades now separate me from my last moments with my parents and I am a very different person than I was when I last saw them. The dead, of course, don't change, but our relationships with them can evolve as we move forward in life. Viewed in a certain light, this book might be regarded as my own attempt to reinter both of my parents in a more dignified setting. However, instead of fancy new burial plots, I will endeavor to remove my mother and father from the frame of victim and perpetrator, where they have remained frozen for the last quarter of a century. In so doing, I hope to see them once again as fully realized people; people who, like each of us, can only respond within the self-limiting framework of their particular culture and era.

Social customs—like the ordering of human beings into artificial hierarchies of value—shaped how my parents viewed themselves and ultimately defined the roles they would take in life. While serfs were freed from their land and indentured servants were freed from their contracts, Black people would continue to live in enslavement. These social customs served to diminish the full potential of their lives through a process we now identify as systemic oppression. My father's experience of oppression translated into several poverties—emotional, financial, educational—to name but a few. Privileged by their race and gender, inequities such as these nonetheless compel many men to enact oppressive actions against those on the lower rungs of the social ladder—women, children, racial minorities—via the perpetuation of aggression, violence, and the withholding of individual liberties. When we are on the receiving end of these oppressions, the result is what we have come to label "psychological trauma."[33]

While the idea of psychological trauma now seems commonplace, the historical development of this modern phenomenon—post-traumatic stress disorder (PTSD)—is fundamental to understanding the crucible of violence and oppression in our country. For those who have experienced violent oppression, understanding the antecedents of these scientific and cultural currents is essential to help orient ourselves in a life turned topsy-turvy. With this understanding, we can find a path forward through the emotional suffering we experience in ourselves and all around us.

Chapter 2

Soldier's Heart

As a boy, I was a passionate devotee of the now defunct genre of film known as disaster movies. They still make movies set against sexy backdrops like the preternaturally tranquil orb of planet Earth where actors like Sandra Bullock fight to "beat the odds" while battling to overcome their "personal demons." Yet the slick veneer of CGI and enhanced quality of script writing have served to stifle many of the campy qualities that once made these films so fun in the first place. The golden age of this group of films lasted for just nine short years and was bookended by the aviation potboilers *Airport,* released in 1970, and *The Concorde: Airport '79.*

Laughing along as Shelley Winters clumsily ascends the artificial Christmas tree from the ruins of the ballroom of the capsized S.S. Poseidon, or watching nervously as the wealthy passengers aboard Jimmy Stewart's luxurious 747 plot their escape from beneath the surface of the ocean, were highlights of my moviegoing childhood that provided a window onto thrilling and glamorous worlds beyond my reach. Each of these films would begin with silly, overly dramatic conflicts and scenes of forbidden love between star-crossed A-list actors. Once a few of these flimsy backstories were established, there would be a grand party used as a pretext to get all the characters together in the same spot while decked out in the outrageous fashions of the day. Then, predictably, an inferno, tidal wave, or earthquake would flip the script, sending everyone scrambling to find a way to survive.

Children never died in these movies, only the valiant or vainglorious —and scads of nameless extras. There would be the tragic but inevitable loss of supporting cast members along the way, but even the lead characters' survival was thrown into question as the story drew closer and closer to the final "Morning After." These movies were like an amusement park ride packed with thrills that would set my stomach churning with anxious fear and delight, but in the end, I would be deposited right back where I started, unharmed. I now see that my affinity with this film genre can largely be attributed to the fact that I remained essentially outside the action, godlike, watching others sweat it out for a change.

Throughout my childhood, I would regularly reenact scenes from these films in my backyard, pretending to be one of the tragically heroic figures depicted on screen. Just like Carol Lynley's character, Nonnie, in *The Poseidon Adventure*, I yearned for an audience to identify with my miseries and to root for me to make it through—even when all hope had been abandoned. Of course, I looked nothing like this vapid damsel in hot pants and knee-high boots (even at the age of seven, my identifications were already trending toward a stereotypically gay aesthetic. While I knew I was different, both my family and I still thought "gay" meant being happy). In the disaster movie of my childhood, I never thought the barrage of unhinged, angry outbursts regularly unleashed by my father posed the type of problem others might be able to solve in the first place. In fact, there was an unmistakable haze of impotent shame that would settle over my family whenever Oscar exposed one of his tirades in public. Growing up in this type of environment, I intuitively related to people whose lives were turned upside down at a moment's notice.

Seeing my father keyed up and strangely enlivened after witnessing one of these lurid extravaganzas, I realize now that I have producer Irwin Allen—and other masters of the disaster genre—to thank for my father's praising of manly sacrifice, and the heartfelt, but seemingly paranoid advice that would be imparted to me as we inched our way toward the theater exit.

"You can't lose your head when you're in a spot like that. Understand? That's the best way to get yourself killed." However, instead of meditating on the appalling contingencies of war—as he had, of course, intended—I would be left imagining something like, "How cool would it be to travel around the world on the *Hindenburg*?!"

To be fair, it was the 1970s. My father had just witnessed three consecutive presidential administrations unnecessarily escalate a war in Vietnam that could not be won, asking for tens of thousands of American young men and women[34] (and over three million Vietnamese)[35] to be sacrificed at the altar to their hubris. He wasn't the only one freaked out by the prospect of his son being sent to fight another pointless war. Throughout my childhood, my mother, Judy, regularly made oddly vague references about sending me to Canada "just in case" and softly sobbed to herself as she drove me to the post office to register with the Selective Service when I turned 18. At the time, the Vietnam War had been over for nearly a decade.

During the summer of 1980, while I was on vacation with my older half-sister, Gail, and her family in Ocean City, Maryland, we went to see the disaster film spoof *Airplane!* This satirical take on the airliner-in-peril storyline serves up conventions of the disaster genre with self-mocking references to the original films—played this time not for drama, but for laughs. During this particular screening, my sister's hysterical laughter was to such an extreme that the ushers were pointing and whispering in amazement. If there was ever more evidence necessary to prove a genre ripe for mocking by a generation raised under the cloud of Watergate and the Vietnam War, I really don't know what it would be. Our brand of humor came liberally dolloped with cynicism—and I ate it up, laughing along almost as hard as Gail.

I can now appreciate that my father and I were experiencing two very different films as we watched these disaster sagas unfold. The earnestness of his demeanor in the wake of these films indicates that these supercharged dramatizations didn't offer the same experience of thrills without risk as they did for me. For Oscar, the combination of overly serious dialogue and harrowing circumstances depicted in these films likely triggered flashbacks to his World War II combat, evoking feelings that rang true to the emotional tenor of these traumatizing events. These experiences and feelings were perhaps too present in his mind to be funny. What was that like for him? Now, sitting next to his son safely in a movie theater sharing a tub of hot buttered popcorn, he was left unarmed against the barrage of memories and images.

As I consider the dimensions of the existential gulf that separated the two of us, I wonder just how a boy like me was meant to discern the wisdom of experience, forged in actual blood and guts, my father was attempting to convey to me, his only son, in those cryptic, post-movie admonishments. It is a painful reality to consider these moments which, though ripe with potential for meaningful father-son connection, were squandered as we rode home from the neighborhood multiplex in awkward silence.

PTSD: The Origin Story

The constellation of symptoms collectively known as PTSD was an essential component in the depression and rage that overshadowed my father's life. I knew he had fought in World War II and that my mother suffered trauma due to the pressures of being a woman in the mid-twentieth century and in the abuse she suffered in her marriage. However, PTSD would only come to be defined in its present incarnation by the psychiatric establishment thirty-five years after the Allied victory in World War II was declared—the same year, in fact, that the movie *Airplane!* was released.[36]

At the outset of writing this book, I thought naming PTSD as the author of my family's tragedy would be sufficient. However, when I started asking myself *exactly* what it was about PTSD that can trigger people to act in bizarre ways, I found myself untethered from solid ground. I discovered that the official recognition of PTSD was the capstone of over one hundred years of intense debate, blind alleys, and leaps of logic that are now largely forgotten.[37] Looking back on that history helped me to look forward—finding greater insight and a broader appreciation of the context that set the stage for my parents' deaths.

■ ■ ■

The development of the disciplines of psychiatry and psychology were driven by the military establishment and the necessities of keeping people ready for war.[38] Throughout history, there were no other circumstances under which the daily lives of great numbers of people were brought under the watchful eye of a highly regulated system of administration. Personality patterns and behaviors disruptive to group cohesion come into sharp relief when bringing together any large group of people. If these groups include young men living and fighting in great peril then it's only natural to expect an amplification of challenging interpersonal dynamics—not to mention any number of troubling psychological issues. For medical specialists, these conditions made for convenient, ready-made subjects of study. Early on, these medical specialists were almost entirely made up of physicians whose primary concern was treating the wounded and returning them to the battlefield as quickly as possible. Consequently, the first theories about the nature of PTSD conceptualized this disorder through the lens of bodily damage. Today, PTSD is understood as a hybrid of symptoms involving the body *and* mind.[39] During the Civil War, Philadelphia physician Jacob Mendes Da Costa encountered soldiers fresh off the battlefield who were suffering with symptoms of dizziness, chest pain, fatigue, shortness of breath, and heart palpitations. This symptom profile was similar to a condition that had first been documented some ten years earlier in British soldiers returning from the Crimean War. With an unintended poetic turn of phrase, Da Costa named this disorder "soldier's heart" (sometimes referred to as irritable heart syndrome), attributing the source of this condition to the effects of "heavy marching, malnutrition, lack of sleep, illness and other hardships" that fighting men regularly endured.[40]

Today, many academics, researchers, and mental health practitioners consider soldier's heart to be a forerunner to PTSD,[41] but like most aspects of this disorder, the picture is not so straightforward. Although Da Costa considered the emotional toll of wartime experience to be a factor in soldier's heart, he viewed this disorder as a purely physiological phenomenon—not a malady predicated on or defined by mental suffering.[42] Nevertheless, the emotional toll of the Civil War did not go unrecognized by the military, physicians, and the public at large. During this period, "nostalgia" was the diagnosis used to identify soldiers suffering from a "pathological form of homesickness tinged with depression."[43] Language like "broke down" and "played out" was used to describe the complicated set of physical maladies and emotional symptoms that plagued veterans long after the war had ended.[44]

During World War I, patients experiencing symptoms of soldier's heart overfilled the three wards of the London hospital where Dr. Alexander Morison practiced. In a 1916 article from the *Journal for the Royal Society of Medicine*, Dr. Morison writes of these wounded, "[A]s far as their hearts are concerned, I have failed to find in them any evidence of exclusively cardiac disorder." In the very same article, Morison's colleague, Dr. O. Leyton presents opposing findings: "I believe that the condition is not due to a single cause, but that the symptoms may arise from a disease of the heart or a disease of the vaso-motor system."[45] The source of their confusion and conflicting assessments is understandable because, in effect, they were both correct. The genesis of PTSD as a discrete, clinically identifiable disorder is marked at every step by furious debates such as these. PTSD appears to me like a giant, mismatching quilt being stitched together at a community sewing bee, with its dizzying array of patterns and materials.

Today, the symptoms of soldier's heart might sound antiquated—more the product of a panic attack or psychosomatic pains—but modern medicine has since linked this Civil War–era diagnosis to very real, sometimes dangerous cardiac issues like mitral valve prolapse and cardiomyopathy.[46] Adding to the growing evidence substantiating the physiological reality of soldier's heart is a 2013 study of nearly 300 sets of twin brothers who served in the Vietnam War. Each set of twins included one brother who was diagnosed with PTSD and one who was not. Over the course of the thirteen years these men were tracked, researchers found that siblings diagnosed with PTSD were "twice as likely to have coronary heart disease as their unaffected siblings."[47]

More Machines, More Problems

After the Civil War, physicians began to devote more and more attention to the growing number of symptoms that occurred in the wake of life-threatening situations. The dawn of the Industrial Age saw the advent of large scale, man-made disasters, which made readily visible, for the first time outside of the theater of war, groups of individuals with no obvious physical injuries who reported bizarre and frightening symptoms after having been struck by tragedy. Railway spine—also known as Erichsen's disease after the Danish-born surgeon of the same name—was an attempt to make sense of these maladies within the context of the newly emerging field of neurology.[48] During the middle years of the nineteenth century, British physicians were regularly being called upon by courts to testify on behalf of survivors of train collisions who were seeking monetary claims against railway companies for their injuries. Providing testimony substantiating the extent of injuries sustained by survivors who suffered wounds that were visible to the naked eye proved to be a relatively uncomplicated matter. However, there were many other claimants who reported physiological and psychological symptoms while demonstrating no outward signs of bodily harm. The fact that the delay of onset for many of these invisible injuries could take months or even years to surface only served to raise the level of skepticism that was leveled against survivors and physicians during the litigation process.

The scintillatingly titled *On Railway and Other Injuries of the Nervous System* is a series of lectures presented by Dr. John Eric Erichsen detailing case after tragic case of railway spine. Like Da Costa's *soldier's heart*, Erichsen saw railway spine as a strictly physiological condition that just

43

happened to be accompanied by symptoms of an emotional nature. Erichsen speculates that symptoms of railway spine might be attributed to the shock of a bodily collision. He believed these shocks—or what he calls concussion of the spine—could lead to the development of lesions in the vertebrae and brain. Erichsen identifies these railway injuries as shocks—not simply to describe a blow to the body—but to highlight the fact that symptoms of railway spine followed a profile like that of "surgical shock." At the time surgical shock referred to symptoms commonly experienced by patients who lost dangerously high amounts of blood during an operation.[49]

While railway spine initially referred to a disorder found in survivors of train accidents, the term was later expanded to include almost anyone who had experienced the shock of a bodily collision. Among the case studies Erichsen presents in his lectures is the story of a twenty-two-year-old man who was struck between the shoulders by a large branch as he fell out of a tree. The details of this accident and the manner by which Erichsen relates this case illuminate the radical shift we have undergone in our understanding of the human psyche, and expose the embedded nature of our current assumptions regarding trauma, PTSD, and the human mind.[50]

While we are given no indication of just what this young man happened to be doing up in the tree in the first place, we do learn that after the fall the patient lost all sensation and movement below his shoulders. Despite these unfortunate circumstances, Erichsen strikes a tone of mild surprise in reporting that after adjusting to his new circumstances, the young man "threw himself into society" and enjoyed traveling hither and yon as he was driven about the countryside in the back of a carriage.[51]

In a strange twist, some six years after the accident, our intrepid paraplegic pays a visit to his local doctor and issues a request with "wonted resolution and energy" that his lower limbs be amputated, to be free of his burdensome legs and to have—wait for it—"more room in his cart for books and other articles."[52] The first good doctor he approached at the County Medical Society declined to proceed. However, our unfortunate patient was eventually able to find an obliging sawbones who was willing to disregard the extreme risk inherent to this questionable procedure. The operation went without a hitch and he healed quickly. This story comes very close to ending on a cheerful note as the young man "resumed the wandering life, and travelled over a great part of the States." However, Erichsen adds a revealing postscript—which should really come as no surprise—sad though it is. The man died one year after his double amputation "of a disease of the liver, brought on by his excess of drink, to which he had become greatly addicted since his accident.[53]

Searching for the Thread

This man's story helps to highlight the conceptual distance we have traveled over the course of just two human lifespans. Today, any child over the age of ten could readily offer up that the legless paraplegic was clearly experiencing some serious psychological issues. And his crippling alcoholism would be a focus of attention rather than a mere footnote. The simple reason for this oversight is that it was not, in fact, an oversight.

At the time of Erichsen's lectures, it would be another thirty years before the word psychology would come to be used in something approaching the framework of our present-day understanding. The scaffolding of this scientific discipline had to be erected before more concrete conclusions about emotional trauma and PTSD could be constructed. The ill-formed nature of the discipline of psychology wasn't the only factor overshadowing early medical case summaries like Erichsen's. Physicians of the day were also influenced by the historically circumscribed interpretation of the word "trauma." Derived from the Greek (*traûma*), trauma traditionally referred to a wounding of the body. It was not until the late nineteenth century that the term was expanded to encompass our current definition, that is, an infliction of a wound upon the mind.[54] The concept of a wound was kept in a phenomenological box whose parameters were defined by physiological processes alone, limiting the way that people looked at their inner world—and the inner worlds of others. The observation that the young man was trying to cure his mental trauma with alcohol couldn't—at the time—fit neatly into any medical discipline's structure.

Was PTSD Invented or Discovered?

There are two schools of philosophical thought that complicate our understanding of PTSD: structuralism and post-structuralism. Structuralism says that the reason Erichsen didn't connect the man's accident to his drinking is because humankind had not yet *discovered* PTSD and its symptoms. *Discovered* is the operative word here because structuralists believe that universal truths exist as discrete phenomena, just waiting for us to put words to them. Structuralism is ahistorical—meaning everything is true in the same way in the past, present, and future. Most modern people fall into this school of thought.[55] On the other hand, post-structuralism is very tied to the chronology. The expression "the whole is greater than the sum of its parts" captures the post-structuralist world view. According to post-structuralists, there is no moment in time when PTSD is unearthed and revealed to the world like some exotic variety of beetle; rather, our notions of PTSD have been invented through synergy—the coalescence of a number of independent factors into a wholly new phenomenon.[56] Each scientific and psychological movement generates new phenomena that could not have existed before. As the realm of the psychological became more ever-present in the public discourse, increasingly elaborate interpretations of our conscious reality emerged—with the quilt of trauma and PTSD being but one outcome.

• • •

The disaster movies of the 1970s highlight the sobering reality that my father and my childhood self existed, quite literally, in different movies. If I put on my post-structural hat for a moment and understand consciousness as very tied to chronology, I can come to understand how differently my father and I conceived of ourselves and how that colored our behaviors. He couldn't conceive of himself as traumatized in the same way that we now understand it, and therefore couldn't understand how that trauma might express itself in his thoughts and behavior. In this way, I hope we can begin to have some compassion for the troubling fact that the fragmentation of self caused by trauma can become malignant—even deadly—when people aren't given the education, tools, and resources to understand how trauma can infect their lives.

Chapter 3

Lepers, and Zombies, and Freud—Oh, My!

Why is it that people like my father don't seriously consider that they are dealing with issues that rise beyond the level of everyday troubles? I don't think it would be a stretch to say that today, the average person on the street has a more radically defined and nuanced understanding of mental illness than most mental health practitioners during the 1950s—to say nothing of doctors and scientists of the late nineteenth century. Yet, much of the conceptual foundation for PTSD was laid over 120 years ago. That doesn't mean all of these theories were off base—in fact, going back to these early sources helps to give greater insight into questions and inconsistencies in trauma theory that still exist today. As we will see, there were also very powerful reasons why people in the not too distant past—and still many today—balked at the suggestion that they had a mental illness. This is problematic because the self-perpetuating process whereby some untreated trauma survivors go on to traumatize others affects not only people on an individual level, but also impacts us on a societal level—reinforcing a culture of collective trauma.[57]

Do We *Really* Know Ourselves?

In 1867, the same year that surgeons like John Eric Erichsen were discussing railway spine, physicians like Edwin Morris were introducing new patterns to the PTSD quilt. Morris proposed that cases of shock were produced by violent injuries or from violent emotions. Puzzling over what structure of the body might be responsible for both emotional and physical symptoms, Morris hit upon the nervous system: "The puzzle is solved once one accepts that fear is simply an assault comparable in its action to a physical blow or injury."[58] These ideas represent a fundamental turning point in history; the ushering in of a new, synergistic conceptualization of human consciousness. Morris writes that, in these moments of shock, our bodies "suspend the faculty of sense and volition" and force the nervous system into prostration.

This phenomenon—the breaking of the everyday flow of awareness—had long been the exclusive domain of the occult and religious ecstasy, not a state associated with the average Joe or Jane. The identification of this prostration—or fragmentation of self—and the meanings attached to this process opened a path for a new category of wounded who would come to be known as "the psychologically traumatized." For our purposes, the fact that in these moments of shock we lose volition raises troubling questions about whether traumatized people committing abuse have also lost their volition. Are they to blame? And if not them, who? What would it mean for the way we dole out justice if we were to conclude that traumatized people who act out violently are not fully responsible for themselves?

As part of the late nineteenth century progression of thought around the newly established domain of the psychological and traumatic experiences, our mental space was replete with specialists like neurologists, psychiatrists, and psychologists playing an increasingly prominent role in interpreting and treating these newly identified (or perhaps culturally constructed) maladies. This, too, constitutes a watershed moment in human history because the medicalization of the mind is an implicit collective confession that we are unable to fully understand the contents of our own minds. While God and Satan (as well as angels and demons) were historically understood to exert varying degrees of outside influence over our behavior, the idea that our minds contained undiscovered dark continents over which we have no awareness would have been completely antithetical to many of our ancestors.[59]

Because of our newly discovered ignorance about ourselves, physicians conversant in these new medical specialties stepped into roles once the exclusive domain of shamans and the clergy. One of these physicians, Jean-Martin Charcot—widely considered to be the father of neurology—conducted work at Salpêtrière, a women's hospital in Paris that he transformed during his tenure into the premier neurological facility of the day.[60] Named for a gunpowder factory that once stood on the site (potassium nitrate—or *saltpeter*—is a constituent in gunpowder[61]), Salpêtrière was initially constructed by order of King Louis XIV in 1654[62] as part of a plan to remove prostitutes from the streets of the French capital.[63] While at first blush this might seem to indicate something of an act of charity on the part of the monarchy, keep in mind that hospitals, up until the middle of the nineteenth century, were nothing like facilities we think of today. They were de facto prisons and work farms where prostitutes and sundry unfortunates like orphans, the poor, and the mentally ill were locked up against their will.[64] While today this might appear to be something of a random grouping of *Les Miserables* to round up and abuse, to the European mind of the seventeenth and eighteenth centuries, the characteristics unifying these diverse populations were self-evident. During that time, each of these groups was perceived by the larger society to be guilty of indolence— that is to say, they were seen as lazy and slothful. Such behavior was considered an affront to the moral sentiments of the powerful bourgeoisie and clergy whose perspectives held sway in the social policing of the French citizenry during this period.[65]

The confinement of social outliers and those who hold the least amount of power in the communal hierarchy was just one manifestation of an age-old human tendency to manufacture bogeymen on which to project one's own psychological conflicts. Before the demise of the stranglehold of religious orthodoxy and the advent of the liberalizing influences of modern-day Western culture, the average person struggled alone with their all too human "immoral" impulses. Tragically for everyone involved, these suppressed internal conflicts had a nasty habit of manufacturing unbearable feelings of shame. These feelings of shame were all but unresolvable given the force of societal judgement and the potential consequence of exclusion from the community during a time when unmitigated interdependence determined not only your ability to succeed, but often, the chances of your very survival.

In the eighteenth century, a confessional technique known as "the cure of souls" sought to address these secrets. Though confession of this sort existed for many sects, this sacrament nevertheless came gift wrapped in the indignant judgment of an uncommonly prickly creator, who in his mercy might forgive individual trespasses—with enough penance—but never get over his creations' initial fall from grace.[66]

Psychoanalysts have a wonderfully useful term known as cathexis, which refers to the investment of emotional energy into an outside person, object, or idea.[67] Throughout history, entire cultures have sought to cope with socially unacceptable impulses—the wildman or devil supposedly inside of all of us—by cathecting their shame-inducing, unresolved conflicts onto disempowered groups. By punishing these scapegoats, the community can breathe a sigh of relief, living, as they do, in a fantasy of having contained the forces of chaos. Nowadays, much of this messy process has been relegated to the legal concept of moral turpitude. Turpitude refers to a depraved or degenerate act or practice. As such, moral turpitude is an act that shocks the public conscience or violates the accepted standards of the community. Today, we enforce our moral climate on a state and social level in the same manner as our ancestors have done throughout recorded history—with imprisonment and/or public humiliation.[68]

One of the clearest instances of collective scapegoating is the treatment of lepers. In his highly influential book *Madness and Civilization*, Michel Foucault proposed that leprosy once served as the embodiment of moral turpitude for medieval Europeans.[69] For Christians, leprosy holds a special place in the imagination owing to a few lines from the

New Testament's Gospel of Matthew. After descending from his Sermon on the Mount, a leper kneels before Jesus and asks, "Lord, if you are willing, can you make me clean?" In response, Jesus reaches out and touches the untouchable leper, curing him instantly of his disfiguring skin condition. Jesus admonishes the man not to tell anyone about the miracle, but the leper turns out to be quite the blabbermouth, telling anyone who will listen about his cure. Word of this miracle transforms Jesus into something of a sensation,[70] attracting massive throngs of groupies who force the savior to hide out in the desert like a troubled celebrity ingenue stalked by TMZ.

Foucault hypothesizes that during the Middle Ages, the story of the fraught relationship between Christ and the chatty leper took on further layers of symbolic meaning. During this period, lepers came to represent a sort of earthly manifestation of God—their disfigurement at turns an embodiment of the Creator's anger with Man and a living expression of his grace toward humankind. Consequently, lepers were rounded up and sequestered in isolated sanatoriums—effectively keeping these wretched souls locked away from family, church, and community for the duration of their lives. Thus removed from the larger community, lepers came to represent "witnesses of evil who accomplish their salvation by their exclusion."[71]

Once leprosy disappeared from the European landscape, Foucault argues that society turned to groups labeled the mad (to which I add misfits/social outliers and the indolent to the list) to maintain the general structure (or symbolic framework) of moral turpitude. In other words, society kept the container (or mental file cabinet) called moral turpitude and switched out the label on the drawer that had read lepers for new and improved versions.[72]

Throughout the centuries that lepers had been incarcerated, the "mad" had lived, for the most part, peacefully amongst the general populace, filling various roles like that of the fool, religious visionary, vagabond, or artist. Many of these groups were even afforded a measure of respect—sometimes inspiring a sense of awe—as these individuals were thought to possess a "hidden knowledge that is unattainable to sane people."[73] This perception lives on in our collective stories; just think of the wisdom of fictional movie characters like Forrest Gump or of how Vincent van Gogh and his visionary madness are regarded today.

Foucault argues that throughout the sequestering of lepers during the Middle Ages, death held supremacy in the ordering of humankind's primal fears. During this period in history, the mad represented those who in their folly did not recognize that the dreaded death was close at hand. However, with the demise of the role of leprosy in the popular consciousness, madness stopped being associated with a generally benign foolishness and came instead to represent death itself. Cast as death and the new embodiment of moral turpitude, the mad were no longer given any measure of respect, much less the sense of religious awe that was once afforded to lepers.[74]

Leprosy's Enduring Legacy

Shame-inducing internal conflicts, with no healthy outlet for transformation, have had the annoying tendency to take corporeal form in arbitrarily defined groups like lepers, the mad, prostitutes, heretics, and the indolent. One might comfortably argue that today in the United States, sexism, racism, homophobia—all the "isms" for that matter—rely on a comparison to an idealized, Platonic form, which is defined as the White, Christian, heterosexual male. Better known as the patriarchy, this pinnacle of our social order is the locus of all power in our culture. If one does not fit this Platonic template, the individual is vulnerable to developing the belief that they are somehow flawed. Often, these individuals are given labels like thug, fag, or bitch to assert the strictures of the patriarchal social order via the spectacle of public humiliation.[75]

Significant implications regarding the power exerted by our patriarchy and the spirit of White superiority lurk beneath the operations of these artificial labels. The American phenomenon of mass incarceration that began under the Johnson administration and escalated precipitously in the 1980s[76] is just the latest permutation of the propensity of great numbers of our citizens to turn unresolved internal conflicts into ritual public demonization of the oppressed. The numbers alone reveal the arrested state of our capabilities to cope effectively with these dynamics: The United States incarcerates more of its citizens than any other country in the world, 698 for every 100,000 people. That's about 1% of the entire U.S. population.[77] Looked at through a different numerical lens, one in every thirty-one Americans is in jail or prison, or under some kind of correctional supervision, such as probation or parole.[78] The phenomenon of mass incarceration is even more alarming for people of color, who are disproportionately represented in these numbers. African-Americans make up 13% of the U.S. population, but 38% of the population of incarcerated people in the United States.[79]

Of course, none of this should be taken as a denial of the existence of mental illness or of the reality of dangerous people who commit acts of violence. Rather, this is an opportunity to reflect on the point that many of the groups we label morally turbid are, by and large, artificial constructs representative of our complicated relationships with our own bugaboos. Beyond these significant ramifications, many argue that in the process of placing outliers and madmen in a box labelled mentally ill, we may have unwittingly cut ourselves off from a vital form of consciousness unbridled from our present-day reality in which predetermined patterns including symbols (e.g., language) and groupings (theories and laws) limit our capacity to understand the universe around us. In short, we are collectively beginning to understand that we must learn from what we deem "madness" or "sick" rather than hide it away.[80] Changing definitions of moral turpitude almost always say more about a culture than the subjects of its derision. The adage rings true: when you point a finger at someone, not only one, but three fingers point back at you.

Hysteria and Hypnosis Take Center Stage
As the medical establishment began to take madness and people's interior lives more seriously, living conditions at hospitals like Salpêtrière

were improved. Many patients were unchained from their beds and provided with medical treatment for the first time in their lives.[81]

Charcot, our father of neurology, is best remembered today for his study of a condition known as hysteria (which he identified as *la grande simulatrice* or the great simulation) and its relationship to the concept of psychological trauma. Charcot single-handedly shaped the construct of hysteria into a medical disorder by discerning a structure from the great number of puzzling maladies found in his patients. According to Charcot, hysterics were characterized by their ability to transform psychological stress into physical symptoms like paralysis, strange muscle contortions, or the loss of normal sensory functioning. Hysterics were also known to suffer from bouts of memory loss as well as superficial, intense displays of emotions. Charcot characterized these hysterical episodes "as moving, with mechanical regularity through clearly delineated phases, each characterized by stereotyped and often grotesque contortions and postures."[82]

Hysteria, derived from the Greek *hystera*—or womb[83]—had historically been viewed as a disorder of the uterus.[84] The Ancient Greeks believed the organ capable of migrating around a woman's body like a pack of wildebeest let loose on the Serengeti. Plato and the physician Aetaeus called these uterine junkets hysterical suffocation. They imagined these migrations exerted pressure on the other organs, resulting in experiential and mood issues like "anxiety, insomnia, depression, irritability, and fainting." To treat this affliction, "The offending uterus was usually coaxed back into place by placing good smells near the vagina, bad smells near the mouth, and sneezing."[85]

Throughout the nineteenth century, the concept of hysteria was, as one historian has put it, "a dramatic metaphor for everything men found mysterious and unmanageable in the opposite sex."[86] Charcot was the first to recognize that hysteria was not limited to females after having observed the disorder in a great many male soldiers.[87] Central to the course that PTSD would eventually take, Charcot concluded, through careful observation of his patients, that hysteria was a self-induced hypnotic state triggered by extreme fear. Because of the supposed parallels between hysteria and hypnosis, Charcot would hypnotize his patients to study their symptoms, turning these sessions into public spectacles. As author Allan Young recounts, Charcot's "Tuesday Lectures were theatrical events, attended by 'a multi-colored audience, drawn from all of Paris: authors, doctors, leading actors and actresses, fashionable demimondaines, all full of morbid curiosity....' In these lectures, Charcot illustrated his findings on hysteria by live demonstrations. The patients he put on display were young women who had found refuge in Salpêtrière from lives of unremitting violence, exploitation, and rape. The asylum provided them greater safety and protection than they had ever known; for a selected group of women who became Charcot's star performers, the asylum also offered something close to fame."[88]

As strange as this might sound, many of the mysterious hysterical symptoms first identified by Charcot can now be found in the *Diagnostic and Statistical Manual of Psychological Disorders* (*DSM-V*), often referred to as the Bible of psychiatric disorders—largely intact—under a diagnosis known as Conversion Disorder. These nervous system disorders are understood to be triggered by emotional disturbances, manifesting in oddly terrifying symptoms like blindness, apraxia (loss of speech), numbness, paralysis, and hearing loss.[89]

While Charcot acknowledged that the mind played a role in these bizarre ailments, he believed hysteria stemmed from internal injuries or hereditary factors.[90] German physician Hermann Oppenheim was the singular voice of the era proposing that psychological factors were the prime instigator of these mysterious disorders, correctly positing that emotionally shocking events can even lead to molecular changes in the brain. Oppenheim coined the term "traumatic neuroses" in his *Text-book for Nervous Diseases for Physicians and Students* (1911), becoming the first to outline an accurate sketch of a psychologically based syndrome that would be refined by science over the years, eventually leading to our current conceptualization of PTSD.[91]

Oppenheim identified symptoms including "unrest, excitement, fear, increased arousal, melancholic mood, irritability and phobias" that correlate to many of the important markers of PTSD as it is currently understood.[92] However, Oppenheim's theories were roundly dismissed at the time. Critics argued that the symptoms identified by Oppenheim were the product of wishful ideas, iatrogenic in origin (meaning they were triggered by the supposed cure), malingering (faking), or the result of unsavory characters trying to collect accident insurance pensions.[93] Charcot also weighed in on the issue, insisting that traumatic neuroses, railway spine, and soldier's heart were not separate syndromes, but rather a byproduct of hysteria.[94]

Given these clues, do we take the post-structuralist view that this cluster of painful thoughts and feelings identified by Oppenheim was always with humankind and give the physician credit for having discovered the new land of PTSD? Or do we take the structuralist perspective which maintains that out of the synergistic chaos of human tragedy a wholly new structure and experienced labeled PTSD emerged?

Traumatic Memory and the Talking Cure

While Charcot had improved living conditions for women at Salpêtrière, he nevertheless treated his patients like specimens, only superficially inquiring into the details of their thoughts and feelings. Taking up the mantle of Charcot, physicians Sigmund Freud and his mentor, Josef Breuer, soon discovered the limitations of the study of hysterics via observation and classification of symptoms alone. In a novel twist, the two decided to start talking to their patients—a lot. Judith Herman observes in her book *Trauma and Recovery*, "For a brief decade men of science listened to women with a devotion and respect unparalleled before or since."[95] Freud called this approach psycho-analysis. The treatment soon acquired the apropos nickname "the talking cure."[96]

Freud and Breuer found that by discussing traumatic experiences in a focused and directive fashion, many of their patients were able to bring about a deeply felt emotional release which helped to free these individuals from the grip of hysteria. All this talking—*and* attentive listening—led Freud and Breuer to conclude that hysteria was not the result of heredity or physical injury, but rather a psychological scar produced through trauma.[97] While hysteria had traditionally been viewed through the lens of emotional and physiological dysfunction, Freud and Breuer noted that hysterics were trapped in a complex relationship with their *memories* of these scarring events, concluding that hysterics suffer mainly from reminiscences.[98] As we will see, Freud's new conceptualization of hysteria (and its relationship to memories) would prove highly influential in the development of our current understanding of trauma and PTSD.

Freud and Breuer's theory of trauma drew significantly from the writings of French psychologists Théodule-Armand Ribot[99] and Pierre Janet,[100] who had independently proposed some years earlier the existence of a new type of memory which they called traumatic memory. Historically, the mechanism of memory had been associated with the act of telling yourself a story about an event you'd experienced and then fitting that story into the chronological sequence of your life. This definition of memory is recognized to be a cornerstone of our capacity to maintain a cohesive sense of self—or personality—and is understood to be the primary reason we can create meaning out of our recollections. Ribot and Janet called these general properties of memory ordinary memory. By contrast, the concept of traumatic memory was something altogether new. In the case of traumatic memory, Ribot and Janet proposed that some events can be so overwhelming in their emotional impact that they alter the functioning of ordinary memory by disrupting our capacity to assimilate and process experiences.[101]

They viewed the process of traumatic memory as an act of concealment whereby information *about* the self is kept *from* the self. This concealment produces something akin to a secret that is kept from the conscious awareness of the trauma victim. Unlike normal memories, which integrate past experiences, traumatic memory is split off from reality. These traumatic memories are like isolated and disowned islands that are cut off from the organizing functions of normal memory. Exiled from the assimilating functions of normal memory, a traumatic memory remains frozen and unprocessed by our normal coping mechanisms.[102] Traumatic memory calls to mind something of a mental version of North Korea, wherein a despotic overlord rules an isolated kingdom marinating in fear and dangerous distortions of reality. These fears and distortions affect not only the people trapped in North Korea, but also set off fissures across the globe to infect people ten thousand miles away with their potent energy.

What, then, distinguishes a traumatic event from the merely awful of everyday life? For Freud, it was a matter of the degree of intensity. He viewed traumatic events as analogous to a psychological attack, theorizing that we experience these attacks as an overwhelming flood of sensory information, so staggering in their intensity that they threaten to destroy our sanity. Freud speculated that our minds are equipped with the psychological equivalent of a knight's protective shield. These shields are automatically deployed during a traumatic experience to help protect us from losing our minds. This protective shield is experienced by the trauma victim as an altered state of consciousness. It was Janet who first linked the stress of overwhelming events to what he called dissociation —a trancelike process that functions as a sort of mental escape hatch that is activated when emotional pain becomes too overpowering.[103]

The Zombie Captains

This trancelike process is akin to the aforementioned "prostration of the nervous system," and can be considered—among innumerable conceptions of trauma—to be the one widely agreed upon detail of traumatic experience. However, if our consciousness is offline, can the traumatized be held responsible for their actions?

My father left the army and re-entered society, got a job, married, started a family, and went to work to support us—at least financially. The fact that he would build this all up over years only to knock it all down in a matter of seconds makes me feel as if he must have not really been in control of his actions. Was that my father's fault? Or his father's fault? Was it the army's fault? Was it the Germans' fault? There is no simple answer here.

We're familiar with the adage that "hurt people hurt people," but what is the mechanism that actually energizes this cycle of abuse? What is happening in the moment someone re-abuses?

In our normal, day-to-day awareness, we experience a seamless integration of memory, individual identity, and perceptions of the environment. In today's mainstream trauma theory, dissociation continues to be understood as a disruption in the normal experience of consciousness.[104] Psychologists understand dissociation to frequently trigger experiences of depersonalization and derealization. In a state of depersonalization, a person has a feeling of being disconnected from themselves, like an automaton, or of watching themselves from a distance (often from above). With derealization, a person experiences a sense of being disconnected from reality itself.[105] Some describe derealization as a dreamlike state or of having the feeling that things are moving in slow motion.[106]

If it's true that a person in the midst of a traumatic event is having an out-of-body experience over which they have no control—then if and when they reenact that event down the line in the form of abuse or violence, are they again having an out-of-body and out-of-control experience? Much of the reason these questions are so difficult to answer has to do with the basic framing of the dissociative experience. Ruth Leys, a professor of humanities at Johns Hopkins University, has written extensively on the role of hypnosis in today's mainstream model of PTSD, pointing out discomforting theoretical inconsistencies inherent to our current understanding of traumatic memory. She wonders if the concept of hypnosis might have a role to play in our mainstream understanding of PTSD. Are victims-turned-abusers really under a hypnotic trance of their past abuse? In the moment they abuse, are they victims once again?[107]

Leys conceptualizes these inconsistencies within the framework of what she identifies as the mimetic model and anti-mimetic model.[108] That is: are people unconsciously mimicking their abusers? Do victims have personal agency during the enactment of their abuse or do they vacate their bodies to become obliging putty in the hands of their past perpetrators?

It helps to think of personal agency as the ability to be the captain of one's own ship, standing at the helm, guiding oneself through life. You're out on the open sea and you have full control. Now, society at large—especially the prison industrial complex and the judicial system— will have us believe that when a traumatized person is committing abuse or violence they are the captains of their own ship, they are fully aware, and yet they still *choose* to *allow* pirates (the dissociative, self-sabotaging parts of themselves) to take over their ship; they do nothing to stop it. That is, they consciously choose to let the pirates steer the ship.

The more troubling scenario is the mimetic model, where the captain of the ship periodically becomes a zombie—they disassociate, falling into a hypnotic trance, losing self-control and personal agency. In this scenario, the trauma survivor has no conscious faculties to stop themselves; in fact, they help the pirates take over their own ship. This is why self-sabotaging behavior comes so *naturally* to traumatized people. This is how my father could end the life and family he had worked so hard to build.

The implications for how we understand human behavior are profound here. If an abuser has agency, they should be held accountable and punished or dealt with as society deems appropriate. If, however, an abuser turns out to not have agency in these moments, then they deserve our pity, support, and understanding, however unintuitive that feels.

These points seem impossible to be proven conclusively, but if you deny the existence of zombie captains then you are also denying the current framework of PTSD. As disturbing as it might seem, much of our contemporary understanding of human psychology is based on this idea. How we deal with criminality and mental health at a legal and societal level has not yet fully reckoned with our scientific understanding of behavior.

We're All Zombies to Some Degree

Most people think we are light years beyond Freud and his antiquated theories involving the "unconscious," "penis envy," and the "Oedipal

Complex,"[109] but the bulk of our everyday understanding of human experience continues to be based on Freud's psychoanalytic theories *and* zombie captains.

The role of psychoanalysis and most methods of psychotherapy are, to varying degrees, a process in which a designated expert (doctor/therapist) helps a zombie captain (patient) to discover things they were concealing from themselves. The expert helps to bring these disowned aspects of the self into conscious awareness where they can be integrated into the narrative of normal memory.[110] After having experienced these important insights into one's interior "dark continents," the zombie becomes human once more.

You would think Freud's insights and novel treatment methods would've been heralded as a breakthrough by the scientific community, but they almost derailed his career before it had even gotten off the ground. Freud published a paper in 1896 called *The Aetiology of Hysteria*[111] that detailed his findings on trauma and the talking cure. The response was a resounding thud accompanied by the chirping of crickets. It seems that in all of Freud's talking to women, a dominant storyline of rampant sexual abuse had emerged. Outlining the sexual seductions of young girls —often perpetrated by close family members—is an explosive topic, even today, but in the sexually repressed atmosphere of late nineteenth century Vienna, these revelations were considered beyond the pale. To recover his reputation, Freud recanted his initial findings, ascribing these abuses to the fantasies of the women. In effect, Freud was claiming the sexual abuse was all in their pretty little heads. Freud soon dropped this line of inquiry into trauma, turning instead to invent his now familiar structural model of the mind that later became better known by its components—the Id (the supposed devil/wildman inside all of us), the Ego (our self), and the Superego (the judgmental Church Lady).[112]

Regardless of the latter-day popular opinion of psychoanalysis, Freud's theories signaled a societal shift of incalculable proportions by turning the spotlight of moral turpitude from external bogeymen (lepers, the mad, and indolent) to our internal conflicts, helping to reduce the shaming and imprisonment of marginalized groups.

Chapter 4

Shocks to the System

At the dawn of the twentieth century, physicians and researchers effectively put a halt to the study of psychological trauma because it was thought to dip too much into the realm of the mystical—jeopardizing the chances of the newly emerging fields of psychology and psychiatry[113] being accepted by the greater medical establishment as a hard science.

The medical model of trauma, with its focus on the body—not the mind—became the order of the day. Judith Herman, a contemporary American psychiatrist and trauma researcher, proposes that the lack of sustained focus given to the study of trauma and PTSD throughout history reflects a larger societal process of silencing and denial that mirrors the process of dissociative amnesia in individual trauma victims. It would not be until after the outbreak of World War I in 1914 that the subject of psychological trauma would be taken up again with any level of urgency by the scientific community.[114]

For nearly two decades after his defeat at the 1890 Internationaler Medzin Kongress, Dr. Hermann Oppenheim—our proposed discoverer of PTSD—abandoned his theory of traumatic neuroses. In the years coinciding with Freud's ascendency, Oppenheim stopped treating working class individuals whose lower social standing had allowed the doctor more latitude in assigning mental health diagnoses. Instead, Oppenheim started treating upper-class patients who would not abide by such stigmatizing interpretations and demanded physiological explanations for their symptoms regardless of their accuracy and efficacy. Years later, while working as an advising neurologist at a large military hospital during World War I, Oppenheim was able to examine great numbers of soldiers returning from the front lines of battle. This newest research cohort enabled the German physician to identify many cases of traumatic neuroses that confirmed his findings from decades earlier. Oppenheim presented his research at a crucial 1916 meeting of neuropsychiatrists where the issue of war neuroses, the general term given to the physical and mental problems found in soldiers, was under debate. Once again, his belief that traumatic symptoms were based in psychological factors was rejected, with the quilt of trauma and PTSD instead taking new directions.[115]

Technology's Contribution to the Story of PTSD

During World War I, the technology of weaponry and the scale with which munitions could be produced multiplied exponentially, outpacing all other previous conflicts at an unprecedented rate. Considering these advances were the same for all parties, they did little to move the needle toward victory for either side. The Allied and Central Powers were evenly matched opponents, with each side dug into entrenched lines of combat. The result was a brutal, multi-year stalemate characterized by a state of near perpetual bombardment.[116]

The very definition of battle changed during the Great War from that of time-limited, hand-to-hand engagement, to one of an ongoing barrage of shells meant to dislodge troops from their dugout positions. Ironclad bombs, sometimes containing up to 200 pounds of explosives, released shock waves equal in force to the weight of ten tons per square yard. Traumatizing events during war transformed from individual skirmishes and hand-to-hand combat to mass traumatizing events that moved through time and space with unrelenting speed and indifference. While the term "shock wave" calls to mind the waves of the ocean that move horizontally across a plane, these blast forces are spherical in shape, behaving like a balloon of gas, expanding faster than the speed of sound, and enveloping everything in their path. Upon detonation of an explosive device, static pressure is generated by a sudden drop in air pressure, creating a vacuum inside these expanding balloons of gas. This process occurs so quickly that a person does not have time to react, much less move. Today, many soldiers call this moment the "thump" for the feeling they get at the center of their chest. Immediately following detonation and the thump, a whirlwind of supersonic wind rushes into the vacuum created, "hurling and fragmenting objects it encounters, weaponizing debris as high-speed, penetrating projectiles [and] lifting human beings or even 15-ton armored vehicles in the air, slamming them against walls, rocks, dusty roadsides." The final effect of the blast is "fire that burns, chemicals that sear, dust that asphyxiates."[117]

Since World War I, physicians have understood that shock waves alone could overwhelm the delicate tissues of the nervous system, sometimes resulting in the bizarre notion of injury—or even death—without visible wounding. Eerie reports began to surface during the war of soldiers being discovered in the midst of their final act, physically unblemished and seemingly alive, but actually frozen in death. A British journalist reported from Gallipoli of having found "in one corner, seven Turks, with their rifles across their knees... sitting together. One man has his arm around the neck of a friend and a smile on his face, as if they had been cracking a joke when death overwhelmed them. All now have the appearance of being merely asleep: for of the seven, I only see one who shows any outward injury."[118]

Physicians theorized that the impact of these intense shock waves had the capacity to overload the natural cushioning effects of our cerebrospinal fluid to penetrate all the neurons of the brain. Aside from the dangerous barrage of shock waves, shrapnel, and other flying objects dislodged by incoming shells, explosive blasts often brought about symptoms that came to be called shell shock. Shell shock was described as a "physical shock, accompanied by horrifying circumstances causing profound emotional shock and terror, which is contemplative fear or fear continually revived by the imagination [that has a] much more intense and lasting effect on the mind than simple shock."[119]

Shell shock is an amalgam of symptoms stitched together from concepts that had lain dormant for more than a generation at the time of their discovery during World War I. Drawing from Dr. John Eric Erichsen and the railway spine era, shell shock incorporates a precipitating event or shock of corporal dimensions, except now the true magnitude of the emotional fallout of these shocks is given equal footing as seen in the use of the terms "horrifying" and "terror." From Pierre Janet and Sigmund Freud we see the recognition that these shocks result in a dissociative memory problem, but with a new wrinkle: instead of the memory of the traumatic event being quarantined from conscious awareness, shell shock places these memories front and center in the consciousness of victims, with these "fears continually revived by the imagination." This phenomenon of uncontrollable recollections has become incorporated into our current conceptualization of PTSD, with its emphasis on ruminations about the traumatizing event and intrusive flashbacks. Finally, with regard to the definition of shell shock revised during World War I, this condition is seen to involve a sustained period of "intense" injury to the *mind* beyond the "simple shock" of a bodily wound. You would think that this amendment would help drive a greater understanding of the psychological dimensions of shell shock and serve as an important acknowledgment of the complexity and severity of these invisible wounds. Alas, physicians and military officials could not reach consensus on the nature of shell shock throughout the duration of World War I. Again, much like in Freud's time, the implications of such a consensus threatened to upend too much of the prevailing systems of thought and control. While the detrimental role of shock waves and cardiac anomalies previously described as soldier's heart were generally well established, the universal acknowledgment of the psychological challenges inherent to shell shock was an altogether different matter.[120] I could have just as well called this book "Swept Under the Rug."

During World War I, our old friend hysteria reappears in the controversies involving shell shock as does a new concept known as neurasthenia. Neurasthenia was thought to be triggered by "exposure to long periods of intense mental and physical strain"[121] and reads almost like our current checklist for depression: "anxiety...; emotional lability and irritability; difficulties sleeping, concentrating, and remembering; chronic fatigue and easy exhaustion; headache; loss of appetite; obsessive interest in somatic states and symptoms [and]; loss of self-confidence."[122]

The overwhelming majority of physicians and military officials would continue to deny the reality of the psychological effects of shell shock throughout the duration of World War I and, as in the case of litigants suffering from railway spine who sought damages against railway companies, injured soldiers were met with similar skepticism and hostile accusations of malingering. The stigma of mental illness was so severe during World War I that most soldiers opted not to seek medical attention from unsympathetic physicians who regarded their symptoms as the moral equivalent of desertion. Following the lead of physicians, the military and public were quick to assume soldiers suffering from shell shock were "cowards," "fakers," or "shirkers" who were to blame for their own problems.[123] Military commanders were implored by World War I physicians not to let the contagion of these "war neuroses" undermine and pollute the ranks of their units. However, what no one could deny is that the practical effects of shell shock were "the equivalent to debilitating wound or injury" which "severely reduced a man's effectiveness as a frontline soldier."[124]

During the most recent wars in Iraq and Afghanistan, improvised explosive devices (IEDs) made blast injuries like those experienced by soldiers in World War I once again a common occurrence. Between 2001 and 2014, nearly a quarter of a million soldiers and veterans injured by IED blasts had been diagnosed with traumatic brain injury (TBI) by the U.S. Department of Defense.[125] These individuals suffer from some combination of "headache, seizures, motor disorders, sleep disorders, dizziness, visual disturbances, ringing in the ears, mood changes, and cognitive, memory, and speech difficulties."[126] It is still not well understood if blast shock waves enter through the skull's natural openings or if the force is absorbed by the chest and abdomen and then transmitted through the vascular system to the brain.[127]

The Department of Defense Center for Neuroscience and Regenerative Medicine Brain Tissue Repository was established under the direction of Dr. Daniel Perl in 2013 to study the effects of these explosive blasts. In a postmortem study of eight soldiers who survived between four days and nine years after exposure, Perl observed that the subjects' "brain tissue [was] as delicate as butterfly wings, spatter-marked as if with buckshot, bearing outright tears surrounded by broken tendrils of scarring or dark clouds of damage looming from the folds and furrows."[128] Perl found "similar severe scarring patterns at the boundaries between tissues of different densities, such as gray matter and white matter, and between tissue and the cerebrospinal fluid that surrounds the brain." Subjects ranged in age from twenty-six to forty-five at the time of death, with five of the eight having died by suicide or drug overdose. Each of the soldiers "had endured headaches, anxiety, depression, insomnia, memory and concentration problems, seizures, and chronic pain" after their blast exposure, up to their time of death.[129]

Utilizing a microscope with a thousand times the capacity of EEG or MRI imaging, Perl and his co-researchers found the scarring extended into regions that mediate sleep, memory, attention span, and emotional control. These processes are all highly correlated with symptoms of PTSD[130]—a diagnosis that has been found to affect nearly 16% of veterans of the wars in Iraq and Afghanistan.[131] Perl's research— admittedly on an extremely small sample size—once again calls into question whether many cases of PTSD might be based in injury to brain tissue and not purely of psychological origin.

A Gentler Approach

The 1916 Battle of the Somme was the largest military offensive by the Allies against the Central Powers during World War I, with an estimated one million soldiers being killed or wounded over the course of just five short months.[132] Astonishingly, this exorbitant sacrifice of lives and resources yielded no material gains for either side. After the Somme offensive, cases of shell shock, already overwhelming in number, went through the roof. In a grudging response to a reality that could no longer be uniformly denied, the British Royal Army Medical Corps set up advanced neurological centers near war zones to assist soldiers with psychological wounds.[133] After a few days of rest, many of these soldiers were once again returned to the battlefield. However, soldiers with the most crippling cases of shell shock were evacuated to England where veterans received treatments like hypnosis, electric shock, and sedation.[134]

Obviously there were better ways to aid these soldiers than giving them drugs and electrocuting them. Dr. W.H.R. Rivers was one of the few physicians treating soldiers suffering from shell shock who sought to apply a far gentler approach.[135] For Rivers, "traumatic memory [was] a system of connected images, associations and emotions [which are] simultaneously a psychological and neurological reality."[136] Rivers believed the symptoms of hysteria and neurasthenia then associated with shell shock could be attributed to the process of repression. Repression refers to the old idea of a buried secret that operates similarly to the example referenced earlier of an isolated North Korea infecting the world with its internal terrors. Rivers based many of his ideas on the evolutionary perspective of mammalian threat management—fight, flight, freeze, or fawn—proposing that the unfluctuating stalemate of World War I left soldiers with a deep-seated sense of paralyzing powerlessness. Cut off from any meaningful action to protect itself—fight, flight, or fawn—"the neurological apparatus switches to the only available response— immobilization," also known as freeze.[137] The unbearable psychological reality of this compromise thus becomes repressed—a secret cut off from the soldier's conscious awareness. Rivers believed these secrets, left to fester, manifest in the panoply of bizarre behaviors and neurological disorders that physically immobilized victims of shell shock: conversion disorders like paralysis of limbs, blindness, and an inability to speak. Rivers' work focused on a particular type of immobilization he called

71

"contractures."[138] Contractures occur when muscles and tendons remain tensed for an extended period as a consequence of a soldier living in a terrorized state of psychological freeze. He believed these freeze responses were abetted and fixed through a process of suggestion in which an individual's thoughts, feelings, and behaviors are significantly influenced by the powerful convictions of others. Suggestion of this sort is similar to the role of the hypnotist as well as our concept of the zombie captain assisting in the pirate takeover of his vessel. People in frozen, contracted, and immobilized states of trauma are easily influenced and controlled, opening the door for even further traumas.

In the treatment of shell shock, Rivers' technique was to talk empathetically with soldiers, much like Freud and Breuer, helping them bring repressed traumatic experiences into conscious awareness and then releasing the associated emotions through the verbalization of these experiences. Today, when we talk about processing emotions associated with trauma, we are referring to a similar method of healing whereby traumatic memories that were split-off during the process of dissociation are reinstated into our cognizance to be integrated and metabolized by the psyche.[139]

Torture as Treatment

During this period in history, animal training was in vogue and a certain Russian psychologist—and dog owner—named Ivan Pavlov was gaining a reputation for teaching the canine set to salivate in response to certain sounds. These animal training fanatics became collectively known as behaviorists and are well known today for their enthusiasm for shaping the behavior of mammals through the administration of pain. Electric current had only recently become available to the average person and behaviorists zealously applied their shocking volts to animals and humans alike.[140] For many victims of shell shock, a disciplinary treatment based on the principles and techniques of animal training was utilized to help alleviate symptoms of hysteria and neurasthenia. A course of treatment would begin with a soldier being kept in isolation and placed on a restricted diet. Esteemed physicians like Lewis Yealland would shout at the patients, left hungry and alone, commanding them to simply abandon their symptoms. If the soldier—now test bunny—did not comply, they would be treated with electric shocks.[141] This was the state of psychology less than one hundred years ago.

The following is a graphic recounting of a four-hour session by Yealland treating a shell-shocked combat soldier who was incapable of speaking.[142] The exchange inspires challenging questions about the nature of shell shock and our current understanding of PTSD:

In the evening he was taken to the electrical room, the blinds were drawn, the lights were turned out, and the doors leading to the room were locked and the keys removed. The only light perceptible was that from the resistance bulbs of the battery. Placing the pad electrode on the lumbar spines and attaching the long pharyngeal electrode, I said to him, "You will not leave this room until you are talking as well as you ever did; no, not before." The mouth was kept open by means of a tongue depressor; a strong faradic current was applied to the posterior wall of the pharynx, and with this stimulus he jumped backwards, detaching the wires from the battery.... [I repeated that] "The doors are locked and the keys are in my pocket. You will leave me when you are cured, remember not before." This evidently made an impression on him, for he pointed to the electrical apparatus and then to his throat. "No," I said, "the time for more electrical treatment has not come. Suggestions are not wanted from you; they are not needed. When the time comes for more electricity you will be given it, whether you wish it or not."

[...] "You are now ready for the next stage of the treatment, which consists of the administration of strong shocks to the outside of the neck; these will be transmitted to your voice box and you will soon say anything you wish in a whisper...." It was not long before he began to whisper the vowels with hesitation.... He... made an attempt to leave the room, and I said firmly to him, "You will leave the room when you were speaking normally...."

I then applied shock after shock to the posterior wall of the pharynx, commanding him each time to say "ah," and in a few minutes he repeated "ah" in expiration. When he was able to repeat the days of the week, months of the year, and numbers he became very pleased and was again quite ready to leave me. I said, "Remember there is no way out except by the return of the proper voice and the door. You have one key, I have the other; when you talk properly I shall open the door so that you can go back to bed." With a smile [the man] stammered, "I believe you have both keys—go and finish me up."[143]

Granted, the description of this sadomasochistic scene sends chills up the spine, but what intrigues me most about Yealland's methods is that they actually worked! Yealland's session with the soldier would appear to endorse the mimetic model of trauma in which the zombie captain of the soldier's ship assists in the pirate hijacking of his vessel. It seems far-fetched to imagine the soldier was consciously aware that he was restricting the use of his voice box given the electrifying torture to which he was subject—not to mention the persistent shame and humiliation of being labeled a mental patient by the military and his comrades. If this premise is, in fact, valid, then a number of fascinating propositions about traumatic memory are implied:

1. There was never any actual damage to the physiological functioning of the soldier's voice box.
2. The conditions of fright that trigger bodily dysfunction are sufficient in themselves to allow for the nervous system to, in effect, "cut off power" to particular parts of the body.
3. Yealland, by virtue of his power over the traumatized soldier, is able to bend the psychological will of his patient and effect changes on the bodily tissues responsible for producing speech.

Physician Joseph Babinski, a former neurology student at Salpêtrière Hospital, had claimed many years earlier that the cases of hysteria put on exhibit during the course of his clinical training "did not arise spontaneously from the patient's conditions, but were the product of external influences vis-a-vis Charcot's own unintended suggestion, mimicry among patients, the intentional and unintentional manipulation of patients by Charcot's staff." Babinski maintained that "symptoms of hysteria are products of suggestion and suggestibility. This disorder is simply a set of symptoms that can be removed by counter-suggestion."[144] If Babinski is correct—and I believe he is—Yealland's cattle prod was effective but not necessary.

Thankfully, most cases of shell shock were not treated with electric shock. Many men were sent out to farms to rest and recuperate. A few small hospitals cropped up to address the needs of the most severely affected cases, where the prescription for care involved rest, playing sports, and gardening. However, the bulk of World War I veterans suffering from shell shock received no treatment whatsoever, with most left with no option other than to accept the shame of the dominant medical perspective and to endure the rest of their lives blaming themselves for having "lost their nerve" on the field of battle.

Chapter 5

Every Man Has His Breaking Point

I was very young—perhaps five or six years old—when I realized my father had killed people. I knew he had been part of the Army Corps of Engineers, but topics like these were seldom referenced and weren't discussed in any detail. I was never told any stories or anecdotes to flesh out the details of his service. The only material evidence of this period in his life was a wooden chest that was kept in the unfinished part of our basement. On the handful of evenings this imaginarium was unearthed by my father, my half-sister, Barbara, and I would stand to the side and watch with guarded fascination as one creepy item of memorabilia after the next was carefully unpacked.

Lurking inside was an enormous red Nazi flag alongside something called a potato masher or *stielhandgranate*, a hand-crafted-looking German grenade with a wooden handle and metal base that looked like, well, a potato masher.[145] Oscar had also kept an olive-green American grenade that always reminded me of the shells of the Teenage Mutant Ninja Turtles. We were assured these munitions were inactive, but I couldn't help but imagine our house being blown to bits as I grasped my teddy bear to my chest while lying tucked away in my bunk bed upstairs.

My father's chest also contained a small stack of glossy black-and-white photos. The surprisingly scrawny young men in the pictures were

very different from the muscular frame of my G.I. Joe action figures—
their passion for cigarettes was unmistakable. Captured in unidentifiable,
often barren rural settings, with neat, squared-off tents lining the
landscape, the expression of these men, barely matured beyond
adolescence, appeared oddly relaxed given their dire circumstances.

How Much Can a Human Being Endure?

Having been driven by the necessity to maintain a robust fighting force
during World War I, scientific investigation into shell shock and
psychological trauma all but ceased with the signing of the Treaty of
Versailles. The outbreak of World War II twenty years later would
rekindle research into trauma and replace "shell shock" and "soldier's
heart" with less poetic, more utilitarian terms like "combat exhaustion"
and "battle fatigue." In World War II, military officials demonstrated a
greater willingness to acknowledge the reality that "psychiatric casualties
are as inevitable as gunshot and shrapnel wounds."[146] The fears provoked
by the lethal dangers of combat were even recognized by many
commanders to exact a toll far greater than the physical and technical
rigors of war. While the emotional strains of battle garnered greater
recognition during World War II, the fact remained that soldiers were
still expected to get back out there and fight.

During World War II, the U.S. Army even adopted the slogan "Every
Man Has His Breaking Point," with inductees being shown training films
depicting dramatized scenes of combat exhaustion.[147] In 1941, noted
psychoanalyst Harry Stack Sullivan joined the U.S. Selective Service with
the intention of creating a screening process that would prevent the
large-scale recurrence of psychiatric cases that had plagued the military
during World War I. Sullivan created these tools based on his premise
that many of the psychological issues experienced by soldiers during
World War I were dispositional in nature. He reasoned that people who
already had difficulty adjusting in mainstream society would not hold
up under the rigors of the military. [148] Although Sullivan's screenings
excluded over two million recruits (or 12% of all men examined), rates

of psychiatric cases were actually *double* that of World War I (which had excluded only 2% of recruits for psychiatric reasons).[149] The Army was, as they say, "not amused" by the dismal performance of Sullivan's screening tools. In a highly public dressing down, Sullivan—and by extension, the entire psychiatric establishment—was severely criticized for the failure of these screenings. Responding to this debacle and under rising pressure to beef up manpower, General George Marshall eliminated the screenings in 1944.[150]

Compared to their British counterparts (who were given four days of rest every two months), American ground troops were pushed longer and harder, remaining in combat for an average of eighty consecutive days. Regardless of the amount of rest they were given, half of all troops were killed, wounded, captured, or missing after only *four months* in action. Over the course of World War II, 1.3 million American soldiers were treated for battle fatigue, with a whopping 37% of *all* ground troops being discharged for psychological reasons. Peak effectiveness for soldiers was found to be attained at the three-month mark. However, after fewer than five months in action, commanders recognized that most soldiers became so "jittery and overcautious" as to be rendered "completely ineffective." And these were not just "weak" men who broke down after their first battle; even the most capable and enthusiastic soldiers became so worn down that they became liabilities to their regiments and the greater morale. PTSD, as of yet, was not a term anyone knew.

While their fellow citizens stayed home and debated what the right course of action was, for the average World War II foot soldier, abstract political principles like the defeat of fascism or the plight of the Jews provided little motivation in their daily struggle to survive. When homes and families are oceans away, finding meaning in the rhetoric of government bureaucrats doesn't come easy. Interviews with American veterans of World War II reveal that fidelity to fellow members of the unit and "making it out alive" were, for most, the primary motivation to fight. Consequently, "the most destructive influence... more powerful than a wound to the body, is the loss of a comrade or a respected commanding officer."[151]

It is a fundamental reality of the military that a soldier's individuality is yielded to the larger functioning of the group. Or, as a commission of military psychiatrists asserted in 1945, "the group life *is* the soldier's inner life."[152] During wartime, this group life is experienced as an existence involving shared "deprivations," coupled with "a string of engagements with the enemy, incidents of narrow escapes, fatigue, hunger, incessant danger, no pause to recuperate."[153] In this daily fight for survival, even loyalty to the greater chain of command can become an empty and meaningless concept. In fact, many World War II veterans described a deep resentment for being subject to the whims of an inept and callous leadership, all the while being made to feel like an insignificant cog in a brutal military machine.[154]

My father had volunteered to be a soldier with the hope of securing for himself a more favorable position than what might have otherwise awaited him if he'd been drafted. The Engineering Corps suited his skills in construction and theoretically offered a glancing bit of cover when compared with the fate of frontline infantrymen. By the time he landed on D-Day, Oscar had already been in the military for two years, first training in Wyoming and then biding his time in Britain as American troop levels built up for the invasion of Europe. Oscar never described the details of his experience on D-Day, even when we visited Omaha Beach, the site where he had landed. Exploring the abandoned German bunkers—with their bird's-eye view of the beach below—was more than enough to fill my twelve-year-old imagination with a sense of the carnage that took place that day. The nearby military cemeteries housed endless rows of ghostly white crosses standing in silent memoriam to the tens of thousands of American soldiers killed in Normandy during World War II. The display was a sobering reminder of just how lucky my father was to have survived.

It might seem weird that he would allude to his trauma at the end of a disaster movie, but remain silent at the very spot where his wartime experiences commenced. However, that's typically how dissociative experiences manifest—they exist in feelings, sensations, and fragments. Without an appropriate facilitator to help guide a trauma survivor through these destabilizing roadblocks, the person can remain frozen in time—perpetually replaying these events in a realm absent the cohesion necessary to share their experiences in words.

Historians generally agree that the Army's coordination of the early morning landing at Omaha Beach was a complete mess. Boats drifted off target. Troops were deposited into chilly, waist-deep water—each weighed down with heavy packs, boots, and weapons. Men had to trudge through strong currents and along sandbars for 100 yards before even making it to shore. In some stretches, the beach was up to 200 yards wide, allowing plenty of time for wave after wave of young men to be deftly mowed down by German machine guns and artillery.[155] Bullets traveling faster than the speed of sound ripped their victims apart before the hiss of their approach could even be detected. Most who survived the initial landing were pinned down all day, unable to move, waiting to be blown to bits by mortar fire. The task of engineers like my father that day was to help land jeeps, tanks, and artillery onto the beach. The infantry was supposed to provide cover to the engineers, but many of the boats ferrying these servicemen landed off target. The units who managed to survive had difficulty regrouping on the beach, leaving the engineers to defend themselves while somehow trying to carry out their mission.[156]

In a sign of the growing public acknowledgment of the psychological wounds of war, *Life* magazine featured an article on combat fatigue accompanied by a copy of a painting by wartime illustrator Tom Lea, entitled "The 2,000-Yard Stare." The image is of a haunted-looking Marine, his gaze at once vacant and intent, his expression conveying great weariness and emotional detachment from the surrounding horrors.[157] Of his subject, Lea commented, "I noticed a tattered Marine... staring stiffly at nothing. His mind had crumbled in battle... his eyes were like two black empty holes in his head...."[158] He added, "Last evening he came down out of the hills. Told to get some sleep, he found a shell crater and slumped into it.... First light has given his gray face an eerie color. He left the States 31 months ago. He was wounded in his first campaign. He has tropical diseases.... He half sleeps at night and gouges Japs out of holes all day. Two-thirds of his company has been killed or wounded... How much can a human being endure?"[159]

During World War II, "cracking up" and "browned off" were two terms used by soldiers to describe men who collapsed under the stress of combat. Those who "cracked" under the pressure were characterized by one wartime physician as "a very weary, dirty and disheveled man sitting with his head in his hands, trembling and jerking muttering over and over, 'shells and tanks, shells and tanks.'"[160] Often, soldiers had to be "strapped down fighting and struggling, attempting to dig in the ground." This was not just exhaustion, but rather a clinical disorder with recognizable stages of progression. During stage one, soldiers were noted to experience increased irritability and sleep problems, often feeling "angry and disgusted with everything—especially the Army;" during stage two there would be a general slowing of thought and physical movement. The soldier might isolate and lose interest in the world, becoming emotionally flat and increasingly dependent on others. Those soldiers experiencing stage two symptoms might also demonstrate confusion, disorientation, and poor judgment along with excessive talking and smoking. Often, tremors and GI problems would accompany these discomforts; during stage three, soldiers were known to "take dangerous chances... run aimlessly about..." engaging in "uncontrollable sobbing or screaming or babbling."

Here, a young World War II soldier hospitalized with combat exhaustion addresses his wartime experience—it's not a stretch to imagine my father saying many of the same things if he'd only been given the right help:

> "How a person feels there at the front I can't explain. You go ahead, but it is just because the other fellow goes ahead. You more or less don't want to show him that you are afraid because

he is going ahead and doing the same thing. During the bombardment—especially through the night, a thousand thoughts go through your mind. You don't have much hope of getting back because you see the friends you have lived with for two or three years and see them knocked out. You don't have much hope... You don't get a minute's rest over there. If it isn't shelling, it's air raids. You are never sure of yourself... The snipers in the trees and machine gun nests... we can't even find them they are camouflaged so well... the bomb explodes, you are confused, and you don't even know where they are coming from. They make all kinds of noise to draw your fire. You don't fire for the simple reason that they want to turn the artillery on you."[161]

What must this war have done to my father? He would have been forced under threat of death—or court martial—to murder enemy combatants, perhaps even kill civilians who were acting on behalf of the Nazi regime. I'm sure he would have been highly conflicted, terrified, and repulsed by being forced to commit these murders—veterans regularly report the faces and mangled bodies of the people they have killed are "permanently etched" into their brains. I imagine he would have regularly seen friends—those he was "really" fighting for—die instantly or suffer from their wounds in unimaginable pain. At almost every moment he would have lived in mortal danger, effectively helpless, surrounded by mud, blood, and the mutilated flesh of women, children, and compatriots. Without a sense of agency or control, he would have been forced to follow the orders of commanders (often against his better judgment) that would regularly put his life at risk. Every part of his existence would be marked by deprivation: of food, sleep, comfort, warmth, and security.

Returning home, Oscar's life was severed from the other survivors of his unit as they each returned to towns dispersed across the country. I'm not aware that he spoke to, much less saw, any of these men ever again. Cut off from the only other people who understood his particular, harrowing story, there was virtually no treatment for what was only referenced in whispering asides as "combat fatigue." Soldiers were told it was best to put the ugly history of the war behind them—in short, to forget. As Judith Herman observed, "many warriors returning home have discovered the myth of the warrior and the actual experience of the warrior are two very different things. One is celebrated and the other is not spoken about."[162]

Oscar was guided by the culture of the American postwar economic boom to put his energies into becoming a family man and breadwinner. My father willingly obliged by jumping with both feet into this all-purpose remedy. This was a man who became a successful contractor and an avowed workaholic, building dozens of spec houses up through the 1960s, after which he transitioned to creating the first generation of gas station mini-marts across the Kansas City area.

Beyond these externalities, what was apparent to anyone beyond the casual observer was that his first marriage to Josephine—and the family they created after the war—constituted a deeply troubled household. This fact in itself is unexceptional. The glossy, superficial nature of 1950s American optimism would be revealed when the children of this era began to come of age a decade later. The baby boomers' radical rejection of their parents' values—along with a vibrant counterculture that prioritized authenticity and personal freedoms—would reshape the Western world and make possible the more equitable society we now take for granted.

Still, my father, like legions of men during the 1950s (veteran and non-veteran alike), physically and emotionally abused his wife and four daughters. Belts were the weapon of choice, and old-school, unreflective parenting was the order of the day. Under this model, children were viewed as "troublemakers" who needed to be kept in line with firm discipline, else they would be overcome by improper impulses and bad habits, only to grow into lazy adults with no sense of self-control. Children were made to complete chores to build character, good habits, and self-discipline. During this era, children were often considered "miniature adults," with an adult understanding of the world, capable of complex manipulations and dark motivations. Often, these machinations were just an elaborate excuse for the adults to lose control, scream, and act violently. Many parents needed no excuse to blow up, making up imaginary violations or lashing out with no warning at all. Physically and sexually abusive parents took this emotionally damaging approach to another level, introducing bodily pain and immoral sexual boundary violations into the mix. The famous "wire hanger" scene from the 1981 Joan Crawford biopic, *Mommie Dearest*,[163] has become a camp classic, but there is an authentic truth in this depiction of a drunken, violent episode of physical abuse. These episodes often appear ridiculous to the outside observer precisely because viewers stand outside the drama, unscathed.

Family and material success didn't soothe my father's troubled mind or the damaging effects of his traumatic wartime experiences. In time, I believe he subconsciously came to blame himself for his inability to experience love and fulfillment—instead of understanding that he was experiencing what can only be described as a medical condition. I can picture him now lying restlessly in the silence of the predawn hours, absently watching the minute hand of the bedside alarm clock, his mind inexorably marching ahead, the rising sun bringing him closer and closer to his daily pantomime of hyper-competence at work and at home. All the while, an ever-growing chasm of desperation and panic stalked the fringes of his consciousness. During the daylight hours, the disgraceful shame of these "failings" pierced the surface of Oscar's awareness in moments when he felt his total authority was challenged. The fragility of his ego was like a flashing neon sign—visible to everyone but himself. Yet, these extremes of anger served as a highly effective deterrent to anyone who dared look too long or too closely for the man behind the mask.

During a few of those sleepless nights, I believe my father must have been conscious of his failure to adapt to life after the war. He may have even been aware of his own culpability in the matter. However, I don't think these were ideas that he could hold on to long enough to be of any real use. Instead, he externalized this pain, blaming others for his unhappiness and unstable sense of self. And the harder he worked, the more he became convinced that his family did not sufficiently appreciate his efforts.

• • •

There was actually one Army souvenir that was never consigned to the basement, but was kept in my father's nightstand, under the sets of slick, short-legged nylon pajamas he favored. The Pistole Parabellum is a recoil-operated, semi-automatic handgun first developed for production in 1900. It is commonly referred to as a Luger, after its designer, Georg Luger, the son of an Austrian surgeon.[164] Luger was a reserve cadet in the Army of the Austro-Hungarian Empire and was recognized early on as a good marksman. He was sent to a military firearms school where he first developed his fascination with guns. After leaving the Army, Luger cast about for a few years as an accountant and social club manager before meeting Ferdinand Ritter von Mannlicher, an engineer and small arms designer of wealthy German descent. Their collaboration on gun magazines helped unlock Luger's innate talent for design. Luger would go on to work for two of the top German weapons manufacturers and live long enough to see his namesake firearm become a staple of the Kaiser's army during World War I. In a twist of fate, Luger would die nearly penniless, after his investments in German war bonds became worthless upon the defeat of the Central Powers.[165]

Besides merely cataloguing these details from the life of Georg Luger, I feel an urgency to interrogate and understand the man who created this killing machine. What kind of man was he? What was the nature of his character? Was he a loving family man—dutiful and steadfast—or was he misanthropic, proud, and vain? Was he an early geek, obsessed with the high-tech gadgets of the industrial age?

During the late nineteenth century, Austrian surgeons like Luger's father were of two camps: the first embraced traditional Austrian multiculturalism and the other embraced German nationalism and anti-Semitism. His dealings with and move to Germany suggest an affinity with the latter. Can we assume his son was indoctrinated with the racial hatred that was consuming Germany?

The Luger continued to be produced under the Third Reich during World War II and was a popular trophy for Allied soldiers.[166] The menacingly sleek profile of my father's impeccably designed Luger told more than words ever could speak of quick, brutally efficient death.

I wonder if, in moments of quiet solitude, Georg Luger ever thought about the people who had been murdered by his machines of death—and those they left behind? What would he think of my father's gun and how it would be used decades later? No matter his feelings, nothing Luger could say now would soften the shell shock in everyone's eyes as I entered the hospital the day my mother was shot through the head by his ghastly invention.

Throughout my childhood, New Year's Eve always went more or less the same way. My family would go out to a movie and a nice dinner. We would return home well before midnight, with plenty of time to watch the crowds on television dance the night away to the Guy Lombardo Orchestra at the Waldorf-Astoria in New York City. The tension between my parents would usually begin to swell around the time the ball was being dropped in Times Square, marking only 11pm in our time zone. My mother would sometimes plead, "Oscar, please, no!" in the minutes leading up to our own midnight bacchanal as my father went to his nightstand to retrieve the Luger. By the time I reached my teens, none of us would follow Oscar out the front door anymore to witness his celebratory ritual. Even as a young boy I clearly remember absorbing my mother's trepidation at the sight of my father's childlike glee as he discharged the Luger into the night sky with roaring pops. Every year we were all hoping he'd stop at just one bullet.

Chapter 6

The Daltons

My father built our home on Blue Ridge Boulevard for my mother, Judy, her five-year-old daughter, Barbara, and myself, then a baby. More than a shelter, he conceived the structure as a cradle for his revised family, and I can sense his aims in projecting a fresh, streamlined image to the world through its design and construction. Like Oscar, I also married and became a home-owning parent in middle age, and I now appreciate how milestones like these can arouse a sense of hope and exhilaration for the imagined life ahead. Only a few years prior, my father had returned from work early to find his previous family home in the process of being hurriedly emptied. Expecting lunch, he instead found his wife and four daughters nervously packing their belongings. After twenty-five years of marriage, Josephine was finally leaving him for good. My father reacted violently, as he had done so many times before, but the severing of relationships that was initiated that day would prove to be a permanent feature in his life.

Americans like to cleave to the conceit that we are built with a "reset button," with most reflexively endorsing the idea that with enough grit and determination we can remake ourselves anew irrespective of our knotty predicaments. My own story is filled with ancestors who were drawn ever westward, entranced by these same hopes and dreams. Yet I suspect many of my kin fared far better than we do today when comparing their imagined futures with the reality of how their lives turned out. Living in an antediluvian age predating mass consumerism, our predecessors existed outside the yoke of advertiser-driven fantasies that now dominate nearly every feature of our present-day reality. Expertly crafted images conjuring up idealized perfection and social media posts capturing staged moments of delight now generate a self-perpetuating, fictitious dogma of rebirth that knavishly fuels the engines of capitalism. Our overloaded and embattled psyches are primed by algorithms to generate wishes based on the sweet spot where unattainable illusions intersect with consumer lifestyle products and services. When we fall short of the mark on the treadmill path to our idealized *new* selves, feelings of disappointment and failure inevitably ensue, creating market opportunity to fill the throbbing gap with yet another new fix. What's more, the lives we lead are at best a mixture of good and bad, and our internal critics are ever on the alert, eager to goad us with self-blame for our perceived flaws. Though the general din of media was significantly diminished when my parents threw their respective hats into the ring to embark on a second marriage together, they were nevertheless responding to similar, unrealistic expectations and constraining internal pressures in the daunting work of resetting their own lives.

Seminal changes like marriage and children signal sharp shifts in trajectory, threading new strands of meaning and texture into a life, but we are born only once, Buddhists and Hindus notwithstanding, and my parents' move into our new home was no different. Along with their furnishings and personal possessions, they each shouldered the weight of previous marriages, burdening the promise of the unblemished rooms with an air of precarity. Plump, blonde and blue-eyed like my father, I was the only thing approaching a blank slate to be found in our new home.

Attendant to the freight of my parents' past, there to greet us on the unscuffed front steps was a new piece of baggage, one that concerned the unconventional physical combination my parents presented as a married couple, its load made heavy by the burden of outside appraisal. Our eyes are trained to seek out familiar patterns to help us navigate the ever-changing terrain of the world. When we find things to be in their presumed order, our bodies react with the lucid, automatic responses of muscle memory. But, when faced with a subject that does not fit a preconceived pattern, our minds will naturally pause on the incongruous object and mark it with a sense of disorientation, irritation, and quite often, critical judgment. My parents' uncommon union presented the world with a particular pattern-disrupting conundrum involving a set of mismatched appearances that challenged outsiders' assumptions about age and the presumed chronological stages of life. Simply stated, if your appearance is too far out of sync with said assumptions, your wife can very commonly—and quite often—be mistaken for your daughter.

Though my father may have been feeling young and optimistic on the inside, his countenance betrayed the full measure of his fifty years. By contrast, my mother experienced no such mismatch between internal and external identities while unpacking her belongings at our new house. At the time, she could still count on just two hands—with a few fingers left over—the number of years since she was spotted by her mother racing her red MG convertible against a Triumph driven by her high school classmate, Herky Davenport, on a densely wooded byway at the edge of the city. Her parents were incensed, but this teenage lapse in judgment would come to appear inconsequential next to the events that would play out over the eight years spanning this youthful fit of exuberance and her move into our new house.

In fairness, my mother was far from wild, and my grandparents, Mildred and Hubert, doted on their only child. But they were living at the pinnacle of the 1950s bourgeois mindset, and girls from "good families" could quickly find the course of their lives altered and fates sealed by an even momentary lapse in restraint. If Judy was secretly racing her car during a school day with a boy whose very name suggested awkward, hip-thrusting abandon in a dim corner of a knotty pine-paneled rumpus room, what else might she be up to?

"Pretty is as pretty does" I once overheard my grandmother say in response to some boy talk going on between my sister and her friend.

Like fingers on a hand, each of these five words coalesced into a slap of powerful judgment, forming an invisible red imprint across the face of my teenage sister. I remember feeling grateful this barb was not directed at me, but shocked by a pronouncement that felt so uncharacteristic of my beloved nana. Up until that point, I hadn't been fully aware of this side of my grandmother and the fact that she did not apply her code of conduct equally between her two grandchildren. She never would have said something so unnecessarily judgmental to a grandson, and it now seems relatively certain that my mother, a dark-haired beauty with bright green eyes and a desirable figure, would have regularly heard this same admonition—and much worse—when she was growing up.

My grandmother Mildred was the youngest of nine children whose parents shared with her, as a child, the nugget that they sat down and cried when her presence was first detected in her mother's womb. It's hard to imagine that the flat, lonely landscape of 1920s eastern Kansas, all blacks and whites like the first reel of *The Wizard of Oz*, ever nourished the state's emblematic sunflowers, much less a kewpie doll of a girl like my grandmother. At nineteen, in a daring stroke of impulsivity of a sort that would later draw her rebuke, she eloped with my grandfather and escaped forever her family's death rattle of a farm.

Hubert was an impoverished farm boy who'd managed two years of college on a football scholarship before being dismissed for an injury that left him unable to play. He had stopped using his given name—the more stalwart sounding "Roy"—as soon as he became an adult, although no one would have ever confused him with his father and namesake, Roy Hubert Dalton. Known to everyone in the family as "Pappy," Roy, Sr. was a failed farmer who served out the remainder of his career as a prison guard at Lansing State Penitentiary, a turreted, stone behemoth, where guards acted as overseers to the forced labor of inmates in the prison's coal mine and farm fields.[167] Diligently malevolent, Pappy brought his work home, tormenting his wife and two children with his abusive words and violent hand.

While the main floor of my childhood home existed in a time warp of 1960s chinoiserie driven largely by my father's tastes, my mother was

92

given free rein to fashion the rooms of the finished basement below into something of a museum that housed well-curated, quaint displays of artifacts from the lives of her ancestors. Compared to the Lewises, the Daltons were a treasury of folklore and family memorabilia. At the time, no one, including myself, ever thought it strange that my mother displayed Pappy's wooden billy club, still rock hard from his days as a guard, on the wall of our downstairs rec room, among the other, more charming keepsakes.

After eloping, my grandparents set up home in Depression-era Kansas City, seventy miles from Linn County, where they had both been raised. By that time, Kansas City had grown significantly from its early days as a crossroads of trails and river landings. The city had transformed itself into a center for processing cattle just off the Chisholm Trail from Texas and as a hub for the management of the historically unprecedented amounts of grain and produce being cultivated in the region. These businesses were highly profitable, but their decidedly unglamorous nature left citizens branded with a congenital self-consciousness at our image as a "cow town" on the national stage. Though these industries are much changed today, just scratch below the surface of any Kansas Citian's default boosterism—mine included—and you will taste the flavor of wounded pride.

In the decade before my grandparents married, giant automobile plants and steel mills named after English industrial Midland cities like Leeds and Manchester had sprung up in the undeveloped land between Independence and Kansas City, populating this once bucolic gap and knitting together a metropolitan community. The young couple first settled in the blue-collar neighborhoods surrounding these plants, my grandfather returning home with holes burnt into his coveralls from sparks that would spray off molten ore as it was poured into molds— after having earned "25 and a half cents an hour" (about $5 in today's currency)—for his labor at Sheffield Steel.

As my grandparents struggled to find a foothold in the early years of their marriage, their poverty afforded them inspiration and a path forward in their embrace of President Roosevelt's progressive policies. Their growing interest in social welfare opened doors to new friendships, leading them both to a lifelong involvement in Democratic politics and labor policy. Hubert took night classes at the local university and remade himself into an influential union representative, helping to negotiate deals with steel corporations during the height of their industrial power. I still feel great pride in the values engendered in this part of my grandparents' story and in their determination to bring dignity and fair reward to the lives of countless poor and working-class families for the first time in history.

Mildred and Hubert's meager finances forced them to wait for seven years to start a family, and when my mother finally did arrive in 1940, complications from her birth nearly killed my grandmother. They were cautioned not to press for more children at the risk of an even worse outcome. And so, my mother would remain an only child.

About ten years ago, I had a small metal tin of 8-millimeter film my grandfather had shot during my mother's childhood transferred to a DVD. I had never seen these images before, and the first time I watched, I was shocked and delighted that a clip had survived of my young mother performing a dance routine on the front porch of her grandparents' home. Watching Judy's determined, awkward moves in a pink, tulle-fringed costume my grandmother had surely made by hand, I immediately welled up with emotion at the feelings of love she would have elicited in those watching her that day. I know it sounds a bit pretentious, but witnessing my mother's plump, young flesh alive, with blood and nerves pulsing beneath, it's not an exaggeration to say that I am reminded of similar figures brought to life in works by Michelangelo. Yet this child was infinitely more valuable and life-sustaining to my grandparents than any old master painting.

Parents with multiple children are said to love their progeny with unequaled ferocity, but only children, like my mother, Judy, and my own daughter, Gemma, encapsulate a fragile totality for parents that is encompassed in a form both vulnerable and powerful—their young owners with but a hint of the life yet to come. Today, I can easily unearth this time capsule moment of my mother with the push of a button, though I seldom do. While it's comforting to be reassured that my mother experienced the profound happiness of being a beloved child, my omniscience regarding the full scope of her life robs me of the overarching sense of promise those watching her in person that day must surely have felt.

A few years after this film was made, my grandparents moved their small family from the working-class east side of Kansas City to an area known as the Country Club District so that my mother could finish her education at the city's best public schools. With dreamy names like Stratford Gardens and Sunset Hill, this collection of green, leafy neighborhoods is centered around a commercial district locally referred to as the "Plaza." The Plaza, an attractive, but bizarre mirage on the architecturally stodgy Kansas City landscape, is a Spanish/Moroccan-designed mash-up that was fast becoming the heart of the city's social life during the 1950s, a period that saw downtown's vitality being siphoned off along the paths of freshly poured concrete highways and into new bedroom communities like the one I would later inhabit on Blue Ridge Boulevard.

My grandparents raised my mother in a handsome, two-story stucco Craftsman in an area known as Brookside. The family now wore nice clothes from upscale department stores, but my grandfather gained a great deal of weight from the stress of his union work, and my grandmother was often left to parent alone because Hubert's work forced him to constantly travel. Completing the household during this period was my grandmother's widowed mother, a cocker spaniel named Cookie, and two TWA airline hostesses who rented the extra bedrooms—giving a sense of the family's tenuous hold on their improved circumstances.

During the 1950s and '60s, my grandparents' role in Democratic party politics reached a series of consequential pinnacles that found the two of them regularly attending national conventions, inaugurations, and teas where they met presidents and other luminaries of the era.

Hubert was made an honorary state Colonel—a specious designation smacking of Dixie-style plutocracy—that came complete with a handsome uniform featuring gold epaulets and an ornate, peaked cap. Tripping over the avalanches of snow that made the sidewalks of Washington, D.C., all but impassable during the week of the Kennedy inauguration, my nana would later regale us with the story of how she had chuckled to herself every time a confused serviceman, unable to place the elaborate uniform, saluted my grandfather just to be on the safe side. Evidently, each time this happened, Hubert snapped to attention to return these salutes with the forced gravity only a civilian in disguise could muster.

These events added highlights to my grandmother's calendar, but they were the exception, rather than the rule of the day. In reality, her time was mostly spent scrubbing, cleaning, and vacuuming her house. Throughout her life, Mildred would work constantly to keep her home in spotless, perfect order. Clothes were washed in a gyrating tub, with each item individually cranked through wringers to squeeze out excess water before being carefully pinned on a line to dry. Everything was ironed—including sheets. Though she was a good cook and enjoyed our smiles of appreciation over her Thanksgiving dinners, preparing food was essentially another household chore for my nana. Nowadays, people crave an open floor plan with their homes configured around the kitchen, but for my grandmother's generation, kitchens were cramped spaces located in the back of houses, out of view. Fine cuisine was the domain of male chefs in expensive restaurants. Cooking for "housewives" was never elevated to the level of artisan craft reflecting a person's individual flair, no matter how hard these women toiled.

Guests were hosted in formal living and dining rooms where meals and parties became an opportunity to showcase your "ideal" home and family. Social gatherings were also a pretext for a demonstration of a woman's polished style for guests to reaffirm through their compliments and superficial banter. During the 1950s, it was the norm for liberal amounts of free-flowing cocktails to loosen social constraints, and conservative, churchgoing Midwesterners certainly did their part to fill out the ranks of the inebriated. However, Midwesterners are relatively private by nature and more likely to sequester their heaviest drinking away from the prying eyes of neighbors and colleagues—keeping loosened tongues, and the deeper, more personal bonds they might have otherwise forged, off the table.

In any event, Mildred and Hubert were Presbyterian teetotalers, a habit that must have surely helped my grandmother to remain focused as she performed her duties as hostess. Mildred was never able to afford outside help like the wealthier women who lived nearby; however, the same appearance of "effortless grace" these women purchased to facilitate their entertainment extravaganzas was publicly demanded of middle-class women like my grandmother.

Life itself, especially for women, was an event where one publicly enacted the style and mores of the social class to which you aspired. While their husbands could gain outside recognition and prestige from their careers, for most women, the sole route to social acceptance was a path paved with exacting attention to appearances and good manners. These self-conscious rituals were particularly effective at masking the insecurities of women like my grandmother—many only a few years removed from hardscrabble, dirt-poor farms like her own. Sadly, the trade-off of pretense for authenticity left many women feeling isolated, judged, and acutely self-critical of their perceived shortcomings.

For girls like my mother, good manners meant restraining yourself and subsuming your impulses. You were to obey the wishes of others. My nana's taunt to my teenage sister, Barbara, those many years later was a call to fall in line with this patriarchal social contract—tantamount to labeling her a slut for acting outside the prescribed code. Luckily, these conventions were beginning to lose a bit of their traction by the time my sister was growing up, but when my mother was a teenager, this perspective represented her only reality. Navigating the scent of sex and the potential loss of a daughter's chance of making a good match are typical refrains for many parents, even today. While the drumbeat of expectations for women sounded more loudly during my mother's youth, I think it was my grandparents' unease with the affluence that surrounded them and their self-consciousness about their own backgrounds that made them even more critical of my mother than they really should have been.

Girls like Judy were raised to be hostesses, maids, cooks, and emotional caretakers to their families. Within these confines, my mother's meager experiments in speed, on the road in her MG convertible, and in her life in general, would remain limited to a handful of impassioned decisions made in her late teens and early twenties. Like nearly all young women growing up prior to the 1970s, she would fall captive to just a few of these impetuous choices and respond with ready compliance as events took on a velocity of their own—constraining her for the remainder of her life, like a butterfly pinned to a mat in a shadow box.

Chapter 7

The Stone Heart

"To the woman he said: 'I will sharply increase your pain
in childbirth; in pain you will bring forth children. Your desire
will be for your husband, and he will rule over you.'"
–Genesis 3:16[168]

"Auuuuuh" was the first word my father ever said to my mother. While
not strictly a word, it was a sound my father often made akin to the
irritating noise kids used to make to indicate that their listener is stupidly
missing an obvious point. Oscar would frequently offer this utterance to
the world, not as a sigh of pain, but as a bland placeholder that would
vary in length, depending on how long he needed to think about his
response to your question. This annoying habit of speech had the
unintended effect of making its speaker appear none too bright, a
condition that was exacerbated by the fact that the sound was typically
accompanied by a slack-jawed facial expression and a disturbing blankness
behind his eyes.

My mother, fresh out of secretarial school, was cold-calling employers
from the Yellow Pages. She had spurred this monosyllabic retort with a
hopeful query about possible work my father might have at his
construction company. Inauspicious as this first exchange may have

been, each of our lives can be traced to similar moments of random conjunction. Nonetheless, it seems extraordinary that from this seemingly innocuous, single decision point, the whole of my existence —and my parents' ultimate fate—tumbled forward.

At twenty-three, Judy was already four years into her marriage to her first husband, Mitchell, and the mother of my three-year-old half-sister, Barbara. There had been a large church wedding followed by a small first apartment. At around the same time Judy and Mitchell were first beginning to plumb the briny depths of the seas of matrimony, my grandparents had helped the young couple purchase a red, barn-themed split level in one of the newly built suburbs of Independence. Though my mother had the unfortunate habit of oversharing with me, even as a child, I don't remember her ever mentioning her reasons for marrying Mitchell.

The two had met at Southwest High, and at the outset, their two-year age difference must have made Mitchell appear quite mature in comparison to my fifteen-year-old mother. They would continue to "go steady" until soon after my mother graduated, after which, Mitchell proposed. Did they decide to marry based on love or merely momentum? Many of Judy's sorority girlfriends had also paired off at around the same age, and by age nineteen, a few of her peers had already married their high school sweethearts.[169] Judy's decision to follow suit was likely made without a great deal of painstaking reflection on serious alternatives like going to college, building a career, or becoming a free-thinking beatnik.

While she must have seen something romantic in her relationship with Mitchell, in her later retellings, all that remained was an acute sense of disillusionment and frustration with her ex-husband's immaturity. Offenses cited—that were appropriate for the ears of children— included calling in sick when he "only had a cold," and eating ice cream from a bowl that he would rest on his chest as he sat slouching on the couch. Translation? Mitchell was not sufficiently ambitious for my mother—less kind interpretations would involve the adjective "lazy." Theirs was the type of breakup where the ex-husband's face is hastily hacked out of the pictures in the family photo album.

It's a telling measure of her naivete that she would have expected so much more out of this young man. It's not as though he were some vile or criminal nogoodnik, but from the start, nothing in Mitchell's story would have suggested an enterprising future. His family was not well off. He didn't attend college and had no clear career path. He was... ahem... "blue collar." Taking into consideration my grandparents' pretensions, Mitchell was an even darker horse. Judy had dated a few of the wealthier boys in high school and had once pointed out to me the enormous, mock-Tudor style mansion of one early suitor. He had gone so far as to present her with a delicate silver "going steady" ring that was kept, until the day she died, in an embroidered satin pouch in the top drawer of her bureau. Riding past the impressive pile where my mother's teenage beau once lived along the manicured path of Ward Parkway (Kansas City's answer to Sunset Boulevard), I couldn't help but ask myself, "What went wrong?"

Like many children, I imagined that a life of immense wealth also equaled a life of great happiness and satisfaction. At the time, it was a secret thrill to picture myself living in mock-Tudor splendor, cared for by my imaginary father. This man would invariably take the shape of an age-appropriate, college-educated, country club member (with great hair) who held an important position at some downtown concern. In this version of life, I envisioned for my mother an existence filled with chummy lady friends who luncheoned together on the Plaza, all the while sharing tips about how to improve their backhands and planning charity balls for the Kansas City Philharmonic over white wine spritzers. However, aside from all these trappings, what I truly wanted for my mother was an unwavering peace of mind—no tears of desperation streaming down her damp, twisted face as I watched her once again lose the daily battle to please my implacable father.

Even from this childlike point of view, I recognized that on paper, my mother had the raw materials to construct a far happier life for herself than the tense, constricted existence we shared as a family. When I was a teenager, my grandmother once made a comment in passing about my mother's "low self-esteem." To my inexpert ears this evaluation had the ring of a clinically based psychological assessment, far different from the off-the-cuff criticisms she normally made. What's more, this appraisal implied a problem that was not speculative or conditional, as in "she seems to have low self-esteem," but rather a diagnosed character trait known to all but myself. My grandmother must have *also* puzzled over why Judy had not been able to build a happier life for herself and had stumbled on this pseudo-psychological understanding to explain her daughter's troubled situation. Nevertheless, I doubt my grandmother would have seen the role of her own judgments and criticisms in this riddle as anything other than encouragement for her daughter—certainly not the undermining agent they represented.

Judy was, at best, an average student, but she was sweet, thoughtful, and funny. She obviously didn't come from a highly educated family or a line of deep-pocketed, would-be bürgermeisters like Kansas City regularly churned out during the first half of the twentieth century. I now understand that most boys who come from a legacy of mock-Tudor mansions most often look to marry girls with a similar pedigree—so who's to say what my mother's chances at a life of even greater privilege ever actually were? A husband with a high-paying, white-collar career certainly wouldn't have assured Judy a ticket to greater happiness—but from this vantage point, it's hard to imagine a worse outcome than the union she shared with my father.

Though it's tempting to conflate some of my own childhood priorities with my mother's, I don't think wealth and its perks were ever a serious goal for Judy. Moreover, I never got the sense that my mother ever felt comfortable in the world of mock-Tudor mansions. I don't think it was by accident that she ended up living her adult life in the homier, blue-collar environs of the east side of Kansas City. Sure, low self-esteem might have been a factor in all of this, but there was much more below the surface.

Regardless of her true aims, an unambitious husband like Mitchell had not been in the home-ec manual for girls like my mother—nor was paid work outside the home. In the year following my sister's birth, Judy began to feel more and more troubled by the picture that was beginning to emerge of a life spent in an ongoing struggle just to attain a bare-bones, middle-class standard of living. To help make ends meet, she took a job in retail, working for Harzfeld's, a purveyor of fine women's clothes where she and my grandmother had been customers for years. Judy later attended secretarial school, learning the basics of typing and shorthand, my nana caring for my baby sister during the long days my mother was kept away from hearth and home.

At the time he received that first call from my mother, Oscar had been married for twenty-five years and was the father of four. Sarah, Kay, and Gail were all adolescents, tightly clustered in age, with Tammy, still a toddler, rounding out the family unit. The family lived in a house my father had built almost ten years earlier on Blue Ridge Boulevard, only a quarter mile to the north from where he would later construct our mid-century modern home.

I seriously doubt the first time my parents met in the flesh they would have glimpsed the future in one another's eyes, but I am certain Oscar would have been instantly attracted to Judy. She was tall, with a curvaceous frame reminiscent of actor Christina Hendricks and her character Joan from *Mad Men*. Naturally, she was hired on. The comparisons to the fictional mid-century advertising agency Sterling Cooper unequivocally end here. My father's construction company was small—a typical day would find him traveling among various job sites, checking in on his crew's progress, and returning to the office in the late afternoons to deal with paperwork and phone calls. The office was a simple two-room affair—the secretary's desk was located in the waiting room near the entryway with a single door connecting my mother's domain to my father's inner sanctum.

It would be many more years before the perfumed-scented title of "secretary"—and its implication of female youth, subordination, and compliance—would be overtaken by the term "administrative assistant" with its reek of organizational flow charts and gender-neutrality. Visitors to my father's office were few and far between, and the secretary was the only other person who worked on site. There is no doubt who made the first move.

At first, there was probably just a well-placed hand and lingering eye contact; later, furtive, fumbling hands; doors locked; unhooking and unzipping; the releasing of inhibitions and flesh for a few moments; the thrill of the forbidden; post-coital awkwardness giving way to routine comfort in one another's company; cycle thrown off by the newly introduced "pill"; missed period; anxiety; swelling abdomen becoming increasingly apparent to all; abortion illegal, dangerous; confusion; promises?

I don't think it would be accurate to say the liaisons that would later develop into a relationship represented a sign of midlife crisis for my father—I believe he existed in a state of perpetual crisis throughout his life. Oscar's new secretary was just six years older than his eldest daughter and exactly half his age. My mother liked to joke that my father had gone off to fight in World War II so he would "have something to do" while she was in kindergarten. Growing up, I found it hilarious that my mother had once been my father's secretary. I used to make jokes about Oscar chasing Judy around his desk just so I could see them squirm. Even as a child, it wasn't difficult to discern that just below the surface, my mother was embarrassed about the circumstances of my birth. But, by God, she tried to put a good face on it—even in her attempts to explain away the fact that Oscar was at Mardi Gras when I was born ("He couldn't have stayed away otherwise"). She would reassure me in those moments that the two had "always planned to have me," but "just not quite so soon." She needn't have worried—I've always felt grateful just to be here— though it would be just as easy to view the very fact of my existence as the bedrock of parents' disastrous marriage and subsequent deaths.

It's not hard to see what Judy and Oscar came to see in one another after the first flush of passion had subsided. Like yin and yang, she wanted a stable breadwinner, and he needed a woman to run his home. Even so, I think it's hard to imagine just how unusual divorce was at that time. While today's national rate hovers around 50%,[170] in 1965, the rate was just 9%,[171] and I think it's safe to say that in the highly conservative

Midwest, the number was much, much lower. No one in Mildred and Hubert's circle would have children divorce for at least another ten years. At first, my grandparents shamed and rejected Judy when she told them she was leaving Mitchell, but seen in another light, Oscar did "fix" many of the financial challenges presented by my mother's first marriage. And after all, my father could have dropped Judy when she became pregnant (though I've often wondered if my being his first male child—after an unbroken line of daughters—had something to do with his decision to marry my mother). Even still, I imagine my grandparents must have despised Oscar, a grown man only a few years their junior, getting his —very young and very married—secretary pregnant. Yet for as much time as we all spent together as a family over the ensuing years, I never heard my grandparents once say a bad word about my father—no matter how abominably he behaved. I wish they had.

When I was eight months old, my parents were married by a judge friend in the old Independence Courthouse, a nineteenth-century Georgian centerpiece of the original town square. My grandfather was the only family member present in chambers during the brief ceremony. My nana was waiting outside, keeping my sister and me quiet. A small family dinner—with only my mother's family in attendance—followed at the Golden Ox, a "nice" steakhouse among the Kansas City stockyards.

At the time they married, my parents' lies were running at a pretty good clip; Mitchell had been led to believe that he was my father. For many years I carried his surname on my birth certificate. The lies kept coming until I was nearly six years old. My sister Barbara and I would spend every other weekend with Mitchell and his new wife, Anna, because my mother was rightly terrified that her ex-husband might fight for sole custody of my sister if he ever learned that he was not, in fact, my father. From as far back as I can remember, I was told the truth—as was Barbara—that Oscar was *my* father. How we were able to keep that secret at such a young age, I cannot answer.

At last, a needle was inserted into my scrawny arm. The blood extracted, undisputed proof of Oscar's paternity. My visits with Mitchell and Anna were immediately terminated. Though I was made to believe that Mitchell was the enemy, these visits had been my reality. While I was relieved at my parents' obvious delight that my custody was settled, I was also saddened by the loss of these visits. I would not wake up to see the light filtering through my navy-colored curtains imprinted with rocket ships or see my group of friends from that neighborhood ever again. Soon thereafter, there was more family court for my half-sister, which culminated in a termination of Mitchell's paternal rights. Oscar then legally adopted Barbara. By the mid-1970s we were a family of four, unmolested by outside forces.

Clearly, Judy and Oscar fought by hook or by crook to make the transition to their "new" lives, and I think these experiences left them both feeling like they had a lot to prove to the world. I imagine my parents' hyper-conscious attention to appearances—including the image projected by our new house—was a means by which they attempted to ballast their severely listing worlds. It all had to look perfect. To appear older than her years, my mother soon began wearing her hair in elaborate configurations, held in place with liberal amounts of hairspray applied during weekly visits to JoAnne's beauty shop.

The extreme shifts in my parents' lives (not to mention their twenty-three-year age difference) appear to have alienated their few friends and acquaintances. They were dropped by most. My mother finally stopped having her remaining friends around for fear they would witness my father's angry outbursts, thus compounding the shame she felt for her newfound role as a victim of abuse. These circumstances eventually led to a state of social isolation that would become chronic only a few years into their marriage. It only made sense that my parents would hide out in their new house, focusing exclusively on raising my sister and myself.

Judy, like her mother, would become a gold medal Olympian of housekeeping—a highly skilled organizer and cleaner of rooms, a champion washerwoman and gardener par excellence. I've always imagined the superficial perfection of our home gave my mother a satisfied sense of efficient productivity that she was otherwise only able to experience in caring for my sister and myself. Besides, housekeeping at least allowed her to feel she was in control of *something*. Over the years, these routines would naturally become wearying, constricting, and dull. Like many wives, Judy was not allowed to "meddle" in our family's finances or to work outside the home. Like many abusive husbands, my father used economic dependency as a means of controlling his wife. My mother once defied this decree by secretly taking a job at a clothing store at the nearby mall. Oscar completely lost it when he found out—"You think I can't support us?" and "You go behind my back to do something like *this*?" Judy soon caved. She would grow into a nervous talker, never comfortable with silence, constantly narrating the minutiae of daily living to a level that I would come to find excruciating. Cleaning and talking. These were the only coping tools available to my mother.

• • •

As a child, it would never have occurred to me to apply the word "abuse" to the fits of rage Oscar used to control my family, but I instinctively understood that his self-serving manipulations kept us constantly fearful and completely under his control. Consequently, the emotional tenor of the house would vary wildly depending on whether he was home. Judy, Barbara, and myself could all breathe freely in the afternoons before his return from work. After school, unmolested by dark energies, I remember contentedly watching reruns of *Gilligan's Island* and *Bewitched* or playing in the backyard with my dogs, an Old English sheepdog named Reggie and a black terrier mutt named Sparky.

As Oscar's 6pm return from work loomed closer, the atmosphere of the house would begin to shift. The instant I heard the garage door begin its ascent, I would beat a retreat to my bedroom, erasing all evidence of my most recent activities so my father would not realize I was fleeing his presence. Then, I would exit my bedroom (as if I had been hanging out there all along) to greet him with a kiss on the cheek—only to make my escape back to my bedroom as quickly as possible. I have no idea which of my parents instructed us to greet my father at the door with a kiss on the cheek, but I do remember this was a chore that was not to be questioned. This ritual was repeated every night before I went to bed, except it took place as my father sat on the couch, stinking of tobacco, an ashtray piled with unfiltered Camel butts on the nearby table. Sometimes he would respond to my kiss by furiously pinching my bottom and telling me, "Don't let the bedbugs bite." It somehow never seemed odd that he never gave me a kiss in return.

Upon his return from work, a VO on the rocks ("with a splash of water") would be waiting for Oscar on the kitchen counter. My mother didn't drink, and she never joined my father as he sipped his Canadian whiskey while reading his newspaper or sifting through the mail in the family room. During the half-hour lead-up to dinner, my mother would remain in the kitchen, holding her breath against a foul mood or heated outburst as she completed our dinner preparations. Though my father often drank more than he should, this is not the story of an alcoholic. VO was only one of an ever-expanding universe of catalysts for his rage. It somehow seems more intentional—and sadder—that he didn't really need alcohol to unleash his anger. If this had been the case, we could have at least imagined his motives to be fogged by drunkenness, offering a ray of hope that Oscar's extremes of emotion could in some way be limited to times when he was under the influence.

Even behind my bedroom door, I was never completely relaxed when my father was around. A portion of my awareness was always tuned to the timbre and volume of my parents' voices coming from the other side of the wall as I busied myself with some distraction. If I heard my father's raised voice and my mother's pleading pitch during the cocktail period, there would be a sickening feeling in my stomach and a jangly sense of adrenaline as it coursed through my limbs in anticipation of my unshielded exposure to the dreadful close quarters of our small kitchen table.

The triggers for his rage were invariably mundane. If he was hungry and thought my mother wasn't doing enough in the lead-up to dinner he'd get in her face and start yelling, "Where's our dinner?" "What have you been doing all day?" "Why didn't you think to start sooner?" Judy learned to be strategic in her attempts to head off these triggers—if she was baking something in the oven, she'd put covered pots with boiling water on the stove so it would be obvious that she was working on our meal. But heading off his attacks was like a game of whack-a-mole. He'd just find something else to pick on. My sister often made herself a target because she didn't like to eat her vegetables. As she moved her food around on her plate, stalling, my father would become more red-faced and belligerent. His eyes would water and his mottled pupil would bug out like a madman as he screamed, "Eat your food, NOW!" threatening her with further punishments if she didn't obey. Sometimes, he'd make her sit on the floor with her plate while my mother and I choked down our food from above.

If my mother tried to defend her, all bets would be off—"This is *my* house!" "*I* pay for this food!" It was in a moment like this that I remember him slamming down a bottle of Tabasco sauce so hard it left a permanent indentation in the table. If he became bored with my sister, he'd start in on my mother again for some minor—or made up—infraction like not picking his shirts up from the dry cleaner. It only made things worse when she tried to reason with him or defend herself. Even if she'd produced a receipt confirming his clothes wouldn't be ready until the next day, it didn't matter. He'd come back with another trivial example of her failings, like his bathroom sink not being spotlessly clean. By then, my mother's tears would be flowing—she'd continue to defend herself or wail out that she didn't understand why he was acting this way. This could go on for days, with dreadful silences punctured by new bouts of screaming. Finally, I would come across them embracing in the kitchen, him kissing her on the mouth and patting her behind. In those moments, the two of them made me sick.

Casino owners love slot machines because it's remarkably easy to make money if you know one thing about people—unpredictable, intermittent rewards will keep a gambler in anticipation of payouts all night. It's just how we're made. Equally insidious is the hardwired, upside-down version of this same dynamic. That is, unpredictable, intermittent punishments keep people in *constant* fear of abuse. Those on the receiving end of Oscar's rage and manipulations were left with two choices—either fight back and make the punishment worse, or recognize the game is rigged and accept there is no way out. I, for one, never fought back. Instead, I would operate in stealth, keeping vital parts of myself hidden, these secrets maintained through subtle manipulations, lies, and half-truths. My mother and sister would often fight back, but in the end, the house always won. Despite their direct clashes with Oscar's verbal assaults, I know Judy and Barbara still felt helpless because the three of us would endlessly discuss his behavior when he wasn't around or become absorbed in "the meaningful eye contact game" as he ranted and raved over some non-issue.

Whether *I* fought back was not really the issue. There was, instead, an implicit understanding that Oscar expected me to follow his lead in the ritual abuse of our womenfolk, as he had most surely done at the knee of his own father. In a twisted reflection of his inherent sexism, Oscar was bestowing what he considered my rightful seat—by his side— at the head of our family table. In this devil's pact I was being offered, I could never rest comfortably in my privileged status as I watched my father regularly tear into the people I cared about most in the world. In fact, I was repulsed by his overtures of male comradeship, embedded as they were in a chilling stew of toxic masculinity. How could I possibly care for—much less love—this man?

Only recently, when impressionistic memories emerge unsolicited, have I realized some strange and novel connections. For instance, from my earliest memory, I loved building with colorful wooden blocks, and it was a revelation when I received my first LEGO set under the Christmas tree. Left very often without a playmate, I needed something to occupy my time for hours at a stretch. My elaborate LEGO projects allowed me to incorporate intricate fantasies into the buildings I constructed, helping me to escape my loneliness so that I might exist— at least for a bit of time—in a better world of my own construction.

LEGO also gave me the opportunity to share something positive with Oscar—*I was constructing buildings just as he did.* While I never lost the thread of memory associated with my nightly retreat to my bedroom upon his return from work, I had, at some point, lost sight of the deep need for a bond with my father that was betrayed by my LEGO projects. I could often gain his attention for a few moments with my latest creation as he made his way to the bathroom to wash up for dinner. After taking my father through the highlights of my project, I would follow him into his bathroom where we would stand side by side at the sink and soap up our hands. Sometimes he would flick a few drops of water in my face, chuckle, and refer to me as "squirt." By the time I was ten or eleven, my collection of LEGO had grown to enormous proportions, and I went about proudly touting my desire to become an architect. Today, I am staggered by my artful compromise. I would refuse to become a contractor—to be "just like my father." Yet, through the vehicle of my LEGO projects, I was toying with the possibility that I might reside in a similar, but adjacent realm to my father as a man.

Beyond this handful of moments, there seemed to be little in our relationship of an intimate nature, and it is probably for those reasons that I did not hold onto many of my father's personal possessions after he died. One of the exceptions was a heart-shaped stone paperweight Judy had presented to Oscar as a Valentine's gift in the early years of their marriage. When I was a kid, this memento of a more hopeful day could be found there among the triangular architect's scale ruler and Newton's cradle (aka "Executive Ball Clacker") cluttering the surface of my father's desk. I don't recall Oscar ever having commented on the paperweight, much less his having shared with me some memorable story about what this object might have meant to him. However, for reasons I've never been able to fully explain, this talisman now conjures in me a visceral sense of my father's presence. Maybe it's enough that the stone heart was always there, inhabiting the single space that was his alone.

A rust-hued crimson, rounded at the edges and about four inches in length, the heart is cut through with discolorations resembling scar tissue. Holding the stone in my hand today, it feels smooth and cool to the touch. I notice delicate, dark strands, much like the black spider veins that have begun to encircle my ankles, threading through the juicy muscle. Today, the lines and curves of the stone remain intact, identical in appearance to the first day that my mother gave it to my father.

• • •

For many trauma survivors, their response to experiencing oppression or violence can mask their broader identity. For my mother—the model of a one-dimensional victim, refracted through the lens of gender bias, stifled opportunities, low self-esteem, and two unhappy marriages—can appear to be all that remains of a vivacious woman who touched people's hearts with her warmth and energy. Having survived various childhood oppressions and the trauma of war, Oscar overcame many challenging obstacles to marry my young mother and take on the responsibility of fathering my half-sister and myself. Practically speaking, it seems to me that it would have been far easier for Oscar to remain single, continue screwing around, and attending Mardi Gras every winter. For that matter, he could have hired a maid, eaten in restaurants, and sent his clothes out to be laundered. Yet if we look at what Oscar *actually* did, he chose to be married, surrounded by his children, in homes he designed and constructed, for the entirety of his adult life.

For trauma victims turned perpetrators like my father, memories of worthy deeds are often wiped out by the heinous acts they commit. Nevertheless, attempting to look at life—much less people—as either "good" or "bad" presents us with a false dichotomy. In fairness, it is abundantly clear that Oscar wanted very much to support our family and to be positively connected with others. And it's not as though he didn't try. Seen from this perspective, the real tragedy of my father's life is the fact that his dysfunctional responses to his traumatic experiences undermined the good he created in the world, and prevented him from ever being truly loved.

Part 2

Where We Went

Chapter 8

Our National Trauma

Examining the role of dissociation and our ever-evolving understanding of traumatic experience provides greater context and insight into how these operations influenced my family's lives—bringing us closer to answering the question of why my father did it. As we have seen, American culture also played a role in determining much of what happened. Though we are White, my family was nonetheless exposed to certain oppressions because in our socio-economic system, all people are ordered into hierarchies of value based on superficial characteristics. This seems to be an unavoidable consequence of being alive.

As I searched for a deeper understanding of why he did it—I pulled the focus of my exploration out from my immediate family to look at how Daddy functions at a societal level. It seems that this hierarchical ordering of all people is how Daddy manufactures traumatic economic and racial oppression. As part of my examination, I look at the role of antisocial personality disorder and what I identify as "ego-driven violence" in American culture. Though I wouldn't characterize my father as someone with antisocial personality disorder, examining this tiny subset of the population is highly revealing of our national character. Most importantly, these individuals wield outsized influence by turning the effects of their own traumatic oppression into a self-perpetuating process that keeps us *all* distracted—and often traumatized—as Daddy amasses more power. Case in point, my distant cousins—people with whom I share a bloodline—were violent Wild West vigilantes who were immortalized in multiple Hollywood westerns.

The Dalton Gang

Men like my father and my maternal great-grandfather, Pappy, used violence to maintain control over others by inciting fear and emotional turmoil in the minds of their prey. Pappy's family were no less prisoners to this dynamic than the inmates he oversaw at Lansing State Penitentiary, subject to the snap of the strap, if not the crack of the club. Viewed within the context of the era in which he lived, the use of these blunt instruments was ordinary and routine. Their use was designed to keep victims obedient and within the fold, where they could remain most useful to the master of the house. Straps weren't the only options in the arsenal of weapons that were dispatched to buttress the power of men like Pappy. Guns were an ordinary feature in farm homes of the era, and their firing was made commonplace in hunting and in keeping control over predators that regularly wandered onto the property to attack livestock. The mere fact of a gun's existence was usually enough of a deterrent to make its use as a tool of enforcement inside the home rare, but certainly not unprecedented.

For the generation of Dalton men immediately preceding Pappy, however, the use of guns against the threat of other humans had become an ever-present reality. The dangerous chaos that accompanied the Civil War and the ongoing genocide of Indigenous Americans often involved meeting threats—whether actual or perceived—to property and kin with lethal force. Set against a backdrop of slavery, racism, and pervasive socio-economic oppression, these catastrophic clashes also served as impetus for scores of trigger-happy, self-appointed defenders of vigilante justice to use violence to rebalance scales they deemed precariously out of balance. At the far reaches of this continuum, gun violence came to entirely govern the dealings of "Wild West" outlaws like Pappy's second cousins, who became notorious for robbing trains and banks throughout the 1890s.

Sifting through long forgotten details in the lives of the four brothers who initially made up the Dalton Gang, I have unearthed a chilling case study in the effects of systemic oppression and narcissistic vigilantism turned deadly. Many historians maintain the Dalton brothers were provoked to action over their anger at not being paid for their work as U.S. Marshals and the greed of railroad robber barons who used fraudulent claims of eminent domain to steal land from farmers. In reality, the Daltons' work went unpaid because they played both sides of the law, even as they'd been sworn to uphold it. While the press that followed the gang's lethal exploits claimed the brothers shared their loot with other victims of financial oppression, the Robin Hood angle would also prove to be untrue. Constantly on the run from authorities, the Daltons had little time to enjoy what fruits their violence could have borne.[172]

Their father, James, and his wife, Adeline, were in the habit of uprooting their thirteen children whenever potentially brighter horizons beckoned, but they were never able to find solid grounding. Kentucky-born James had been a saloonkeeper in the town of Westport—a stopover on the Santa Fe Trail that would later be absorbed into the expanding boundaries of Kansas City—before relocating his family in the "Indian Nations" territory near present-day Tulsa, Oklahoma. When James was unable to eke out a living in the inhospitable Sooner landscape, he moved his family to a rented farm near the tiny city of Coffeyville, Kansas—a town that would later make headlines as the location of the last stand of his son's infamous gang. In the final days of his life, James had intended to stake a claim of his own on 160 acres back in Oklahoma, but he died en route from Coffeyville. Adeline and her children persisted, settling for a time on the newly acquired land at the banks of Kingfisher Creek, living in a cave-like structure known as a "dugout"—a filthy, damp space carved out of the soil and a common accommodation for impoverished settlers on the Great Plains during the nineteenth century.[173]

Frank, the eldest Dalton brother, became a U.S. Marshal, but not far into his career, he was shot to death by the gang of horse thieves he'd been charged with apprehending. Brother Bob followed in Frank's footsteps to become a Deputy Marshal in charge of keeping order over the lands of the Osage Nation in Northeastern Oklahoma. In a foreshadowing of the spree of narcissistic violence to follow, Bob murdered a rival for his sweetheart's affection based on a series of trumped-up charges. Bob would eventually be discharged from his command for illegally selling liquor to members of the Osage Tribe he'd been charged with protecting. Bob's younger brother, Grat, became a Deputy Marshal in Arkansas, but was soon dismissed after being accused of taking bribes and stealing horses. Emmett, one of the youngest members of the Dalton clan, became a cowboy at the Bar X Bar Ranch in Oklahoma. It was here that Emmett became acquainted with "Bitter Creek" Newcomb, "Blackface" Charlie, and Bill Doolin, colorful-sounding characters who would later help round out the ranks of the Dalton Gang.[174]

While out on bail and awaiting sentencing for the various charges the government had lobbied against them, Bob, Grat, and Emmett all fled together to their brother Bill's ranch near Paso Robles, California. On the way, the brothers pulled off their first robbery at a gambling house in Silver City, an isolated mining town on the western fringes of the New Mexico Territory. At the time of their stopover, Silver City was enjoying a boom whose conclusion would be signaled a few years later by a flash flood that would carve a fifty-five-foot trench down the path of the town's main street. Like the better-remembered mining towns of Tombstone and Deadwood, Silver City was widely known for being flush with cash from its namesake product. Saloons and gambling halls lined the streets, attracting outlaws like Billy the Kid and Butch Cassidy. Had Sheriff "Dangerous Dan" Tucker, a lawman said by many to exceed the fierceness of his peers, Wyatt Earp and Wild Bill Hickok, been on patrol when the Daltons rolled in, the gang's career in crime might have been nipped in the bud there and then. However, in a scene reenacted in countless Western pulp novels, the brothers, likely playing one of the popular card games of the era like Faro or Chuck-a-luck, became increasingly suspicious about their streak of bad luck at the tables. Convinced they had been duped, the sore losers relieved the house of its cash at gunpoint, then rode out of town, unmolested, to continue their trek westward.[175]

Their brother Bill was a respected rancher and family man who had become an impassioned member of the Populist Party during his time in California. The Populist movement was a political revolt led by farmers who banded together in the 1890s to address the long-term, debilitating effects of drought and falling crop prices. Populists, or the "People's Party," felt Republican and Democratic politicians had been ignoring the interests of farmers for far too long. They held these party members culpable in facilitating the exploitative tactics of money lenders, grain elevator operators, and railroad robber barons who had all contributed to the ongoing hardships of farming families.[176] Populist Party members cast an impressive 8.5% of the votes in the 1892 presidential election for their candidate, James B. Weaver,[177] but this was not nearly enough to secure his triumph in the contest between the big-tent candidates, Grover Cleveland and Benjamin Harrison.[178]

The U.S. had been sliding off the economic rails since Barings Bank of London, the world's second oldest merchant bank, nearly imploded after its investments in Argentine wheat collapsed in 1890.[179] When other European investors awoke to the fact that they were similarly over-extended in the over-inflated commodities markets, they too started making huge withdrawals of U.S. gold. These events triggered a run by depositors on American banks, culminating in what became known as the Panic of 1893.[180] Twelve days before the inauguration of Grover Cleveland, the powerhouse Philadelphia and Reading Railroad went into receivership. With drought-related failures of wheat crops spreading to the U.S., the country fell into an economic depression equivalent in scale to that of the Great Depression of the 1930s. Farms were wiped out, 500 banks failed, and 15,000 businesses went under.[181]

Wanted Dead or Alive

In 1891, the four Dalton brothers joined forces for their first train robbery, the results of which were a complete disaster. The Southern Pacific railway train they'd chosen to hit was making its way to Los Angeles through the rural San Joaquin Valley when the brothers intercepted its path near the small community of Alila. When a railroad engineer refused to tell the gang where cash and other valuables were secured, they shot him in the stomach. Finally locating the correct carriage, they found the car defended by an armed guard who—not surprisingly—opened fire.[182]

Frustrated, the gang fled with nothing to show for their efforts. Grat and Bill were later apprehended by a posse sent to round up the robbers. Bill was later acquitted because his friends from the local Populist Party came to his defense, but Grat was found guilty and sentenced to twenty years in the pen. While being transported by rail to prison, Grat reportedly lifted the keys to his handcuffs from a dozing deputy and—like a scene out of some Yosemite Sam cartoon—leapt out the window of the moving train, escaping into the San Joaquin River below.

Brothers Bob and Emmett had been able to elude authorities and the two returned to Oklahoma where they hooked up with several of the former Bar X Bar cowboys to begin a successful year-long run of train robberies. After making his daring getaway, Grat made his way back to Oklahoma and rejoined brothers Bob and Emmett to take up with the reformulated gang on their crime spree. The jewelry and cash of the passengers had now become fair game, with more and more innocent people being killed or wounded along the way.[183]

Brother Bill, the onetime rancher who had been acquitted in the initial attempt on the Southern Pacific train, also returned to Oklahoma, but joined up with a new gang, dubbed the "Wild Bunch." Sometimes known as "the Oklahoma Long Riders" for the full-length duster coats they favored, the Wild Bunch was organized by former Bar X Bar cowboys and original Dalton Gang members Bill Doolin and Bitter Creek Newcomb.[184] The Wild Bunch—not to be confused with Butch Cassidy's "Wild Bunch," who operated in Wyoming—would go on to become one of the most successful and bloodthirsty of the outlaw gangs in the twilight of the American Wild West era, inspiring directors like Sam Peckinpah and Clint Eastwood with their badass look and lethal attitude.[185]

One by one, each of the members of the Wild Bunch would eventually be picked off by the army of deputies who had been charged by U.S. Marshal E.D. Nix to hunt them down.[186] Some say a lovely fifteen-year-old girl named Rose Dunn, dubbed "the Rose of Cimarron," betrayed her onetime paramour, Bitter Creek Newcomb, to help her brothers —yet more former bandits turned deputies—collect the reward that had been levied on Newcomb's head. There were whispers that Rose lured Newcomb to her family's ranch where he and fellow gang member Charlie Pierce were promptly shot to death by Rose's brothers.[187] And yes, the brothers did, in fact, end up collecting the reward money for their bounty.[188]

In 1894, Bill Dalton was finally tracked down by marshals at the Houston Wallace ranch near Pooleville, a small Oklahoma town near the Texas border. Early one morning, Bill was outside playing with some children when a young girl who happened to be milking cows in a field nearby spotted two members of the posse on her way back to the house. Pretending not to notice the men hiding in a ravine, this cool-headed lass warned Bill of the marshals' presence upon her return. In response, Bill ran into the house and fetched a pistol, then jumped out the back window, attempting to flee. He didn't make it far before the marshals demanded that he surrender. In reply, Bill shot at the two men and missed. The marshals returned fire and Bill was shot to death.[189]

The Younger Brothers and the James Gang Join Forces

Though their origin story differed in the details, the Dalton brothers wouldn't have had to look far for a useful model of the outlaw lifestyle. *Their* infamous cousins were known as the Younger "boys,"[190] and twenty years earlier had been the recipients of the nation's rapturous attention. They rode alongside Jesse James and his brother Frank for a daring and deadly tour of bank robbing spectacles.[191] The four Younger brothers were well-educated and hailed from a prosperous Lee's Summit, Missouri, farming family. Though their Kentucky-born father was a Union sympathizer, he owned two slaves and was often harassed by abolitionists known as "Jayhawkers" from across the nearby state line in Kansas. The Jayhawkers frequently raided the Younger farm, vandalizing and stealing property in the process. These actions undoubtedly turned the allegiance of the Younger brothers against the Jayhawkers, but it was only in the traumatic aftermath of their father being killed by a Union militiaman that they came to detest abolitionists—and the Union—with a violent vehemence.[192] From Hammurabi's Code[193] to the Bible's Book of Exodus, the law of an eye for an eye is well established.[194] At this stage, it's not a stretch to empathize with the Youngers—feeling under siege and vulnerable—their worst nightmare having come true.

However, a strategy of tit for tat is doomed to fail. On an individual level, avenging the trauma of a murder with more killing won't provide the bereaved with what they need most—a sense of meaning in a needless death. On a collective level, an eye for an eye only serves to escalate traumatic violence in a never-ending loop of retaliation and revenge. Murder and needless death are tragic, but responding by enacting more violence against perpetrators is ineffective as a long-term deterrent. Even if the sides are unevenly matched, great damage can be inflicted on the powerful. Just think of the trauma perpetuated, en masse, by a handful of people during 9/11.

In response to their father's murder, the brothers retreated to the forests and backcountry of Missouri to join with other young men in waging guerrilla warfare on Union-supporting civilians and troops in a melee of vigilante terrorism, fighting on the side of the Confederacy in the vicious border conflict that raged in that state throughout the Civil War. These fighters, known as "Bushwhackers," grew out of the inveterate southern sympathies of settlers from Kentucky and Virginia who had first established slave plantations along the snaking path of the western half of the Missouri River in an area of the state that was then known as "Little Dixie."[195]

In a state so divided that there were two governments operating simultaneously under the opposing flags of the nation, the Bushwhacker movement created terror and mayhem in the civilian population by murdering and scalping(!) Union supporters, often using the pretext of war to settle personal vendettas with violence.[196] It was during these hostilities that the Younger brothers first met Jesse and Frank James.

Both sets of brothers thrived under the tutelage of the most celebrated of the Bushwhackers, William Quantrill, a man so savage he would eventually prove too much for even the Confederates. As a child, Quantrill distinguished himself for the creative ways in which he would torture small animals, sometimes tying the tails of cats together to watch the animals fight one another to the death. Quantrill had initially formed the Bushwhackers because he felt the Confederate Army was not sufficiently fierce in prosecuting the Civil War. He was clearly not alone in his sentiments, having attracted many of the most psychotically violent young men in the state of Missouri. Quantrill was finally excommunicated from the unofficial corps of the Confederacy after leading the ambush and murder of 190 civilians—many, young boys—in Lawrence, an abolitionist stronghold 40 miles across the state line of Kansas.[197]

To surpass the reputation of the James-Younger Gang, the surviving Dalton brothers came to a violent end when they attempted the simultaneous robbery of two banks on the main square of their former hometown of Coffeyville, Kansas, in 1892. Though they'd attempted to disguise themselves with false beards, the brothers were immediately recognized by a local man. Word spread quickly around the busy town square that the Daltons were in the process of robbing two nearby banks. To bide time for authorities to intervene, a quick-thinking teller fabricated a story that his safe was on an automatic time delay and told the gang they would need to wait ten minutes for the vault to unlock. This stalling tactic allowed for several of the citizens of Coffeyville to rush inside Isham's Hardware store to arm themselves for the defense of their town. In the end, Bob Dalton, Grat Dalton, Bill Power, and Dick Broadwell all died, as they say, "in a hail of bullets," unleashed by townspeople as the gang attempted to make their escape. In the process, the gang murdered four defenders of the small town and wounded many others.[198] Emmett, the youngest Dalton brother, survived despite being shot twenty-three times.[199] He would serve fourteen years at Lansing State Penitentiary,[200] the *same* Kansas prison where his second cousin, my great-grandfather, Pappy, would later wield his wooden billy club among the cell blocks thirty years later. Upon being pardoned, the now retired outlaw made his way back to California, settling this time in Los Angeles. Emmett would live on to become an even bigger outlaw celebrity in his own right, penning (in what is surely a ghost-written manuscript) *Beyond the Law.* In 1918, Hollywood would turn this largely fictional, self-serving account of the Dalton Gang into a movie – *with Emmett playing himself in the title role!* [201]

●●●

Because of exploitative governmental policies that concentrated resources, power, and wealth at the top rungs of the social hierarchy, during the final decades of the nineteenth century, people on the lower rungs—like the Dalton family—were forced to live like primordial men in their earthen caves. The harsh realities of an inequitable society have always been self-evident to poverty-stricken families like the Daltons. As the hardships of financial oppression mushroomed for middle-class families over the course of the 1890s, many became increasingly resentful of the politicians and policies favoring the elite that had helped get them into this mess. Sound familiar?

As with scores of other hard up and troubled young men, Grat and Bob Dalton learned their skills from the violence innate to law enforcement. Like many lawmen, they became accustomed to exploiting the blurry line between right and wrong, especially when they were the only authority figures for miles around. It should come as no surprise that some number of citizens, witness to our culture's exploitative systems of governance, and having known little but the trauma of a life of poverty, would attempt to violently seize power and resources at their first opportunity.

In his book, Emmett portrays criminality in Wild West lawmen as the norm—as do most current movies and television shows—peddling this myth as a rationalization for his brothers' actions. However, the fact that Bob and Grat Dalton were both brought up on charges for their misconduct tells us a different story. Likewise, the drastic nature of their flight to California reveals the true gravity of the consequences that were likely to befall the brothers for their unlawful transgressions.

It would follow that the circumstances of financial oppression may have served as motive for the Dalton brothers to rise violently against the state and its elite. Even if they were trying to stick it to the all-powerful banks and railroads by making off with a bit of their cash, the gang nevertheless murdered innocent bystanders who had the misfortune of finding themselves in the wrong place at the wrong time. What's more, the Dalton and James Gangs almost always targeted small banks financed by deposits from local citizens—average people—farmers, teachers, and small businessmen. In the days before the FDIC, the citizens in Coffeyville—and towns like it—confronted bank robbers not just in defense of their town, but to keep from having their hard-earned savings wiped out.

Ego-Driven Violence

Lining your pockets with cash is a logical response to financial oppression —it answers an obvious practical need. One could even argue that the Bushwhackers were being similarly practical in laying waste to anyone suspected of supporting the Union. Yet, I am convinced that there is something more lurking beneath the surface here. I call that extra something "ego-driven violence." Ego-driven violence is the byproduct of the gnawing insecurity of men who dwell too long on the limits of their control.[202] Those who exhibit these tendencies are narcissistic and self-involved, with low levels of empathy for their fellow humans.[203] Unable to see beyond their own feelings, wants, and needs, they view themselves as victims, justified in their violent actions.[204] For them, life is a zero-sum game.

Extreme cases of ego-driven violence, like those of the Wild West outlaws and the Bushwhackers of the Civil War era, might now be diagnosed with antisocial personality disorder. However, most of us know them by their mainstream labels, "sociopath" or "psychopath." People with antisocial personality disorder can appear quite charming on the surface; however, their true agenda is to manipulate situations to their own advantage.[205] Most consider themselves to be the sole arbiters of justice.

In an 1872 unsigned letter to the *Kansas City Times*, Jesse James portrays himself as an innocent victim of persecution, in fear for his life, despite unequivocal evidence of his murderous bank robbing rampages. Playing on the sympathies of his fellow defeated Confederates, James writes, "Just let a party of men commit a bold robbery, and the cry is hang them, but President Ulysses Grant and his party can steal millions, and it is all right. It is true, we are robbers, but we always rob in the glare of the day and in the teeth of the multitude; and we [only kill] in self-defense [when] men refuse to open their vaults and safes to us [...] Some editors call us thieves. We are not thieves—we are bold robbers. It hurts me very much to be called a thief."[206]

I share the story of the Dalton Gang and other Wild West outlaws to illustrate how the dual identity of a trauma victim-turned-perpetrator operates on our national stage. The dangers are manifest: a sociopath's ego-driven violence can be spun into a thrilling and entertaining yarn— much like the one I just shared; traumatic oppression is used as justification for the continued perpetuation of violence, racism, and other atrocities. Emmett Dalton's star turn was not without precedent. Provocateurs with public platforms, eager to further their own agendas, craft messages to stoke the flames of division. Jesse James was made the darling of many pro-South newspaper editors until he met his end at the hands of a fellow gang member enticed by the sizable bounty offered for his leader's capture. An 1874 article entitled "Missouri's Gay Bandits: The Genuine James Boys and One of the Youngers"—from the dubiously titled newspaper *The Lexington Caucasian*—captures the spirit of the transubstantiation of savage, ego-driven violence into a glamorous underdog's tale of adventure:

In all the history of medieval knight-errantry and modern brigandage, there is nothing that equals the wild romance of the past few years' career of Arthur McCoy, Frank and Jesse James and the Younger boys.... Their desperate deeds during the war were sufficient to have stocked a score of ordinary novels, with facts that outstrip the strung-out flights of fantasy. Their fierce hand-to-hand encounters... their long and reckless scouts and forays, and their riotous jollity... all combined to form a chapter without a parallel in the annals of America.[207]

Today, we see these same forces at work in the glowing endorsement of vigilante justice throughout the country. What's more, the dark skills of the sociopath are a boon to many businesspeople and politicians. The Bushwhacker movement and the narcissistic rationales deployed by Wild West outlaws vividly demonstrate the outcome of allowing psychopaths to join forces to run rampant over our communities—the result is the perpetuation of trauma, oppression, terror, and anarchy.

Given these contingencies, how is it that ego-driven violence continues to be accepted—and even *encouraged* by our culture? Why was the Populist Party not swept into power on a tidal wave of support? Why do so many of our fellow citizens condone the violent storming of the U.S. Capitol in 2021 to halt the ratification of a free and fair presidential election? What strange sorcery is afoot?

Chapter 9

Oppressors—
Unwitting and Otherwise

As Plato famously observed, "Wars are occasioned by the love of money,"[208] and the defining conflicts of the early American Republic generally adhere to the spirit of this maxim. However, there were other, essential motivations that enlivened the Revolutionary and Civil Wars that went beyond the purely financial—and it's the unique alchemy of these considerations to which we owe many of the traumatic societal oppressions we experience today. The conflict over who would direct the future of a small agrarian colony on the fringes of established global power centers would provide the catalyst for British colonists to launch the American Revolution, but in a happy accident of history, these grievances over tariffs and taxation coincided with a movement that was just beginning to chip away at the unquestioned legitimacy of divinely sanctioned authority. In the century preceding the Revolutionary War, this new type of thinking, based on reason and the scientific method, was coming to be known as the Age of Enlightenment.[209]

Monotheism had been the name of the game in the Western world for nearly two millennia, but during the Enlightenment, people were beginning to challenge God's place at the center of the universe, and in the process, the scale of domination held by church and monarchy had begun to shrink.[210] Humanism, the celebration of human dignity, beauty, and potential, had risen to prominence during the Italian Renaissance three centuries earlier, but these ideas found new expression during the Age of Enlightenment. The new religion of humanism would ultimately place man's needs foremost above all sentient entities to empower marginalized groups who had historically been oppressed by traditional authority, bringing into creation the modern, scientifically focused Western civilization we know today.[211] The American Revolution and its founding documents seamlessly blended the financial with the philosophical, elevating Plato's dry, straightforward manifesto of war into a complex philosophical discourse on the matter of individual self-determination, autonomy, reason, and progress.

Like the rebel colonists who were concerned with gaining control over their financial fates during the American Revolution, the sons and daughters of the Confederacy initiated their split from the Union based ostensibly on the "love of money." Cotton products were the literal fabric of the Southern economy and accounted for nearly 60% of American exports at the start of the Civil War.[212] While the North profited enormously from banking and textile production associated with the cotton industry, for the South, this crop was the undisputed king.

Fundamental to the continued success of "Dixie" was the plantation system, and the millions of people living in enslavement who were essential in cultivating and harvesting this labor-intensive crop. Not only was slave labor key to cotton production but the monetary investment in people living in enslavement was estimated to be *seven times* the total investment held in all banks across the United States at the start of the Civil War.[213] While the South fought to maintain an economic system rooted in cotton and slavery, the full fury of narcissistic rage that was unleashed across Dixie during the Civil War cannot be explained by financial motives alone; it was also a manic defense.

"Manic defense" is a fancy term used in psychoanalytic circles to describe a particular type of strategy people employ to cope with fear-inducing thoughts and feelings. This strategy is largely unconscious, meaning the operations involved in managing these fears occur automatically within our psyches and, for the most part, are not available for analysis within the range of our day-to-day awareness. The operations of the unconscious, known as unconscious processes, consist of repressed emotions and subliminal perceptions that drive many of our outward feelings and actions.[214]

A manic defense is said to be one type of unconscious process used to cope with fear-inducing thoughts and feelings.[215] In that sense we can say a person is employing a strategy to psychologically *defend against* a troublesome aspect of the mind (remember Freud and his psychological shields?). One strategy utilized in manic defense is distraction. In this context, distraction is a frenzy of energy directed to outward actions whose overarching purpose is to divert conscious awareness from a fear-inducing stimuli. Another tactic of the manic defense involves maintaining a set of convictions that stand in direct opposition to the fear-inducing stimuli. These machinations often involve frantic efforts to control others and outward demonstrations of contempt for the fear-inducing elements the individual is seeking to control within themselves.[216] To illustrate, think of J. Edgar Hoover, the former head of the FBI, who instigated the persecution and purge of gays from the government up until his death in 1972, all the while conducting sexual relationships with other men.[217]

Southerners rightly feared violent reprisal if their slaves were ever freed—after all, that's most likely how *they* would have reacted if the situation were reversed. However, men like William Quantrill and other defenders of the South committed atrocities against abolitionists, civilians, and Union soldiers not just to maintain their safety and livelihoods, but also as a desperate bid to rebalance their imperiled sense of self-respect by acting on the operations of a societal manic defense. Fundamentally, these individuals were attempting to avoid consciously recognizing the humiliating reality that they had made themselves sucklings whose very existence depended on leeching sustenance off the scarred brown breasts of the twelve and a half million human captives they had enslaved and brutalized over the previous two centuries.

Everyone's a Little Bit Racist

Among these tragic consequences is the small, sad reality of my own family's racism. Like tens of millions of Americans living today, the Confederates were defending a way of life and attitudes held by many —if not all—of my own ancestors. Though no living member of my family would have ever endorsed the idea of people living in enslavement, there persisted, during my childhood, ugly language, stories, and asides that revealed the not-so-distant effects of our predecessors having fought to the death to maintain their right to own other human beings.

I remember the story of the water ladle, told in a spirit of hilarity, which concerned the large ceramic urns that were filled with cool well water to keep the people living in enslavement and other workers refreshed during their long days in the fields. Instead of cups, a single ladle was provided from which all were expected to drink. It seems some great-great-grandfather, whose name is now lost to time, always took pains to drink from the part of the ladle nearest the handle to keep his mouth from touching the lower area of the cup where the people living in enslavement commonly placed their lips to drink. One day, while taking his usual draw from the ladle, one of "his" women living in enslavement happened to witness this curious exercise. At this point, the storyteller assumes bug eyes and mimics a minstrel inflection for the punchline, which has the woman laughingly exclaim, "Massa Dalton, you drink up thar at da handle just like I does!" Of course, the great-great is so shocked and horrified by the woman's disclosure that he thereafter has an additional urn set up for his personal use.

I don't remember the first time I heard this story, but I've no doubt that I would have laughed along with everyone else at the "antics" of our great-great. Most members of my immediate family were not natural storytellers, and there was a time when I lived for tales like these. As any parent knows, children will ask again and again for their greatest hits in your repertoire of careworn narratives, sitting in rapt attention as the familiar details unfold. I can only believe that I must have asked for the story of the water urn to be repeated several times over the course of my childhood to be able to recall the details so vividly today. The images evoked were of another world, so seemingly different than my own, as to be ripped out of the pages of a storybook. Looking back, I think what stood out most was how these words stimulated my sense of the peculiar. It seemed impossible that anyone in my family had been connected to characters who felt so fanciful.

While everyone laughed at the shock my ancestor must have surely felt in having his best laid plans go awry, no one remarked on the implication held in consensus that the woman in the story was so ignorant that she didn't know that she was disparaged by her master. I guarantee you it never occurred to them that this woman may have known fully well why the great-great was drinking from the top part of the ladle. My family's reflexive sense of superiority was so well reinforced that they were blinded to the possibility that the woman might have gotten a laugh out of making the master retch in disgust and knew the only way to get away with a prank like this was to play dumb.

Young children learn to communicate in a world that is mainly constructed of references to events that occurred before they existed. They are by design accepting of what they hear due to the sheer amount of data they must absorb and the limited number of sources available to provide information. A child's primary task is to construct a working model of the world so that they can act with increasing levels of independence.[218] Early cognitions depend on the quick and dirty, not a subtle, objective parsing of the fears and prejudices held by their family members. For many years the story of the water urn was nothing more than another story that was incorporated into my mental model of the world to which I gave no serious reflection. This entire process is succinctly summarized in the song "You've Got to Be Carefully Taught," from the 1949 Rodgers and Hammerstein musical *South Pacific*:

> You've got to be taught to hate and fear
> You've got to be taught from year to year
> It's got to be drummed in your dear little ear

You've got to be carefully taught

You've got to be taught to be afraid
Of people whose eyes are oddly made
And people whose skin is a different shade
You've got to be carefully taught

You've got to be taught before it's too late
Before you are six or seven or eight
To hate all the people your relatives hate
You've got to be carefully taught[219]

Two Steps Forward; One Step Back

My mother, Judy, would have been told the story of the water urn at around the same age as I had been when I first heard it, but over the course of the twenty-five years that separated our childhoods, some things had changed for the better. Around the same time *South Pacific* was playing on Broadway, my mother was in her final years of elementary school, and just sixty miles away, thirteen Black families were filing a class action lawsuit against the Topeka Board of Education challenging the enforced segregation of public-school students.[220]

Typical accounts of "Black" schools in the 1950s include a pattern of dilapidated buildings with children of all ages packed onto wooden benches; shoddy, out-of-date educational materials; and curricula designed to train farm and service workers, not future scientists and businesspeople.[221] A little girl named Linda Carol Brown, who was just three grades below my mother, is the best remembered of the students because her family's surname came first alphabetically among the plaintiffs in the suit. The basis of the Browns' complaint was summarized as such: Carol walked six blocks to catch a bus that then drove her one mile to her "Black" school, whereas there was a "White" school seven blocks away to which she was denied entry because of her race. While the slightly tangled logistics of Carol's commute don't appear to be an example of extreme hardship on par with that of other Black students of the era, that wasn't really the point.[222]

The Browns' suit was just one of the many test cases being put forward across the country by the National Association for the Advancement of Colored People (NAACP) to challenge the legally mandated division of public institutions and facilities by race into "separate, but equal" spaces.[223] The Browns were arguing that all families, regardless of race, should have an equal say in where their children attend school. In fact, many now say that the Topeka Board of Education did a respectable job of providing something close to an equal educational experience for its Black students. Carol's mother, like many other Black Topeka parents, even felt "Black" schools were a superior option for their children because they were staffed by well-trained Black teachers who were highly dedicated to their students' success. After desegregation in Topeka, many Black students fared far worse due to the racism or disinterest of their new, White teachers. Regardless, after desegregation, great numbers of other Black students across the country had access to quality instruction and educational materials for the first time, leading many to improved opportunities and better jobs as adults—not to mention the tremendous psychological benefit of having legal protections against their treatment as second-class citizens.[224]

The Topeka chapter of the NAACP had organized the Browns and other parents for the class action suit in the tradition of the "Comité de Citoyens," a mixed-race, New Orleans civil rights group that had been instrumental in putting forth the case the Browns were now seeking to overturn. *Plessy v. Ferguson* had started as a test case by the Comité to challenge the Separate Car Act, passed in 1890 by the Louisiana State Senate. The Separate Car Act required White and Black people to travel in separate railway cars, and was one in a number of reversals and setbacks for Black people as racially motivated White people began to reclaim the power they had ceded during a period that has become known as Reconstruction.[225]

New Orleans, a city that had traditionally allowed the races to mix more freely than in other locations throughout the South, was especially hard hit by the new law. The city was well known for its extreme parsing of racial identity, with special rights and designations for people of mixed blood. There were Creoles, which referred to Louisiana-born persons with some combination of Spanish, French, African, or Indigenous-American blood. There were also "quadroons," whose racial heritage was one-quarter Black and three-quarters White. Homer Plessy was an "octoroon," meaning his racial heritage was seven-eighths White and one-eighth Black. Nevertheless, Plessy was considered a Black man under Louisiana state law.[226]

These designations might seem ridiculous today if not for the fact that Louisianans' hyperconscious attention to their racial makeup was a reflection of the centrality of the role of racial identity in determining one's legal rights and social standing in the wider world. In a foreshadowing of Rosa Parks's bus ride in Montgomery, Alabama, some six decades later, the Comité had urged Plessy to take a seat in the "White" car of a train to establish a test case to challenge the Separate Car Act. When asked to vacate his first-class seat for the "Colored" car, Plessy refused and, as planned, he was promptly arrested.[227]

As the Comité had hoped, Plessy's case challenging the Separate Car Act went all the way to the U.S. Supreme Court, but the results for anyone "legally" Black were catastrophic and far-reaching. The Court's 7-1 decision in *Plessy v. Ferguson* (1896) held that "segregation did not in itself constitute unlawful discrimination."[228] In writing for the majority, Justice Henry Billings Brown stated that the Thirteenth Amendment, which had abolished slavery, did not imply a "general legal equality" for Black people. Regarding the Fourteenth Amendment, which states, "nor shall any state ... deny to any person within its jurisdiction the equal protection of the laws," Billings maintained that the intent of the protections of the amendment should be limited in scope to the concept of "legal" equality only, and was not, in any event, meant to "prevent" racial discrimination.[229] The court's ruling also provided ample leeway for states and local police to enact laws requiring racial separation. Billings had the indecency to add in his ruling that the court's decision did not imply that a particular race was "marked with a badge of inferiority."[230] In the lone dissenting opinion, Justice John Marshall Harlan argued "the Constitution was color blind and that the United States had no class system. Accordingly, all citizens should have access to equal rights."[231]

It's No Joke

Thomas Dartmouth "Daddy" Rice was a Caucasian actor who became wildly popular with White, Northern audiences in the first half of the nineteenth century for performing in a burnt-cork blackface mask and shabby clothes. Rice maintained his character, "Jumping Jim Crow," was based on his firsthand observations of Black people during the time he'd traveled with touring theater companies throughout the South. White actors performing in blackface predated Rice's routines, but never to the degree of acclaim given to the character of Jim Crow. Rice would become known as the Father of Minstrelsy for his buffoonish witticisms paired with idiosyncratic jigs and songs, all making for a demeaning, over-the-top caricature of Black people's supposed behavior.[232] Later in the nineteenth century, the character of Jim Crow would come to signify a derogatory catch-all term for a highly subservient, stereotypical Black man, and a reference point for an assemblage of laws and White customs that reinforced a system of American apartheid—a traumatically oppressive caste system that had been given the stamp of approval by the highest court in the land.[233]

Only two decades before Plessy took his seat in the "White" car of a New Orleans train, it had seemed the promise of true equality for Black people under the eyes of the law was close at hand. The Civil Rights Act had been enacted by the United States Congress in 1875, ten years after the defeat of the South, and the freeing of over four million people living in enslavement. The Civil Rights Act represented a high-water mark of legislation for the equality of the races. It granted Black people equal treatment in the use of public transportation and other accommodations as well as the right to serve on juries. Though this was just one step in addressing a series of traumatic oppressions that had been perpetuated against Black people since they were first kidnapped from their homelands in West Africa, the Civil Rights Act signaled an intention by the U.S. government to be held accountable for a promise proclaimed by the Declaration of Independence a century earlier.[234] Rejecting the control of their English king, this document held out a pledge to all Americans that states, "We hold these truths to be self-evident, that all men are created equal, that they are endowed by their Creator with certain unalienable Rights, that among these are Life, Liberty, and the pursuit of Happiness."[235]

These words, of course, were penned by Thomas Jefferson—our third President—noted humanist, diplomat, and all-round Age of Enlightenment poster boy, who sired at least six children with Sally Hemings,[236] one of the over six hundred Black people he held in enslavement during his lifetime.[237] This inherently incompatible fusion of values was not unique to Jefferson and is, in my humble opinion, the bedrock of the American delusion and the formula of our discontent. At the outset to the American Revolution, clear-sighted British author and abolitionist Thomas Day observed, "If there be an object truly ridiculous in nature, it is an American patriot, signing resolutions of independency with the one hand, and with the other brandishing a whip over his affrighted slaves."[238]

Segregation: It's a Beautiful City for the Privileged Few

Kansas City has long promoted itself as the "City of Fountains." "More fountains than in Rome!" we would report to visitors, the earnestness of this claim only serving to reinforce the depth of our parochialism in this tone-deaf comparison. Many of these fountains are in neighborhoods constructed during the "City Beautiful" movement that took place at the beginning of the twentieth century. The movement's development of landscaped parks and wide, tree-lined boulevards attracted the construction of fine homes and apartment buildings in their vicinity, transforming cities that had heretofore been collections of grimy, ad hoc conglomerations of factories, homes, and businesses.[239] Racial covenants —both explicit and unspoken—in which White Christians arranged to resell or lease their property only to other White Christians, dominated these "City Beautiful" neighborhoods up through the 1960s.[240] When I was growing up in the 1970s, many of these once "genteel" areas had experienced a near uniform degree of White flight a generation earlier and were now almost exclusively inhabited by Black people—who also happened to make up nearly a third of the city's population.[241]

It would not be an overstatement to say that Linda Carol Brown was responsible for the contours of the landscape I took for granted as a child. The Kansas City metropolitan area stood at 1.2 million inhabitants by the mid-1970s,[242] and had become characterized, like many other American population centers, by a predominantly impoverished Black central core surrounded by ever-expanding concentric rings of newly constructed White suburbs. *Brown v. Board of Education* had been unanimously defeated in the U.S. District Courts in 1952, opening an important path for the suit to be heard on appeal by the U.S. Supreme Court. Thurgood Marshall, Chief Counsel for the NAACP Legal Defense and Educational Fund—who would go on to become the first Black Supreme Court Justice in 1967—was one of the lead attorneys for the plaintiffs.[243]

In 1954, the court at last reached a decision to overturn *Plessy v. Ferguson* by ruling in favor of the Browns. The newly appointed Chief Justice Earl Warren wrote in the unanimous ruling, "[W]e conclude that in the field of public education the doctrine of 'separate but equal' has no place. Separate educational facilities are inherently unequal."[244] While this ruling related only to public schools, the court had opened the door for the rights of Black people just far enough to allow for the implication that their decision could be applied to all public facilities. In response to this call to rebalance the longstanding injustice of enforced segregation, White people in Kansas City—and across the country—voted with their feet. They would not abide by their children being bussed across cities to attend schools outside their comfort zone, or to live in close proximity to "people whose eyes are oddly made... and people whose skin is a diff'rent shade." Central cities were abandoned by White people seeking out the presumed "safe" predictability of neatly ordered suburbs. This "White flight" decimated central city property values—undermining the tax base and starving central cities of revenue for schools and other infrastructure.[245]

■ ■ ■

Throughout my childhood, my father kept a strange-looking metal sculpture on the coffee table in the waiting room of his office suite. He had picked up the piece at an amateur art show and was likely drawn to the work for its construction-oriented theme. Whenever I visited his office, I would entertain myself by examining the artwork's tiny abstract figures, caught frozen in time, as they ascended ladders to various platforms and lean-to shelters that clung to the vertically inserted pieces of metal. About three feet in height and anchored on each end by two large stones, his curiosity had been titled *Urban Renewal* by the artist after a concept in city planning popular at mid-century. Urban renewal effectively meant the razing of huge sections of inner cities and erecting cheaply constructed, totalitarian-style apartment blocks in their place. The concept was popularized by car-mad urban planner and development czar Robert Moses, whose wrecking ball most notably plowed through eighty acres of the Lower East Side of Manhattan. In place of established neighborhoods, Moses erected massive red brick apartment blocks in the shape of "plus" signs. Moses is also responsible for knitting together the New York City region with bridges and highways. He would have built an eight-lane highway straight through Soho if not for the efforts of grassroots preservationists.[246]

Urban planners in Kansas City—and most other large cities— followed Moses's lead by demolishing block after block of inner-city homes, cleaving communities with wide, unapproachable concrete highways. In a half-hearted measure to address the corrosive neglect of neighborhoods—each on a downward race to the bottom as more and more businesses moved to the suburbs, and once beautiful residential structures fell into disrepair—cities would create new infill housing which came to be known as the "projects."[247]

As a child, I remember riding through the heat-wilted streets of summertime Kansas City where temperatures regularly exceed the 100-degree mark. The windows of our air-conditioned car were rolled up as we passed through the former "City Beautiful" neighborhoods, their fountains brimming over with brown skin in various states of exposure, young children squirming and splashing gleefully, enlivened by the refreshing plumes of water gushing from the monumental jets. Inside, we would pick out the largest and most exposed bodies to "poke fun" at, making comparisons to baboons in the same way people have recently done with memes related to the Obamas.[248] "They just don't know how to take care of things" would be the self-assured "tut, tut" of judgment coming from the mouths of the adults inside the car. If you had challenged them, they would have expressed with certainty that their opinions were well-founded facts. While it would be easy to shrug off this scene with an air of entitled liberal superiority, you must understand, they had been "carefully taught."

Though most members of my family were dyed-in-the wool Democrats, they existed, like President Nixon's "Silent Majority," in an echo chamber of bias informed by the operations of a societal manic defense that maintained the illusion of White supremacy. Of course, none of this excuses our behavior, but we have to grant that even if members of my family had worked to forge relationships outside their insular circles, they still would have faced an uphill battle to see non-Whites with anything approaching a clear sight. Back when Russian trolls referred only to unfortunate-looking little men who lived under bridges composing morose poetry in Cyrillic script, White people nonetheless found themselves manipulated by ubiquitous propaganda campaigns designed to fuel their highly negative projections about other races. Organizations like Tammany Hall and newspaper chain owners like William Randolph Hearst leveraged the weaknesses inherent to members of any dominant racial group by playing on their fears of powerlessness and subjugation. Despicable, spiritually bankrupt individuals such as these have churned up paranoid anxiety in dominant social groups throughout the ages in a self-serving effort to gain, consolidate, and maintain their own, *individual* power.

The hypocrisy of White humanists like Thomas Jefferson howling at the moon about the rights of man—all the while maintaining a system of legal ownership over Black people—finds its antecedents in the operations of a societal manic defense that continues to make its presence felt today from Ferguson to Charlottesville. The conviction that certain humans can be divided into categories constituting a lesser species of being, existing only to serve the needs and fancies of their "masters" can be traced to the feudal caste systems of Europe's Middle Ages, and is reflective of the hierarchies found throughout the animal kingdom. Any illusion that these predilections died out with the South's surrender at Appomattox—or over the course of the tenure of the now dead Voting Rights Act of 1965, or the two-time election of President Barack Obama—must be dismissed out of hand. Distilled from the same venom that drove the hypocrisy of the founding fathers and the slave-owning Confederacy, sanctified American archetypes like "the rebel spirit" (a code word for White supremacy) have continued to give societal carte blanche to outlaws, tycoons, and small-minded people to inflict traumatic, ego-driven violence on any person or group they might wish to subjugate.

The entire Western genre—including sagas like the Dalton Gang's movie debut—are romanticized depictions of the rebel spirit, providing blanket validation for attitudes and expressions of traumatic oppression that continue to co-opt the humanistic ideals of the American Revolution. The ongoing propensity for large numbers of Americans to fetishize vigilante violence and White supremacy serves only to make banal the most grotesque and perverted aspects of humanity. Today, this dystopian vision of human relations and its embrace of Libertarian/Ayn Randian "rational self-interest" dogs our democracy. All the while, we slide more deeply into a dangerous morass where even the most even-tempered among us are unable to mobilize the most basic of these insights to reach individuals blinded and deafened by the effects of pride, fear, poverty, and media disinformation. We're *all* rightly terrified—but for different reasons. On some level, it feels as if our inaction is also an embrace of our captors, which facilitates our own oppression. This may seem unlikely or inconceivable, and to go against everything we know about human beings, and yet...

Chapter 10

Hostages

I will never forget the feelings of confusion and fear when my mother suddenly stopped the car to scold me as we were driving away from my grandparents' house.

"He is my father, and you will not treat him like that! Do you understand, young man?"

She had just picked me up from a visit with my nana and grandpa and something I'd done was apparently very bad. She was very angry with me—an unusual event. I was four or five years old and did not normally get scolded. I was a good boy. I kept my head low. I wanted nothing more than to please the adults in my life—especially my mother. I would have agreed with anything she said at that moment, just to see her look at me again like I was the little boy she loved.

It seems that during my visit, I had once again been intentionally ignoring my grandfather, Hubert, choosing instead to focus my attentions on my nana. This avoidant behavior was nothing new. I was exceedingly shy as a boy. I would avert the gaze of most adults and often ignore their friendly attempts to draw me into conversation. I wanted nothing more than to be invisible during those moments where I was the focus of attention, hoping against hope that the big people would just go about their business if I acted like they weren't there. My conduct proved to be a source of embarrassment for my parents, who found my actions disrespectful, their interpretation only serving to make me feel even more odd and ashamed about my anxious reticence.

I was particularly withdrawn around men. Though it took many years to fit the pieces together, I now see that the real culprit in my rejecting attitude toward my grandfather was my mistaken assumption that my father's frightening inability to control his anger was a quality shared by all men. I learned to give the adult members of my own gender the widest possible berth as a strategy to maintain some measure of control over putting myself in harm's way.

While fight and flight are our most widely recognized responses to threat, the third option, freeze, stands as a well-tested, time-honored defensive strategy in the animal kingdom.[249] Though I could never have articulated it at the time, I now see that I instinctively adopted this "deer in the headlights" strategy to manage my overwhelming feelings of fear when confronted with Oscar's rage. While I might have appeared inert to outside observers, my interior would roil with destabilizing emotional turbulence in those moments when my father's anger was on display. Neurologist Pierre Janet first pointed out that many victims dissociate during these intervals of abuse, with minds "vacating" bodies to take on the role of a detached observer who watches the scene unfold at a "safe" distance.[250]

Over the years, my mother, Judy, enjoyed recounting the story of how she had "laid down the law" with me over my insensitive treatment of my grandfather. In her version, this scolding was a well-deserved and character-building lesson for young Timmy that demonstrated her ability to set firm boundaries with her children. She was still relatively new to her marriage with Oscar and did not yet have the psychological savvy to see the connection between my avoidant behavior and my fear of men. While Judy absorbed the punishing impact of my father's anger on a daily basis, she did not yet fully calculate the weight of this burden on the lives of her two children. Well into my teenage years, my mother would still sometimes blame herself for my father's outbursts, half blind to the parallels between Oscar's behavior and those of her own grandfather, Pappy. Happily for me, Pappy's ruthless hand shaped his son Hubert into a big-hearted man who was nurturing and gentle with me. But, as we'll explore in the coming pages, survivors of childhood abuse just as often go on to perpetrate more violence as adults.

Hubert was fascinated with every aspect of our family history and often jokingly referred to us as the "Dalton Gang." Throughout my childhood, he even kept a commemorative plate depicting scenes from the family heist gone bad on a bookshelf next to his favorite, overstuffed green leather chair. Whenever my family happened to be dropping by, we could usually find my grandfather perched in his armchair, eager to host my sister and me in what he referred to as the "nest" of his lap. I regret that I was never completely comfortable basking in the warmth of Hubert's attention; only now do I fully grasp the reality that the love my grandfather felt for me was a rare experience in my upbringing, not to be revisited in quite the same form ever again. I ask myself why some survivors of childhood abuse like Hubert can keep their experience of violence on a shelf, limited to a commemorative plate, while others go on to use it as a model for their own ego-driven violence? And how is it that some number of those who once committed violent acts come to abandon their destructive ways for good? These are questions that I've been forced to try and answer in one way or another since I was a small child. What happens at that fork in the road where people seem to "choose" the path of violence or non-violence?

Cycles of Misery

The concept of the cycle of violence is one way we have tried to understand the antecedents of human cruelty, and it is by now familiar to most people not the least because this model tells us something we all intuitively understand—that violence begets violence. Cathy Spatz Widom was one of the first researchers to rigorously examine the effects of childhood maltreatment on adult behavior, and her 1989 study on child abuse and criminality has emerged as a highly influential framework for understanding this phenomenon. Widom's research involved an exhaustive examination of over two decades worth of case files relating to abused and neglected children. Among the many unsettling findings, Widom noted that the experience of childhood abuse and neglect increased the probability of juvenile arrest by nearly 53%. Most critically, Widom found that adult survivors of childhood abuse and neglect are 38% more likely to commit a violent crime when compared to those who experienced no such childhood traumas.[251] A more recent study, examining data from the National Longitudinal Study of Adolescent Health (2012) echoes Widom's findings, concluding, "childhood maltreatment roughly doubles the probability that an individual engages in many types of crime."[252]

Many in the public sphere took Widom's study as a blanket validation of the effects of the cycle of violence; however, the picture is not so straightforward. First of all, Widom emphasized that while there exists the widespread belief that violence begets violence, "the majority of abused and neglected children do not become delinquent, criminal, or violent."[253] Secondly, it is extremely difficult to study the intergenerational transmission of abuse and trauma because multi-determined variables like poverty, genetics, positive social supports, and physiological disorders can often lead researchers to confusing and sometimes contradictory findings.[254]

The mechanism by which the cycle of violence operates has been conceptualized in a number of ways by more recent researchers: those who emphasize the importance of social learning hypothesize that children observe and then imitate their caregiver's response to stress and conflict. In this manner, childhood maltreatment operates as a sort of training ground for future abusers in the sense that violent reactions modeled by caregivers come to be seen as acceptable methods for coping with anger, fear, and other internal tensions; in contrast to social learning theory, social control theorists believe we humans just have a natural appetite for criminal behavior. This theory posits that childhood maltreatment prevents abused children from developing positive social bonds with their caregivers, placing these individuals at a higher risk for perpetrating violence as adults. Social control theorists maintain that it is the experience of positive social bonds with caregivers that offsets these innate criminal inclinations, helping to restrain children from committing violence against others.[255] Social-psychological strain theory focuses on the role of extreme stress in triggering developmental delays and other issues in brain functioning "that may permanently alter the way that individuals respond to environmental stimuli..." suggesting that "maltreatment could predispose a child to risky, self-destructive or aggressive behaviors."[256] Current research also demonstrates that genes, in combination with certain environmental factors, can lead to neuropsychological issues like ADHD and low levels of self-control, each of which has been identified as a significant risk factor in violent behavior.[257]

While the cycle of violence has helped illuminate the underpinnings of criminal behavior, this model has had little to say about the perpetuation of spousal battery and child abuse that remains, by and large, hidden from public and legal scrutiny. Those working in domestic violence treatment circles often look to the power dynamics of abuse to help explain the actions of these perpetrators. According to this line of thinking, adult survivors of childhood abuse commit acts of violence against family members to cope with the repercussions of *their own* abuse.[258] It's now well understood that nearly all survivors of abuse are left with an overpowering sense of shame because of their victimization —many even describe the feeling that they are "less than human." Those survivors who go on to perpetrate abuse often develop the false belief that the commission of violence provides a kind of "immunity" against further exploitation and shame. These distortions can be traced to the moments of their own abuse; many victims assume that their perpetrator, though cruel, is at the very least a person to be reckoned with—someone who would never allow another individual to violate their integrity as a human being. As a result, some survivors who later perpetrate violence desperately crave a taste of what it is like to be totally in control of another person. Their aim is to hold the same level of absolute power —and its imagined freedoms from exploitation—they believe their own perpetrators experienced during the enactment of their abuse.[259]

Most perpetrators live in psychological torment, existing in an emotional wilderness, set upon an unending, futile quest to quell their internal terrors by enacting cruelty upon others in the misguided hope of finding safety from their shame once and for all. It should come as no surprise that violent perpetrators find no long-term escape from their nightmare lives so long as they continue to harm others. In fact, each new act of violence serves only to reinforce the frightening reality that these individuals are incapable of managing even their own impulses. In the end, there is only more suffering for perpetrator and victim alike.

The DSM, The Vietnam War, and the Establishment of PTSD

Human violence, fueled by the cycle of violence, poor social modeling by parents, extreme levels of stress, genetics, or the misguided desire of abuse victims to gain mastery over their pain may well be sufficient to explain the behavior of the outlaws, rebels, and run-of-the-mill domestic abusers in our midst, but what is the role of PTSD? Does PTSD *cause* violence?

Before we can answer that question, we must take a detour to examine the forces that shaped our current conceptualization of the disorder after the conclusion of World War II and the eventual recognition of PTSD as an "official" clinical diagnosis in 1980.[260]

As we have seen, the horrors of combat were the primary lens through which medical science first came to identify and catalog the effects of traumatic experience. In the relative peace between World War II and the Vietnam War, the quilt of PTSD was effectively abandoned much as it had been in the period between the two world wars. Much of the reason for this abandonment can be attributed to the fact that Freudian psychoanalysis came to dominate the field of psychological inquiry during the postwar, mid-century era. These elaborate theories of the mind are primarily concerned with internal psychological "conflicts" and early childhood relationships with caregivers. While the reality of trauma was not denied, the emphasis of treatment fell to vanquishing problematic coping tools—or defenses—that prevent the patient from functioning at more sophisticated levels of emotional development.[261]

Another reason the quilt of PTSD was abandoned at mid-century is because many leaders in the field of mental health turned their attention to the establishment of the first Diagnostic and Statistical Manual of the American Psychiatric Association in 1952. The first two editions of the DSM were assembled by psychiatrists involved with directly treating the mentally ill. Their goal was to give a common language to our perplexing behaviors and untidy minds. By the third iteration of the DSM in 1980, the direction of the manual had been wrested from psychiatrists and other clinicians by academic researchers. These researchers were concerned with creating structure out of the morass of theoretical approaches and nomenclature that had continued to plague the field. What emerged was a cookbook of mental disorders made up of standardized ingredients (i.e., symptoms) that would come to influence every nook and cranny of our lives today.[262]

Before the advent of the PTSD diagnosis, the troubling "image of the 'crazy Vietnam vet'—angry, violent and emotionally unstable—had become an American archetype."[263] To illustrate the pivotal impact the PTSD diagnosis has made on our culture, author Allan Young recounts the story of Sarah Haley, a psychiatric social worker who worked at the Boston VA Medical Center during the early 1970s. Haley was assigned to meet with a veteran who disclosed that he'd been a member of an infantry platoon that had murdered hundreds of civilians at the village of My Lai. Although he had been present, he claimed that he had not fired on the villagers. Following the massacre, the patient related that his fellow soldiers warned him he would be killed if he revealed these events to anyone. While the patient maintained his silence, he'd recently experienced a mental breakdown. He reported feeling overcome by feelings of terror, couldn't sleep, and now believed the members of his platoon were plotting to assassinate him. Haley, who was unfamiliar with the My Lai massacre at the time, accepted the veteran's story at face value. A short time after the interview, she presented her case notes and conclusions at a VA staff meeting:

"The staff assembled to discuss all the information and reach a diagnosis and treatment plan. When we met, the intake log already had a diagnosis [for this patient] filled in: paranoid schizophrenic. I voiced concern. The staff told me that the patient was obviously delusional, obviously in full-blown psychosis. I argued that there were no other signs of this if one took his story seriously. I was laughed out of the room."[264]

The perception in Congress, the VA, and veterans service organizations was that the new diagnosis was a product of "self-serving psychologists and psychiatrists who, having opposed the Vietnam War, were now out to milk the VA further."[265] Fortunately, "the same issues that provoke comments like these... had the effect of mobilizing support for PTSD in other circles, including the American Psychiatric Association."[266] The implications of an approval of the PTSD diagnosis by these powerful organizations was potentially costly and far-reaching— it would mean the VA would be obligated to provide services well beyond the scope of anything they had ever before delivered. The tide finally turned in the late 1970s when the director of the VA was replaced by its youngest ever administrator. This change in leadership was reflected in Congress, which was welcoming younger and more progressive members sympathetic to the plight of Vietnam veterans. In 1980, these forces aligned and the VA at last recognized PTSD as a compensable disorder.[267]

Below is the most current installment of the diagnostic criteria for PTSD:

Criterion A

You were exposed to one or more event(s) that involved death or threatened death, actual or threatened serious injury, or threatened sexual violation. In addition, these events were experienced in one or more of the following ways:

→ You experienced the event

→ You witnessed the event as it occurred to someone else

→ You learned about an event where a close relative or friend experienced an actual or threatened violent or accidental death

→ You experienced repeated exposure to distressing details of an event, such as a police officer repeatedly hearing details about child sexual abuse

Criterion B
You experience at least one of the following intrusive symptoms associated with the traumatic event:

→ Unexpected or expected reoccurring, involuntary, and intrusive upsetting memories of the traumatic event

→ Repeated upsetting dreams where the content of the dreams is related to the traumatic event

→ The experience of some type of dissociation (for example, flashbacks) where you feel as though the traumatic event is happening again

→ Strong and persistent distress upon exposure to cues that are either inside or outside of your body that is connected to your traumatic event

→ Strong bodily reactions (for example, increased heart rate) upon exposure to a reminder of the traumatic event

Criterion C
Frequent avoidance of reminders associated with the traumatic event, as demonstrated by one of the following:

→ Avoidance of thoughts, feelings, or physical sensations that bring up memories of the traumatic event

→ Avoidance of people, places, conversations, activities, objects, or situations that bring up memories of the traumatic event

Criterion D

At least two of the following negative changes in thoughts and mood that occurred or worsened following the experience of the traumatic event:

→ The inability to remember an important aspect of the traumatic event

→ Persistent and elevated negative evaluations about yourself, others, or the world (for example, "I am unlovable," or "The world is an evil place")

→ Elevated self-blame or blame of others about the cause or consequence of a traumatic event

→ A negative emotional state (for example, shame, anger, or fear) that is pervasive

→ Loss of interest in activities that you used to enjoy

→ Feeling detached from others

→ The inability to experience positive emotions (for example, happiness, love, joy)

Criterion E

At least two of the following changes in arousal that started or worsened following the experience of a traumatic event:

→ Irritability or aggressive behavior

→ Impulsive or self-destructive behavior

→ Feeling constantly "on guard" or like danger is lurking around every corner (or hypervigilance)

→ Heightened startle response

→ Difficulty concentrating

→ Problems sleeping

Criterion F
The above symptoms last for more than one month.

Criterion G
The symptoms bring about considerable distress and/or interfere greatly with a number of different areas of your life.

Criterion H
The symptoms are not due to a medical condition or some form of substance use.[268]

The aperture on traumatic experience has continued to widen well beyond the scope of combat over the various iterations of the DSM. As we can see, the DSM-V now recognizes exposure to any event involving "death or threatened death, actual or threatened serious injury, or threatened sexual violation" to be triggers for the array of symptoms now associated with the disorder. While "aggression" coupled with "risky and self-destructive behaviors" are now well-established components of PTSD, it would be inaccurate to broadly characterize PTSD as the "root" of violence. Rather, PTSD might better be regarded as a catalyst of these behaviors. After all, it only makes sense that a person living with PTSD could be depleted and angry much of the time. To cope, many reach for drugs or alcohol to numb the pain. Naturally, the introduction of these substances leads to further emotional dysregulation and stress.

Recently, a special category of PTSD has been identified for children age six and younger and, "angry and aggressive behavior, including extreme temper tantrums" is included as part of the symptom checklist.[269] If you will remember the case of Randy, the tiny, tortured bully from my elementary school days, a lot of us—children included—reflexively intuited what his home life was like and reached the very conclusions Cathy Spatz Widom reached long before her research on the effects of the cycle of violence was ever published.

. . .

Although I lack a verifiable narrative of my father's childhood, it's clear that Oscar was a victim of the cycle of violence. My intuition tells me that my grandfather, O.F., physically and emotionally abused his wife and son. Even though my grandmother, Ethel, was also being abused, Oscar may have viewed his mother's inability to shield him as a betrayal. As a result, my father came to believe, from a very early age, that his emotional needs were of little consequence to both of his parents. Such neglect is a virtual guarantee that a child will develop low levels of self-esteem and deep reservoirs of shame. As he grew into a young adult, Oscar's culture reinforced the idea that Ethel was yet another "useless" woman. Losing both parents to relatively early deaths, my father was forced to shoulder his childhood emotional trauma alone, without hope for resolution or reconciliation. While the actual details of Oscar's childhood will remain forever cloaked in mystery, the effects of his wartime combat brook no doubt as to the influence of PTSD on the course of his life. Miraculously defying death during World War II, Oscar returned home to create a life that held great promise for rich, meaningful experiences—experiences that he completely undermined with his rage and abuse. Angrily giving up on the possibility of receiving authentic love from the family he alienated, I believe Oscar decided to settle for second best—to garner the fear, admiration, and envy of others. Consequently, my father continued the cycle of violence with his own children.

In the person of my grandfather, I was provided with a model of how to put an end to this cycle of misery. Having grown up under the abusive hand of his own father, my grandfather took a different path, keeping his embrace of violence on a shelf as he cuddled nearby with his grandchildren. Hubert, like many survivors of childhood abuse (myself included), must have made a vow to himself to never, *ever* become like his father. Instead, we make a choice to identify with the other abused members of our families, rejecting, deep in our hearts, men who could have been so much more than our "daddies." They could have been our fathers.

Cults and Domestic Concentration Camps

When Patricia Hearst, granddaughter of famed megalomaniac and fake news pioneer William Randolph Hearst, was kidnapped at gunpoint from her Berkeley, California, apartment by members of the left-wing Symbionese Liberation Army (SLA) in 1974, the nation was stunned when images emerged three months later of the college sophomore cradling a cocked, semi-automatic carbine at her chest during the robbery of a San Francisco bank. The SLA had been organized only a few months prior to Hearst's abduction and was led by escaped convict Donald DeFreeze. DeFreeze had previously been implicated in the kidnapping of a synagogue caretaker and had, up until recently, been serving time for a Los Angeles bank robbery that ended in a shoot-out with police. To say that DeFreeze "escaped" from prison would be giving more credit to his cunning than would be strictly appropriate. He had actually walked away unnoticed while performing a work detail outside the perimeter fence that surrounded the minimum-security prison where he was being housed.[270]

DeFreeze was born in Cleveland, Ohio, and was one of eight children. He'd reportedly been severely abused as a child, having his arm broken on three separate occasions by his father as "punishment." DeFreeze dropped out of school in the ninth grade and soon developed into a violent young man with a fascination for guns and homemade bombs.[271] Many have come to believe that DeFreeze (a Black man) was a police or intelligence informant who was being paid to infiltrate the Black Power groups that were flourishing in the late 1960s.[272] DeFreeze and the group of White, Berkeley-based Marxist activists who formed the SLA were intent on overturning the capitalist economic system through force. They'd already murdered an Oakland School District Superintendent—and seriously wounded his deputy—whose only crime against the "People" had been his onetime endorsement of the creation of ID cards for students.[273] In an irony apparently lost on members of the SLA, DeFreeze had appropriated the term "Symbionese," which refers to the process of biological symbiosis in which organisms coexist in a state of harmonious and mutually beneficial interdependence. The group's goal was to bring about an economically and socially equitable society that would be achieved through the radical redistribution of wealth—eliminating prisons and monogamy as part of the bargain.[274] Like the outlaw gangs and Bushwhackers a century before, the SLA's narcissism was such that they appointed themselves the ultimate arbiters of "justice," and anyone who stood in their way, even innocent bystanders, were subject to the wrath of their ego-driven violence. The SLA symbolically chose April 15th, Income Tax Day, for their "appropriation" of monies from the "corrupt capitalist state"—as represented by a branch of the Hibernia Bank in the sleepy Sunset District of San Francisco, only a few miles from the apartment where Hearst had been confined since her abduction.[275]

Around 9:45 that morning, Hearst entered the bank with three of her armed abductors. As instructed, she took up a position in front of a security camera that had been previously identified for the express purpose of capturing her actions during the heist. For her close-up, Hearst did not disappoint. She kept her gun aggressively trained on bank employees and identified herself as "Tania—Patricia Hearst," declaring at one point, "The first person puts up his head—I'll blow his motherfucking head off!" Two unfortunate customers who entered the bank as the robbery was in progress were wounded by one of the nervous abductors cum bank robbers. The heist lasted all of two minutes, but the images of Hearst, in her awkward brown wig, were destined to become an enduring symbol of the 1970s, as footage from the bank security cameras was endlessly looped on television news programs and splashed across newspaper and magazine covers.[276]

The unprecedented level of attention focused on this event was further multiplied by the wildly conflicting perspectives about what viewers were witnessing in the images captured from inside the bank that morning. Many felt Hearst was being coerced into her participation in the robbery. As proof, they pointed to their perception that one of the abductors had kept their gun pointed at Hearst throughout the robbery. Others felt just as strongly that they had observed Hearst acting on her own volition during the heist, and a tape recording released by the SLA one week later seemed to confirm this conviction. On the tape, Hearst claimed full responsibility for her actions and asserted her unequivocal allegiance to the SLA. She went on to take cheap potshots at her fiancé, Steven Weed, who had been tied up and beaten by her abductors during the kidnapping. It had been their wedding announcement—published complete with Hearst's home address—that had led kidnappers to her door. In the days after the robbery, Weed had been an outspoken defender of Hearst's innocence, maintaining publicly that Patricia had been manipulated into compliance through force. Many other defenders of Hearst's innocence—including her parents—felt her words on the tape recording sounded scripted and rehearsed, the tenor of her voice flat and disembodied.[277]

The following month, two of Hearst's abductors were caught shoplifting at a Los Angeles sporting goods store. As they were attempting to escape detainment by the store manager, Hearst, who was waiting outside, unloaded her automatic weapon across the storefront. Hearst and her abductors then made their getaway—which involved no less than the hijacking of two separate cars. One of the hijacking victims later remarked on Hearst's polite demeanor throughout his ordeal during which the famous kidnapping victim expounded on the effectiveness of cyanide-tipped bullets.[278]

The next day, Los Angeles police officers surrounded the apartment where DeFreeze and five other members of the SLA were gathered. As television news cameras broadcast the gun battle live, a fire was ignited by one of the canisters of tear gas police had lobbed into the hideout. As the building was consumed by flames, DeFreeze shot himself. His five companions died in the firefight. Hearst was not in residence at the time but was instead watching events unravel on a motel television set, twenty-five miles away, near Disneyland. Hearst would be on the run and in hiding with two of her remaining abductors for more than a year before she was finally rescued—or captured depending on your perspective—and put on trial for her crimes.[279]

While in custody, it emerged that Hearst had been blindfolded and locked in a closet where she was verbally and sexually abused for the first two months of her ordeal. After being allowed out of the closet, Hearst was raped by two of her abductors and repeatedly told she would likely be killed if she did not fully embrace the SLA and its mission. Hearst complied with these demands and embraced the SLA's doctrines— sometimes with the exuberant vigor of a religious convert—rechristening herself Tania, after an Argentinian-born, ethnic German comrade of Che Guevara who had been killed in the celebrated Communist's ill-fated attempt to overthrow the Bolivian government in 1967.[280]

In presenting Hearst's defense, attorney F. Lee Bailey—who had risen to prominence defending the Boston Strangler and who would go on to help defend O.J. Simpson in 1995—made the concept of Stockholm Syndrome widely known for the first time.[281] Stockholm Syndrome was a term coined in the period following yet another bank robbery in which four Swedish bank employees were taken hostage and held for six days in the vault of Kreditbanken on Norrmalmstorg Square in Stockholm. The robbery received an unprecedented amount of media attention, being the first ever extended event covered live on Swedish television. Police finally dislodged the captors with the use of tear gas. None of the hostages were seriously harmed during their extraction. It later emerged that during their ordeal, the hostages had come to empathize with their armed captors and had even come to feel fearful that police intervention would put them in harm's way. In the subsequent trial, the former hostages refused to testify against their captors.[282] "Brainwashing" some called it.

At the Hearst trial the jury didn't buy Bailey's rationale for Hearst's participation in SLA violence, and in the end, she received a seven-year sentence—serving less than two years before being pardoned by President Carter. The jury's decision didn't change the fact that the concept of Stockholm Syndrome had resonated with great numbers of the public. The idea that a brutalized kidnap victim, in fear for her life, might respond by giving her mind and body over to her captors rang true to many trauma survivors watching these events unfold.[283]

Four years before the Hearst kidnapping, the bloodthirsty murders of pregnant celebrity actress Sharon Tate—along with four of her friends—by members of the Charles Manson "family" tipped off a decade of national fascination with cults. Many of those in support of Bailey's defense of Hearst were already beginning to connect the dots between the concept of Stockholm Syndrome and the type of cults led by powerful, charismatic leaders. These cults would reach their horrific zenith in 1978 with the forced suicide of over nine hundred followers of Jim Jones, leader of the Peoples Temple, in the small South American nation of Guyana.[284]

Key to unlocking the enigma of Stockholm Syndrome and the power of cult leaders like Manson and Jones is the concept of "Identification with the Aggressor," first described by Hungarian analyst Sandor Ferenczi, an acolyte and member of the inner circle of psychology patron saints Sigmund Freud and Carl Jung.[285] Identification with the aggressor refers to a survival strategy Ferenczi identified in children undergoing traumatic abuse. In response to these incidents, Ferenczi believed a child may split off from reality and cease all thoughts and perceptions, becoming completely passive. Under this spell, children submit to all of their parents' "desires, or even anticipating them, and eventually realizing that he can find some satisfaction in this."[286] Many followers of Ferenczi's work went on to apply the concept of identification with the aggressor to circumstances experienced by adults who are exposed to traumatic abuse.[287]

These theorists have observed that adults can revert to a childlike state of defenselessness and passivity in situations where they are made powerless by a complete loss of control over their personal safety. To adapt to ongoing traumatic abuse, it's been hypothesized that victims fuse their identity with that of a charismatic, seemingly all-powerful leader. With an individual's volitions and sense of self effectively erased, the motivations of a parasitic group or the needs of a cult leader are embraced by the victim as their own. Victims often feel gratitude for "favors" they are granted by those in power—small things like being allowed to live.[288]

Existing in these asymmetrical power arrangements, it's believed that victims strike these self-destructive compromises to create an illusion of safety and protection for themselves by obeying the whims and commands of the leader. The unconscious cycle of passivity and pleasing of aggressors can continue ad infinitum, with fewer and fewer reinforcements of actual threats necessary to maintain this agonizing stasis. Obedience and loyalty to the leader or group can sometimes persist long after the actual danger is lifted.[289] In domestic violence treatment circles, this dynamic is summed up with the dictum, "one beating is good for all year."

Beyond statistical outliers like SLA kidnappers and cult leaders, the concept of identification with the aggressor finds everyday expression in the cycle of violence that occurs inside countless homes around the world.[290] Noted trauma theorist Judith Herman aptly identifies these arrangements as the "small, hidden concentration camps created by tyrants who rule their homes."[291] The concept of Battered Woman Syndrome (BWS) hinges on identification with the aggressor, keeping people of all gender identities in relationships with abusive perpetrators when common sense would seem to dictate running very quickly in the other direction. With BWS, the perpetrator and victim follow a repetitive, seemingly scripted pattern of behavior: first, the perpetrator explodes in a fit of rage and/or physical/sexual abuse; in response, the victim crumples in pain and despair; next, the perpetrator apologizes profusely, promising never to be abusive again; remarkably, the victim believes this is the sign they have been waiting for—that their abuser has finally seen the light and he will walk the righteous path from here on out; finally, the victim identifies with the pain and remorse of their perpetrator, feeling sorry for their abuser—often blaming themselves for having triggered the violent outburst in the first place. These steps can be repeated over and over again. For far too many victims, this lamentable dance never ends.[292]

Do Victims of Trauma Possess Free Will?

At the core of our understanding of concepts like Stockholm Syndrome, Identification with the Aggressor, and Battered Woman Syndrome are troubling questions involving the degree to which a victim of violence can exert a fully realized sense of volition or "free will" within the context of their abuse. Though most choose to look past these inconsistencies, I believe these theoretical conflicts are worth examining in some detail because they help explicate the fiercely differing perspectives regarding victim culpability that surfaced in the travails of Patricia Hearst and in the crimes committed by cult members like the Manson Family. Although these questions might be impossible to answer conclusively, they are nonetheless pivotal to our consideration of the full dimensions of the antecedents of violence, traumatic experience, and PTSD—to say nothing of the implications of responsibility with regard to my own parents' murder/suicide and the tide of politically based, ego-driven oppression sweeping over our country.

The concepts of Stockholm Syndrome, Identification with the Aggressor, Battered Woman Syndrome, "brainwashing," and the "mesmerizing" power of cult leaders each find their fountainhead within the framework of the mimetic ("zombie captain") model of traumatic experience. As we have seen, each of these concepts is grounded in the mysterious world of Charcot's hysteria and Janet's concept of dissociation. In rendering their "guilty" verdict, the Hearst jury rejected our (now) mainstream conceptualization of traumatic experience, concluding that Patricia made a fully conscious choice to facilitate the terrible crimes of her abductors—saying, in effect, that during the ninteen months between her SLA kidnapping and her arrest by authorities, she was not like a person under hypnosis, she was *not* a zombie captain, she had full agency.

In 1953, Nobel Peace Prize recipient Elie Wiesel published an autobiography entitled *Night*, which documents his experiences as a Nazi concentration camp prisoner during World War II. Living in the shadow of the smokestacks of the crematoria, Wiesel, a kindhearted and highly devout fifteen-year-old Jewish boy, transforms, in less than a year, into a man capable of making dark, inhumane calculations in his daily fight for survival. Summoned to visit the camp dentist, Wiesel learns that the man—a fellow Jew—planned to extract his gold crown under orders of their Nazi commanders. Over the course of two weeks, Wiesel begs off, claiming to have a fever. Shortly thereafter, Wiesel learns the dentist's office has been closed and that the dentist is about to be hanged. "It appeared that he had been dealing in the prisoners' gold teeth for his own benefit. I felt no pity for him. In fact, I was pleased with what was happening to him: my gold crown was safe. It could be useful to me one day, to buy something, some bread or even time to live. At that moment in time, all that mattered to me was my daily bowl of soup, my crust of stale bread. The bread, the soup—those were my entire life. I was nothing but a body. Perhaps even less: a famished stomach. The stomach alone was measuring time."[293]

As callous as Wiesel's calculations might appear to be in the case of the dentist, one incident in particular stands out in my mind because it puts into sharp relief the dicey implications of victim culpability in the midst of traumatic experience. Wiesel shares the story of the day that his father and he were being forced to load heavy diesel engines onto a waiting train. In the process, the Kapo—a Jewish overseer—begins to beat his beloved father with an iron bar for being too slow. "You old loafer!" he started yelling. "Is this what you call working?... At first, my father simply doubled over under the blows, but then he seemed to break in two like an old tree struck by lightning." Wiesel shares that in the moment, he *blamed* his father for having invited his own beating. The son remains mute and on the sidelines, *not* contemplating intervention. In fact, Wiesel tells us that he even considered running away. Wiesel concludes, "What's more, if I felt anger at that moment, it was not directed at the Kapo, but at my father. Why couldn't he have avoided Idek's wrath? That was what life in a concentration camp had made of me."[294]

Was Wiesel the captain of his ship at that moment, making a calculated decision—based on clear-sighted logic—that "if I intervene on my father's behalf, I will not stop the violence—in fact, I will be beaten myself"? In other words, did he have the same ability to exercise a fully conscious choice—as you are now presumably capable of doing as you read this book—or was he in a state akin to hypnosis (or dissociating), identifying with his aggressor, a zombie tacitly endorsing and facilitating his captor's brutal abuse? Some theorists argue that in the latter case, the victim still holds some degree of responsibility, implying that victims—even if they are in a dissociative state—are complicit in helping to facilitate the violence against themselves because *there is no part of their being that is rejecting their abuser.*

No one disputes that under conditions of extreme fear and powerlessness victims of trauma do, in fact, consciously help perpetuate harms against themselves and others, compelled, as they are, by the necessity to survive their traumatic circumstances. However, many, if not most, are understandably alarmed by a proposition that implies that victims are in any way complicit—much less *responsible for* their abuse—or the abuse of others. Nevertheless, this is the inevitable outcome of our understanding of traumatic experience, grounded as it is in the concept of the zombie captain/dissociative state.

Internalized Oppression and Vanishing Identities

My mother, Judy, like most women brought up during the middle years of the twentieth century, had no shortage of psychological captors—her parents, suitors, other women, the patriarchal social order... the list is long. While she was not physically held hostage, these aggressors dominated an outsized sphere of influence within the realm of her decision-making and self-image. The small-minded judgment of insecure women, her parents' criticisms, class consciousness, and gender bias—all jealously dictated how she would feel about herself. From an early age, love and bondage became inextricably intertwined, her identification with her aggressors encompassing her psyche slowly and methodically, but with unyielding persistence.

Like the Hearst jury, many of us are loath to acknowledge just how little control we have over our own lives. In reality, our every decision is influenced by tidal cultural forces and the unconscious operations of our individual psyches. Owning a gaudy plate commemorating a bank heist in which four innocent people were murdered or displaying your grandfather's prison billy club in the family rec room suggests an ear accustomed to the background noise of perpetual violence—*of cruelty made quaint*. As television and movie westerns played nonstop in the background, my grandfather and mother were desensitized to the full magnitude of the violence that surrounded them because racism, guns, and ego-driven violence were portrayed as ordinary—even valued fixtures of their family and culture.

What's more, the enduring racism of my mother's ancestors kept alive the precept that human beings could be classified by a wholly fictional, artificially derived system of value based on a person's race, reinforcing the supposition of White supremacy in the process. Humans have existed on the slippery slope of these categorizations perhaps for the entirety of our existence, throwing people of color, women, members of the LGBTQ community, and random out-groups (like lepers and the mentally ill) off a cliff (or down a well) whenever it was expedient—or even just "for the hell of it, bro!"

If the dominant culture—and everyone you know—holds the presumption that a person's humanity can be prioritized based on genetic and predispositional variations over which they have absolutely no control, then it is not a huge leap to dismiss any artificially labeled group as "less than"—*even if you include yourself as a member of one of those groups*. For my mother, the background noise of White superiority, as damaging as it was to others, helped to facilitate the seemingly casual, but bedrock idea that women are of inherently less value than men. My grandmother was not far off the mark in her diagnosis of my mother's "low self-esteem," but the implication that she was to blame for her predicament would be unfair. I believe the concept of internalized oppression, a process recognized to trigger internal conflicts and poor self-regard, would be a more accurate summation.

In many ways, Judy was an uncommonly strong and resilient individual, but her vision of herself and the world was, shall we say...

seriously hindered by her upbringing and her culture at the time she came to work as a secretary for my father in 1962. At that moment in history, a single woman couldn't get a bank loan or obtain a credit card. In the world where she grew up, the formal institutions of slavery and indentured servitude had been abolished, but for women like Judy, their choices and identities were still largely the property of men. For confirmation of this proposition, all you had to do was look at her checkbook—the single name in the upper left corner read "Mrs. Oscar F. Lewis."

Chapter 11

The Flood

Outside, the fierce morning heat is releasing the moisture that has been trapped in the sodden soil all night, cloaking the approaching noonday bright in a residue of oppressive dampness. Throughout the previous spring, torrential rains lashed the Midwest, and today, one full week after the Fourth of July, there is still no end in sight. The airwaves are full with coverage of the swollen Mississippi River over on the other side of the state. Hundreds of levees have been breached. Footage shot from helicopters passing overhead vividly captures the magnitude of the catastrophe. Entire communities have been swallowed up by a noxious stew of mud, sewage, and agricultural pollutants, with the encroaching tide stretching deeper and deeper into the adjacent flatlands each passing day. To provide a broader context and identity to these developments, the news media christens this disaster the Great Flood of 1993, breathlessly pronouncing the deluge to be "a once-in-a-century event."[295]

That Sunday morning I'm inside, recovering from a night of drunken conversation and feverish copulation with a closeted cattleman named Matt. While there was an indisputable chemistry between the two of us, we were not "dating," per se, and the chances of our becoming a couple seemed, at best, a long shot. Over the previous two years, my laissez-faire approach to our liaisons had worked wonders to disarm this cowpoke's native panic of people harboring designs for complicated emotional entanglements, providing unfettered access to a breed of man that sparked spine-tingling currents of reverential desire deep in my core. I particularly liked the fact that Matt's labor relied more on his hands than his mind, and aside from his sexual preferences, he was not dissimilar to my father and the crew of construction workers he'd overseen at job sites. Like these men, Matt seemed to have claimed his seat at the head of life's table without a trace of self-consciousness or internal conflict. No whiff of unnamed burdens hidden beneath the surface here.

For closeted men like Matt, the mingling of male entitlement and "good ol' boy" masculinity works wonders to vouchsafe one's heterosexual status and keep gossip to a minimum—but only up to a certain point. In a couple more years, this paradox in Wranglers would be fast approaching that pivotal mid-thirties cutoff whereby the continued absence of female companionship can topple even the most sincere of deceptions.

I no longer remember my reasons for abandoning Matt's cozy bed in the first hours of that Sunday morning to pour myself into the car my parents bought for me after I'd totaled my mother's Cutlass a year earlier. Our nights together were infrequent, and I loved cuddling up with Matt, taking in his scent and the shape of his body against mine as I drifted in and out of sleep. The memory of my recent skid off a misty road into a fire hydrant one drunken 3am should have been more than enough to make almost anyone think twice about navigating the hour drive back to Kansas City from Matt's rural outpost.

Fate gave me a pass—as it does more often than not—during those particular predawn hours. The room where I would awaken, unscathed but for a hangover, was the basement bedroom of my childhood home on Blue Ridge Boulevard. What initially stirred me from sleep for the second time that morning was the sound of my parents arguing from the kitchen above. Through the scrim of my grogginess, I could make out that my father was shouting, in the hoarse, croaking voice characteristic of the elderly, that my mother had done "nothing" to observe Father's Day, three weeks prior. Judy countered, in her tear-choked, beseeching tone, these entirely false accusations, presenting relevant evidence to the contrary; there had been a special dinner, a homemade dessert as well as cards and praise for my father—now just a few months shy of his seventy-sixth birthday. They went back and forth like this for far too long, determinedly retracing the same steps in this pathetic, age-old dance.

During the two years I'd been living back at my parents' house, these arguments had seemed less frequent compared to my childhood recollections. However, I was convinced my parents had only become more adept at hiding their worst behaviors out of a fear I would become so alienated by their fights that I would leave Kansas City for good. The previous evening, nothing seemed out of the ordinary as I passed through the family room on my way out to the garage. Oscar was sitting on the sofa watching television. Judy, already dressed for bed in a full-length floral robe, was stretched out on a wicker chaise nearby. My mother glanced over the top of the newspaper she was reading and peered at me from above her half-glasses, smiling affectionately as she said goodbye to me for the last time.

By that evening, it was starting to feel like an eternity since the day my parents welcomed me back from my time on the road with a sigh of relief and a grunt of ambivalence. Like most adults who find themselves unexpectedly rooming with their aging children, Judy and Oscar had been understandably—but quietly—incredulous that my trajectory from college optimist to mid-twenties flop could be measured in just eight short years. With a succession of apartments in Miami and Boston quickly fading into the haze, no doubt their Flying Dutchman had finally landed with a thud. With not much to show on my resume besides an English degree and a string of jobs waiting tables in nice, but not very fine restaurants, I was now existing in a twilight world of low-paying service jobs, my only respite being Stoli tonics and a promising stint as the new face on my hometown club scene.

In fairness, I had finally begun to make some tentative inroads into a more substantial life by enrolling in several psychology classes at

UMKC with the hope of resuscitating my flaccid GPA. Though my family had indulged my recent whim to become a commercial aviator by bankrolling my training for a private pilot's license, this latest venture was gaining some serious momentum, and looked to be building into a legitimate stab at grad school. Surprising everyone, including myself, I was succeeding in my most recent studies with a focused determination that had been noticeably absent throughout the duration of my undergraduate career.

My negligible list of accomplishments up to that point could be chalked up to the fact that the true nature of my vocation during those seven years away could not have been listed next to a bullet point on my underpopulated resume. Like most gay adolescents, I had missed out on a host of key social experiences most straight teens take for granted. After graduating from high school, I'd craved, more than anything, distance, and time away from everything and everyone I'd ever known so that I might let down a few of my heavily fortified defenses. In other words, I had had some catching up to do.

Before I Knew I Was in a Closet

As a boy, I'd been able to overcome—under the right circumstances—my initial childhood reticence to become a funny and outgoing kid, full of curiosity and creativity. Throughout elementary school, I functioned relatively well within the protective confines of nurturing female educators, perfecting my act as the teacher's pet over my six years at Chapel Elementary. During those relatively happy years, I developed several close friendships with boys who displayed a temperament similar to my own. At recess, we'd play made-up fantasy games—that never involved balls—and laugh together over our latest "Wacky Packy" trading card finds. A few of us would even become Scouts together but leave the organization behind when our den mothers yielded their cubs to the purview of the packs of Webelo fathers.

I now appreciate many of these self-selecting friends must have also developed same-sex attractions later in life. However, at the time, none of us could have imagined the cluster of preferences and interests we shared would ever evolve into something that would be linked to sex. By virtue of its emphasis on activities that do not adhere to traditional gender norms, and a less aggressive manner of being in the world, relationships like these can prove extremely fragile over the long haul of adolescence. Eventually the imperative to fit in or die, the ugly mantra of all teenagers, eclipsed my own needs, and extinguished all but one of these important bonds forever. As the Japanese proverb succinctly exhorts, "The nail that sticks out gets hammered down."

Like countless numbers of gay teens preceding me, most people probably never even registered the moment when the funny, amiable kid everyone had come to know turned—once again—inward, quiet, and sad. After my transition to Pitman Junior High, it was not unusual for me to speak no more than five words throughout the course of a school day. I would refuse to join clubs and couldn't have imagined joining a sports team. At lunch, I would sit silently at one of the cafeteria's long communal tables hoping against hope no one even looked my way. During those interminable hours I mostly just watched and observed. I watched with particular interest as the boys who had shunned me after our mothers stopped arranging our playdates went about the highly rewarding work of consolidating their red-blooded heterosexual identities—identities that seemed to be validated by the world every five minutes. I wonder, who among us would not succumb to an uncomfortable envy—or in my case, a masochistic idolization—of boys whose innate qualities of personality yielded such vigorous and unflagging nods of approval from the world?

Every day, I would don a straitjacket in the futile hope I could conceal unacceptable parts of my personality from the shame-inducing glare of the world. Every day, I took the forty-five-minute bus ride to school, all the while the boys behind me, who had gotten high at our bus stop before boarding, flicked the back of my head with their fingers, finding endless ways to assert my status as a "faggot." Other classmates looked on in weary fascination, no doubt relieved they were not the focus of this attention.

After getting off the bus, first period gym class held unprecedented opportunities for yet another group of bullies to taunt me while clothed *and* naked. The sound of two dozen pairs of sneakers slamming clumsily up the staircase from the frigid, subterranean locker room created a deafening, metallic drumroll that would transform into a muffled roar as we made our way onto the gym's hardwood floor for the inevitable warm-up exercise of "murderball," my twelve-year-old self feeling like nothing short of a Christian set loose on the floor of the Coliseum.

The word "bullying" existed during my adolescence, but the far-reaching impact of this type of abuse was roundly ignored by educators of the day. Without the psychosocial framework—and YouTube campaigns—that have emerged in the ensuing years to help properly contextualize these experiences, the self-hatred and confusion of gay teens—and other nails that stuck out—found fertile ground in the isolation of our days. We understood with every fiber of our being that we represented a pulsing, throbbing target, open to attack if we didn't perfect the art of making ourselves invisible. We knew that we would truly rather die than let our parents know our secret burden. We convinced ourselves, based on years of hard evidence collected in covert watchfulness, that if we ever exposed the extent and nature of our pain, then the jig would *really* be up. After all, the teachers at Pitman saw the abuse firsthand and pretended not to notice. The willful negligence of these authority figures reinforced what we feared most in our hearts: we were shameful beings, unworthy of protection from the terror visited upon us from God's favored children.

The overall effect of this type of bullying is mercilessly malignant to a child's self-esteem. If the theme of your bully's chant concerns a truth you are desperately trying to conceal, a part of your mind tells you, "Yes, he is right. And if he is right, I am deserving of this punishment." With daily repetition, the bully's taunts can become internalized—indistinguishable from your own thoughts and feelings. As a result, a stink of shame takes hold of your being. You come to blame yourself for something you didn't do because it is universally decreed that you are, without a doubt, repugnant.[296] This is where the line is crossed between "regular"—albeit hurtful—bullying, and the type of traumatizing bullying that warps the fledgling self-concepts of defenseless children.

In the beginning, the look of shame in the eyes of a victim is sufficient to prop up a bully's anorexic self-esteem, but these abusers can quickly develop an unstoppable drive to mainline the hard stuff. Most bullies will go on to crave the added high of seeing their gladiatorial thrusts and parries witnessed by an audience. And it's not just the cheers of validation by the spectators in the box seats that bullies eat up. More than anything, bullies come to crave the reflected glory of their kill mirrored in the eyes of the assembled crowd. The looks of shock, horror, and amusement on the faces of an audience act to highlight the scale of their latest transgression and confirm the magic of their twisted superpowers.[297]

It seems almost comical now, but my parents' only response to the trauma of those two years of junior high was to force me to work out every week at an inner-city boxing gym. Aside from the mix of self-consciousness and randy fascination I experienced in such a venue, I was against this intervention from the start—primarily because the workouts conflicted with Captain and Tennille's television variety show. I can still see Oscar (my mother never brought me—this was the realm of men) looking on with an air of studied neutrality from across the gymnasium as I attempted to mimic one of my trainer's moves. I will say on my father's behalf that he was adept at concealing his disappointment for this effeminate, skeletal specimen of manhood fumbling through his routines in the ring. After nearly a year, the program was mercifully dropped without further comment.

Oh, Yes, They Call Him the Streak!

When authentic expression of core components of the self are rigidly suppressed, these needs can often make their presence known by other means—actions that can be risky, behaviors that can be wrongly labeled as disturbed or perverse. Not surprisingly, if a person comes to believe their innate libidinal impulses are unacceptable to the outside world *and* they are given poor models of managing powerful emotions, weird things can happen. Case in point—during the same time that I was being bullied at Pitman Junior, I developed a habit of public exhibitionism. Those who lived through the 1970s will remember that "streaking" was something of a national craze for a few years—some random guy had even run buck naked past the rows of bubble-topped hair dryers at JoAnne's beauty shop, my mother's longtime salon. By comparison, I took great care not to be seen. I would find secure cover, then pop out or sprint for a distance when I was reasonably sure no one would be passing. In the moments leading up to my exposure, my heart would race with dizzying feelings of fear and elation. I was doing something that felt dangerous, even titillating. The places where I chose to expose my... compulsion... were telling: behind our A-framed Methodist church; at my father's office building; in the field behind Chapel Elementary; even on Blue Ridge Boulevard, in front of our house in the dead of night. Only after a bit of therapy as an adult was I able to recognize that these transgressions were really all about breaking boundaries. I was demonstrating to myself the ferocity of my spirit and the reality that I was not fully owned by the people who filled these institutions.

At about the same age, I also began to set leaf fires. One Easter Sunday, a fire I'd set got out of control, incinerating a winter-parched shrub at the side of our house. Celebrating inside, my family was drawn into the front yard to investigate exactly why so many people driving by on the street outside were slowing down to look at our house. When confronted, I lied and said I'd seen a stranger lurking around. They didn't believe me. The matter was dropped. I didn't get help. Even if they had sent me to see a therapist, I don't think I would have dared to share anything remotely relevant—at least not at first. In any event, these experiments in exhibitionism and pyromania came to a halt by the time puberty fully hit.

Fortunately, I was a good student and able to leverage this fact to my advantage, making the case with my parents that I should be sent to a private school because "I was not learning enough" at my local public torture chamber. Judy and Oscar seemed to jump at this proposition. Within six months, I found myself starting my freshman year at the Barstow Country Day School, twenty miles—and a world away—from my eastside Kansas City neighborhood. Aside from Denton—my single self-selecting boyhood friend who had stuck around—I would never see any of the kids I had grown up with except in sporadic, anxiety-inducing long-distance sightings at the mall. My transition to Barstow would become the first in a series of self-imposed exiles and transformations I would initiate whenever I felt the pressure of my life becoming too much. It would take many years before I would come to recognize the collateral cost of these actions and the hard reality that I couldn't outrun my own shame.

The Preppy Transformation

"The" Barstow School was established in 1884 by two Wellesley alumni as the first independent college prep school west of the Mississippi. The current incarnation of the school was constructed on forty acres of cropland at the southern fringes of the city in 1962. Today, the school has been encompassed by affluent suburbs, and is reached by a private drive that curves along an expansive field hockey pitch before terminating at a looming brick-and-iron entry gate meant—no doubt—to evoke the well-known McKim, Mead and White "Johnson Gate" that opens onto Harvard Square in Cambridge.[298]

At the time we were touring private schools, Barstow was the only secular, coeducational institution of its type in the area. Though I'd not yet read *Lord of the Flies*, I'd instinctively refused to consider the rival, all-boys Pembroke Day School, for a very real fear of jumping out of the frying pan and into the fire. (At that stage in my life, I'd never met a red herring I didn't like and I was more than willing to let my enthusiastic endorsement of a coeducational environment stand as a hopeful sign to my parents that I harbored a budding fascination with the fairer sex.)

In one of the many handbooks we were sent outlining the ins and outs of my nascent "country days" at Barstow, I was informed that the school's dress code for boys forbade "uncollared" shirts and "blue jeans"—essentially the bulk of my wardrobe. In anticipation of the big move, my mother took me on a shopping spree at the local mall. Being no stranger to leisure suits—and having absolutely no sense of what I was getting myself into—I selected several snazzy combos from the Merry-Go-Round, a popular retail chain. For those who don't remember, Merry-Go-Round outlets were designed to resemble a carousel-themed nightclub, with pastel-lit interiors illuminating the racks of glossy fashions inspired by the beat of the disco music that pulsed throughout the stores. My perilous flirtation with these fashion "don'ts" could be attributed, in part, to a vacation I had taken earlier that summer. Jammed uncomfortably into the back of a TWA 747 at the start of our European "grand tour," I'd watched with rapt absorption my first in-flight movie, *Saturday Night Fever*, projected onto the bulkhead screen several rows ahead of me. The sound and look of John Travolta's Bay Ridge, Brooklyn, filled my senses. The frank sexuality of disco music set my heart aflame—as did my newly chosen polyester dress shirt imprinted with Erte-inspired representations of the Chrysler Building. Within days of starting at Barstow, I would beg my parents for more and more shopping sprees to correct my initial misstep. Predating by several years the 1980s "Preppy" explosion and Ralph Lauren's ubiquitous polo pony, I would become an adept disciple of a new look. For all intents, I was a native speaker in the coded symbols of wealth, fluent in the language of colorful Izod knit shirts, Brooks Brothers khakis, and Sperry Top-Siders—worn sockless, in all weather, of course.

The bullying stopped at Barstow. No one ever said a word about my preliminary disco inferno. There were only thirty kids in my class, and most were fairly well-behaved—at least to my face. Yet, invisibility remained my go-to strategy, and I avoided, as much as possible, interacting with the more popular kids, finding some solace in the handful of highly intelligent geeks and tech crew nerds at the school. I still felt lonely and isolated, but relieved to be left to my own devices. Once I started to drive, my friend Denton and I would seek out the only area in Kansas City that had any resemblance to a happening urban hotspot by going to Westport (where James and Adeline Dalton, parents of the Dalton Gang members, had once run a bar) on the weekends. We would haunt the aisles of Penny Lane Records and Whistler's Books before taking in a film at the Bijou, a refurbished art house repertory theatre. Often, we would stay for a midnight screening of the *Rocky Horror Picture Show*, racing into the aisles to show off our moves during the "Time Warp," and finding desperately needed liberation in shouting out silly (and filthy) ad-libs into the darkened space.

For each of us, the fundamental realities of survival dictate that we make ourselves of some value to heterosexual men. And when a boy—let's call him Tim for the sake of familiarity—longs for a rageful father's love and protection, it's almost inevitable that he'll grow into a young man with an aching need for male acceptance. As I finished out my final two years at Barstow, alone and in secret, I would haunt large gyms and sports facilities. Most attendants would just wave me past the check-in desk because I looked like a nice kid who belonged there. I would then make a beeline to the locker room to undress, shower, and hang out in the sauna or jacuzzi. I would discreetly—I thought—stare at the naked men, practically willing some wayward soccer dad to make a move. No one ever did. Alas, there existed no suburban Kansas City version of the Village People's YMCA—if there were, believe me, I would have found it.

Man Up, Tim

As an adolescent, the painful rejections and traumatizing bullying by my male peers conveyed the message that I was not a "real" boy, but rather a pathetic half breed—part man, part woman. "Real" boys were assertive, confident, naturally athletic, with voices held at a deep register. Emotions and movements of the body were carefully measured, with extreme expressions of feeling reserved for the domains of anger or rooting for the home team.

Though much of the world continues to claim otherwise, it should be obvious by now that one's sexual preference doesn't automatically imply the absence or presence of any particular constellation of characteristics. I feel these points bear repeating because many women may not fully realize—and most men forget—the extent to which certain habits of life are ruthlessly drilled into boys from the time they are born. Any deviation from these artificial norms quickly draws aggressive retaliation and threats of exile from the group. The fiery pitch of hostility visited on gay boys by other males stems from the perception that we are dangerous betrayers to our sex. Our experience is further devalued because it is characterized as "womanly" (read: feeling-based)—still considered the sine qua non signifier of interiority in our society. Any major deviation from these culturally reinforced gender and sexuality scripts is tantamount to challenging the idea that we are, by divine right—and God's will—to be ordered into hierarchies of value. These challenges to identity represent an existential threat to the patriarchy's position at the pinnacle of our societal pyramid—and in this mainstage dogfight, there will be no sharing of power.

When you have been cast out of the circle of men at an early age and then bullied for your differences, a young man can come to fetishize certain qualities of the sex to whom you are naturally attracted. It's not a stretch to find yourself sitting in a sauna fantasizing about unicorns— ghost figures who embody inherently incompatible dualities—the completely "straight" man who will desire me and love me as his partner. Without opportunities to test out these daydreams with appropriate peers as you grow into a sexual being, these unicorns can swell and morph in the shadows of the imagination. You can come to fetishize characteristics you have been bullied into believing that you lack— covertly embracing a highly traditional, rigid interpretation of masculinity in the process. This is a sign that the patriarchal power structure has permeated your very being and created an intolerable state of internalized oppression.

I would eventually find proxy "daddies" like Matt who were responsive to my advances, but I now recognize my fantasies of these men did not bear up under the level of mature scrutiny I now possess.

The total assumption of privilege that so drew my avid hunger can only be truly accomplished by a heterosexual man; those like Matt who contorted and concealed defining—but ultimately inconsequential—aspects of their biology are, in fact, prisoners serving life sentences. Furthermore, as we have seen in the case of my own father, being a "daddy"—or any bona fide member of the patriarchy—doesn't exclude a man from pain and suffering, much less the experience of trauma and PTSD. The price of remaining an unwitting foot soldier drafted into a lifelong battle to maintain the control of the patriarchy is dear. The responsibilities of maintaining the illusion of being a "real man" (and all that it entails) regularly crushes men, creating ripples of collateral destruction across the world.

The Final Weeks and Hours

After about ten minutes, my parents' argument over Oscar's Father's Day celebration that I'd overheard from my basement bedroom that Sunday morning in 1993 died down. I heard footsteps heading toward the garage, and then the diesel engine of the old orange Mercedes clattering away as it was backed out of the garage. It was not uncommon for my mother to leave the house when she became overwhelmed by my father's behavior.

Aside from their current dispute, I will grant that the energy and direction of the two months prior had been unusual. That period involved two foreign vacations—each with very different meanings. My mother, grandmother, and sister had only just returned from a tour of Great Britain. This was the first time just "the girls" had ever gone on a vacation together. In response to being "excluded" from Judy's vacation, my father had taken a Caribbean cruise, alone.

Oscar had never gone on vacation alone. He clearly wanted to demonstrate his independence in a fit of bravado by going off on the cruise, though no comment was ever made by the rest of the family regarding this fact. Literally and figuratively at sea, I believe he must have felt lonely, old, and pathetic. He probably sensed what a desperate move the whole trip had been. At seventy-five, he was really showing his age—he had shrunk considerably and often appeared a little wobbly.

During the previous five years, Judy had taken over managing my grandmother's comfortable estate (Hubert had died of cancer six years earlier, courtesy of Philip Morris), and had been on something of a mission since that time to help her Depression-era mother "enjoy" her money "while she still could" (Mildred had footed the bill for the British excursion). Naturally, my mother, being an only child, was set to inherit all my grandmother's assets. Judy's relative youth in comparison to her mother and husband was becoming increasingly evident during those final years, and the trajectory of her life, after their deaths, was coming more sharply into focus with each passing year.

Upon reflection, these divisions had been growing for several years. At some point during my time in college, my mother had begun sleeping in my childhood bedroom. She had redecorated, filling the space with Dalton family heirlooms, including a massive oak headboard my sister had used while she was growing up. In response, my father had pasted over Barbara's yellow apple wallpaper with a masculine grass cloth, transforming her old room into his den.

In the weeks leading up to the trip to Britain, it had been Barbara who had been alert to the danger my father posed. Chatting with her in the living room of her new condo, she'd confided—apropos of what, I don't remember—"I'm afraid he's going to kill us all." I must have taken this statement seriously, because I repeated this fear to my friend Ned not long after. Prompted by these anxieties, I'd even checked to see if the Luger was still in his nightstand during the time the girls were away on their trip and my father was out of the house on some errand. I found the pistol where it had always lived, with a fully loaded clip inserted into its grip.

After the garage door went down and my mother drove away, the house was silent. I heard no stirring or movement by my father from above. I was tired and hungover. I went back to sleep. I woke up about an hour later and turned on the nearby television to help ease myself into the day. The AMC cable channel was playing the movie version of *Fahrenheit 451*. I tuned in partway into the story. I had a mild interest in

186

the movie—it had been something my tech crew, computer geek friends had raved about at Barstow. Sci-fi was never my genre, but gazing at the screen, I found myself becoming drawn in by the movie's goofy, 1960s style of futurism and stilted dialogue.

My parents' argument that morning felt unsettlingly familiar to me. Oscar's casting around for some criticism, some invented reason, or minor detail writ large to prove he was uncared for, unloved, and unappreciated. It was true, we didn't love him, but at least by our words and deeds we mostly went through with a show of caring. So here we have my father, Oscar Lewis, blinded in his final hours by the spell cast by his wartime PTSD and unaddressed childhood traumas, like one of Charcot's hypnotized patients at Salpêtrière Hospital, giving the crowds a shocking taste of the bizarre.

Listening to my parents' argument that morning, I couldn't, for the life of me, understand why my mother still became so hooked into his manipulative rantings. Was she, in those moments, a zombie captain helping to facilitate the pirate's takeover? Or was she fully present—coolly calculating that her best move was to try and reason with her perpetrator so she might negotiate a better outcome? I now understand, after twelve years of marriage, something I could not possibly have grasped lying there that Sunday morning: when you live side by side with someone for years and years at a time, the ties that bind run deep. So deep, in fact, that the sense that the two of you constitute separate ships can quite often appear to be untrue.

Dark and cool against the noonday heat, my room was illuminated only by the diffuse light emanating from a tiny, curtained window and the television in the corner. The silence of the house upstairs was abruptly broken by a sound I couldn't recognize. Within half of a second, my own, hungover brain filed through a long list of possible sources for the sound I'd just heard. Though there was no record on file of previous occurrences, my brain spit out what it thought was a solid match in under a second flat: *The porcelain vase from the front hall table shattering as it hit the slate floor.* A few moments later, I heard the same noise again.

Chapter 12

Execution

On July 11, 1993, a few minutes after noon, I awoke to a dream world that felt more like a Dali concoction with time and space dripping off its matrix. I was already awake watching *Fahrenheit 451*, and now I had been awoken again. Before this moment, my consciousness had presented itself as a seamless, integrated unit of thought, feeling, and observation all working in tandem to mediate my actions and feelings. Now, my awareness felt like a Mr. Potato Head assembled by a distracted toddler. My vital body parts were all tacked on haphazardly, my eyes, arms, legs, and ears akimbo. Each part of me seemed to be plugged into the wrong hole, creating a reflection of myself that looked familiar but wasn't quite myself. Something had just happened upstairs.

> **Action:** "Is everything okay?" I call out.
> **Observation:** No response.
> **Thought:** *Odd.*
> **Action:** Putting on my white terry cloth bathrobe.
> **Observation:** Silence except for my footsteps on the stairs.
> **Action:** Passing through the family room.
> **Observation:** MacDuff (our West Highland terrier) frightened and barking toward the bedrooms.
> **Action:** Walking toward the bedrooms.

Thought: The smell of fireworks?

Observation: My father lying on his side on the hallway floor.

Thought: My father has killed himself.

Feeling: None.

Thought: Luger? Yes, right there.

Thought: This is it. This is really happening. He is finally gone. This is how it finally ends. This is how it happens.

Thought: He has killed himself.

Feeling: None.

Observation: He's lying outside my childhood bedroom.

Observation: MacDuff barking from inside the bedroom now.

Thought: No, can't be. She left in the Mercedes.

Action: Turn around.

Thought: She's not even here. I heard the engine as she left.

Action: Going back down the hall, through the family room to the garage.

Thought: This is really happening.

Observation: There is the Mercedes.

Feeling: Afraid.

Thought: I don't know what to do.

Action: Going back through the house.

Observation: MacDuff still barking.

Observation: Father's body.

Thought: Body? Okay, my father's body.

Observation: No movement w*h*a*t*s*o*e*v*e*r.

Observation: Blood soaking into the carpet by his head.

Observation: MacDuff still barking.

Thought: I DO NOT, <u>ABSOLUTELY</u> <u>DO</u> <u>NOT,</u> REPEAT <u>DO</u> <u>NOT</u> WANT TO LOOK IN THERE.

Feeling: The bottom of the world has dropped out. It's gone.

Thought: I have to do something.

Action: Peeking around the corner.

Observation: My mother is in a sitting position with her legs out in front of her on the heirloom Dalton bed set. She is slightly slumped with her back against the giant oak headboard, her pink sleeping mask covering her eyes. There is a patch of blood at her left temple.

Observation: MacDuff leaping around the bed barking. Barking.

Thought: *911.*

Thought: *Call 911.*

Action: Go to the wall phone in the kitchen.

Feeling: Calm.

Observation: I'm feeling calm and clearheaded.

Thought: That's odd. I shouldn't feel this calm given what's just happened.

Thought: My father shot my mother and then shot himself.

Observation: I shouldn't be calm.

Thought: He shot Mom in the head and then shot himself in the head.

Thought: *911.*

Thought: I'm in the house with two people who have been shot. I have to talk to the 911 dispatcher, and I will sound calm. That is not good. The police will come.

Thought: This is good that I'm calm. I can think clearly about what to do.

Thought: I need to make myself sound upset on the call or they will think I had something to do with this.

Action: Dialing 911.

Observation: A woman picks up. "911. What's your emergency?"

Action: Trying to sound upset and overwhelmed.

Thought: Is this convincing?

Feeling: She is very nice.

Observation: I'm starting to get emotionally hooked to the feeling of acting like I'm upset, but I'm not yet actually upset.

Thought: I think she knows I am afraid. What I just described to her was frightening. She says the ambulance and police are coming. Good. This is working.

Thought: Am I afraid?

Action: She's staying on the phone with me until they get here. I'm really glad to talk to someone.

Feeling: Completely alone.

Action: I ask, "Will they come in with their guns drawn?"

Observation: She says they will make me come outside with my hands on my head before they come inside. She says not to make any sudden movements.

Feeling: Scared of the police.

Observation: The dispatcher is reassuring. The police arrive more quickly than I thought. One squad car. They park on Blue Ridge, not in the circle driveway that leads right up to our front door. Two male officers in blue walking across the front yard. Guns in holsters. They ring the fucking doorbell! MacDuff's barking increases pace if that is even possible.

Action: Letting them in.

Thought: They seem weirdly casual.

Feeling: Relief at not being shot or publicly humiliated in our front yard.

Action: Directing one of the cops toward the bedroom, the other directing me into my living room.

Observation: The energy and pace of the cop in the back picks up. He is on his walkie-talkie sounding hurried. Voices back and forth on the device. The two cops confer outside my visual range. Ambulance arrives. Then another. News trucks across the street. Doors slamming. A cop starts asking me questions.

Action: I am answering.

Observation: Huge, collapsible stretchers coming in through the kitchen. There is a hustle of people as the house fills up. The nice cop tells me to stay with him in the living room. The stretchers are going out.

Thought: Mom would be so upset if they scratch the walls.

Action: I ask, "How are they?"

Observation: I hear, "We don't know." Female cop brings me MacDuff.

Feeling: I am so happy to see him. I feel so bad for what he's been through.

Action: Hugging him. Trying to calm him down.

Observation: More people filling the house. A few in uniform, but most in plainclothes. Some in jackets and slacks. Coming in and out of the front hall. Cars slowed down outside. Police directing traffic on the road.[299]

The female cop remains in the living room with the original cop. She's really nice, too.

Action: Approaching my neighbors Marge and Fred in the garage.

Thought: Fred is a physician. Five years earlier he gave my father CPR amid a catastrophic heart attack and saved his life.

Observation: Orange Mercedes sitting there still.

Thought: Fuck. He shot her.

Observation: Dressed up. Sunday. Embrace Marge. Snotty tears on her dress. The social interaction is pulling me out of Dali's world.

"He shot her!" my voice says.

"I knew it was bad, but I didn't know it was that bad. Do you know how they are doing?"

"No, I don't know how they are doing. I don't see how they could be alive. He shot her in the head."

"He must have had some issue with his brain to do this."

Action: I'm looking at Fred like he has lost his mind.

"We'll go to the hospital and see what we can find out."

"Can you take MacDuff to your house?"

Action: Going down to the basement bedroom to make some calls.

Thought: How am I going to tell Nana? How can I possibly tell her what just happened?

Feeling: I feel so horrified for her.

Action: Trying Barbara. No answer.

Feeling: Needing to talk to Barbara. Needing to see Barbara.

Action: Calling Barbara again. No answer.

Action: Calling my sister Gail. My brother-in-law, Bill, picks up. Telling him that I have something really important to say and that he should be on the phone at the same time as Gail.

"You're joking, that's not right. He's joking, right, Bill?"

"No Gail, he's not joking."

"We're flying out ASAP."

Action: Calling my friend Ned. He is on his way.

Feeling: I want to talk longer. I feel cut off. I need to talk longer, but he is on his way now.

Feeling: Very alone.

Action: I take off my robe and I get dressed.

Observation: The questioning has resumed in the basement rec room—aka the Dalton Family Museum. It's the two nice cops, one male and one female.

Action: Ned arrives.

Thought: How did he get in?

Action: Being helpful. Cooperating fully with the authorities because I have nothing to hide, I explain that my fingerprints will be on the gun. I tell them why. I start smoking.

Thought: I have never smoked in my parents' house.

Feeling: Weird to smoke, but I keep doing it. This is what a person under extreme duress is supposed to do.

Thought: Where's Barbara?

Action: I can't reach Barbara.

Thought: How am I going to tell Nana?

Observation: Someone told me that they sent my father to the Independence Sanitarium and my mother to Research Hospital. Separate hospitals seem entirely appropriate.

Action: Agreeing to everything the police ask me. Agreeing to have my hands tested for gunpowder burns.

Thought: Nothing to hide here, officer.

Observation: Pappy's wooden billy club hanging nearby. They tell me I will have to go downtown to make a formal statement.

Ned brings word back.

"Your father is still alive. Your mother is still alive."

Thought: How does he know these things? Is he magic?

Feeling: Dazed.

Thought: What? How can it be.

Feeling: Disbelief.

Thought: Oh please. Oh please. This all could be overcome.

Observation: I'm told I must go to the station with the two detectives. Nobody asks me if I want to go to the hospital. Nobody says I'm under arrest. Nobody tells me I don't have to go with them.

Action: Telling Ned to alert my therapist.

Thought: That's what people under extreme duress do, right?

Action: Sitting in the back of an unmarked police car for the long ride downtown.

Observation: It's daytime out.

Feeling: Very nice to be out of the house.

Observation: Quiet.

Observation: It's Sunday afternoon.

Observation: The two detectives are chatting casually.

Thought: Do they know what just happened?

Thought: Is this what their weekends are usually like? Going to murder scenes?

Action: Entering the old Art Deco police headquarters downtown.

Feeling: Curious. Looking around. Never been here before. Taking on aspects of an adventure.

Thought: I'm a tourist in my hometown.

Observation: Why aren't I at the hospital?

Thought: Why am I all alone?

Thought: The Menendez brothers.

Observation: Questioning. Questioning. Answering. Questioning. Answering. Bathroom.

Action: Looking at myself in the mirror. Branding this moment in my brain.

Thought: Remember, Tim. You were here in the bathroom of police headquarters. This is happening. Don't ever forget.

Action: Riding home.

Observation: Late afternoon light.

Observation: Therapist and Ned waiting for me. Father dead. Mother in ICU on life support. Not looking good.

Thought: Best that he is dead. Not surprised he didn't make it. If he had lived and she died, then....

Action: Pretending to be the patient. It's me and not me.

Feeling: Sorry for spoiling my therapist's day all for nothing.

Thought: I really should be breaking down since she's made all this effort.

Observation: "Research Hospital."

Thought: God. Mom always joked, "Don't ever let me die there." Seriously. She hated Research Hospital. I don't remember why. More important things to worry about now.

Observation: Nana is in the waiting room. Lots of people are there. A combination of family and friends that you would never expect to see all at the same time except at a wedding or a funeral.

Observation: Everyone regards me with hushed awe. They think I have a story to tell. They think I know "what the hell happened?" This is the question on all of their minds but they are too polite (and too scared for my mother) to ask. God knows what they are thinking about my father.

Thought: I'm not alone. Finally.

Feeling: Relieved that I don't have to break the news to Nana myself.

Thought: She might be feeling ashamed in front of them.

Observation: Mom in ICU. Horribly swollen face.

Observation: Hair a mess.

Observation: Weird rising and falling in her chest.

Observation: Tubes.

Observation: Beeping.

Observation: Lots of activity outside. Mom has no brain activity, I'm told.

Feeling: So, so sad for her. So indescribably sad for her.

Action: Nana hugging me as we look down on my mother.

Feeling: Guilt. Guilt. Guilt.

Action: We found Barbara.

Feeling: Relief. I need to see Barbara. Only she gets it.

Action: Barbara and I embracing and crying in another room. Just the two of us.

"What are we going to do?"

"I don't know."

"You might as well all know I was with father, Mitchell, and his family today since everything is now out in the open."

"Okay?"

Thought: Fine? Good for you?

Feeling: Confused.

Thought: Who cares about that now? The only people who that might really matter to are dead and dying? How is this affecting her?

Observation: Doctor. "No hope, no need to make decisions tonight. Organs?"

"53, diabetic."

"I didn't realize she was that old. Thanks anyway."

Thought: She'd be glad for the compliment.

Observation: I'm told that Ned and my mother's childhood friend who I haven't seen in years have hired a special company to clean up the house and dispose of my mother's bloody mattress. It's a day for revelations.

Feeling: Guilty and grateful.

Thought: I wonder where you'd find someone to do something like that.

Action: Saying nothing except "thank you" for probably the hundredth time today.

Observation: Everyone goes home.

Action: Sleeping at Ned's. No more memories from that day.

Observation: Next day. Hospital. Same room No more hope.

Action: Barbara and I approving removal of life support after a brief discussion.

Feeling: Acutely aware of this being a moment I will never forget.

Action: Surveying everything from outside myself and dully taking notes in my head.

Observation: My actions, just pretend actions, not connected in the *right* or expected way to my feelings. My brain is analyzing to make sure my actions are the *right* actions, actions I will be proud of when I look back on these events.

Thought: I will look back on these events again and again for the rest of my life.

Observation: Barbara and Nana standing next to each other, watching from across the bed from me.

Action: Sitting beside the bed, putting my head on her lap and my left arm around her in an embrace.

Thought: That's what I'd want her to do for me if the situation were reversed.

Feeling: It doesn't feel like her body. It's lumpy.

Thought: *Focus.*

Observation: Doctors and nurses fiddle with devices and leave the room.

Thought: Why are Barbara and Nana standing so far away. Why aren't they touching her? How can my entire relationship with my mother be over? What does that even look like?

Part 3

Where We're Going

Part 3

Where We're Going

Chapter 13

The Anatomy of Tears

"Don't fear the reaper. Come on, baby take my hand,
we'll be able to fly..." –Blue Oyster Cult

The last major event on our family's monthlong European grand tour in 1978 was a visit to Pompeii. The day before we were supposed to go, I'd woken up with a stomach bug that had forced me to remain in bed while my parents ventured out to explore the gardens and fountains of Villa d'Este at Tivoli. Though I'd enjoyed some aspects of my day, pretending to be Eloise "alla Romana," ensconced in our faded dowager of a grand hotel overlooking the Via Veneto, we were scheduled to fly home the following day and I wasn't about to miss my chance to visit the ruins of the doomed city. I was still feeling a bit unsteady on my feet as we emerged from our bus to join the herd of tourists being corralled about the archeological park by their guides. With the elongated profile of Vesuvius languidly presiding over the horizon, we trudged gamely through the maze of streets, awed by the vast scale and quality of preservation of this two-thousand-year-old marvel. At the end of our tour, as we were headed back to the bus, our group was diverted into a large, shed-like structure topped with haphazardly placed sheets of corrugated metal. As my eyes began to adjust to the diminished light inside, I was able to make out long rows of shelves containing dozens of Roman-era amphorae—the all-purpose, jumbo version of our ubiquitous two-liter bottles. Lining the dirt floor were scores of broken columns and other architectural features that would have been the highlight of any museum collection back home. Incredibly, scattered among these treasures, my now fully dilated pupils detected what appeared to be a fever dream of haunting corpses, emerging as if from Dante's lowest circle of hell. It was as though the golems of Jewish folklore, constructed from the muck and clay of the earth, had suddenly taken on fully human attributes. Clearly, we were looking at the bodies of those killed in the eruption in 79 AD, but how was that possible?

Earlier that day, we'd learned from our guide that experts have no shortage of competing theories about the circumstances by which the victims of the eruption met their end, with gruesome tales of suffocation, "flash frying," or being crushed by boulders topping out the list. Regardless of the precise cause of death, the bodies of the citizens of Pompeii remained where they fell as the city was buried under nine feet of ash. These layers of ash eventually hardened into a type of stone known as pumice, entombing the city—and everything it contained—until excavations were begun in the eighteenth century.[300] While poking around the ruins of Pompeii in 1863, archeologist Giuseppe Fiorelli discovered that the corpses of the victims of the eruption had left spaces in the hardened stone before decomposing. In a stroke of mad inspiration, Fiorelli began filling these voids with plaster. Incredibly, macabre statues of the dead, frozen at their moment of death, emerged. Most are in the prone position, with chests and legs flat against the ground, heads tucked down. One poignant figure sits with their legs drawn up to their chest, hands clasped at the face, as if in prayer.[301] Fiorelli's clever handiwork captures something of the ineffable—yet just one look at these tragic figures transmits an unmistakable mammalian message. These creatures have, without a doubt, given up on the project of life.

Coming across the haunting accounts of incarcerated murderers collected in James Gilligan's *Violence: Reflections on a National Epidemic* many years after my parents' deaths, the memory of these plaster figures immediately sprang to mind. In his capacity as a psychiatrist and longtime director of the Massachusetts State Prison System, Gilligan had the opportunity to speak at length with a number of inmates serving time for crimes of extreme violence. The common theme that unites these disparate stories is the fact that these men, like the victims of Vesuvius, have also given up on the project of life, becoming what the author describes as "the living dead." Like the citizens of Pompeii, each of these killers unwittingly found themselves living atop an active volcano, with mentally ill and drug-addicted parents erupting with life-threatening and perverse extremes of abuse—think serial rape, ongoing murder attempts—which were seldom acknowledged much less discussed. Instead of being entombed under layers of solidified ash, these men had been buried under a barrage of powerful communications that conveyed the message that they were worthless human beings, incapable of being loved.[302]

Complying with these negating messages, these trauma survivors came to generalize the dynamics of their abuse onto the world at large —shunning life-redeeming bids for comfort, support, and validation from others. This self-destructive path, while an ostensibly rational survival strategy, has the long-term effect of deadening all warmth and positive emotions within them. For human beings, dwelling in these emotional deserts can become so intolerable that many prefer their own deaths—and the deaths of others—to the continuation of the torment that the rest of us refer to as life. In the most cogent summation I have come across regarding the motives of killers like my father, Gilligan concludes, "The living dead need to kill others, because for them, the most unendurable anguish is the pain of seeing that others are still alive."[303]

To illustrate the extent of this anguish, and the level of distorted thinking taking place in the minds of these men, Gilligan offers the perspective of one killer who proclaimed, "The people I murdered had murdered me. They murdered me slow like. I was better to them. I killed them in a hurry." Not surprisingly, Gilligan added that "the suicide rate among men who have just committed murder is several hundred times greater than it is among ordinary men of the same age, sex and race."[304]

Given my father's diminishing capacities, it's not likely that he would have been physically capable of killing every member of our immediate family. Moreover, the full impact of his homicidal acts would have largely fallen flat without leaving behind those of us who held a significant personal stake in the outcome of his actions. Though he left no note or other indication of his motives, his actions spoke unequivocally to our punishment for our perceived betrayals... for having "killed" him "slow like." However, as his final argument with my mother over Father's Day demonstrated, he had, by the end, completely lost touch with reality, imagining slights and rejections that never occurred, but nevertheless felt totally real to him.

How Is the Son of a Murderer Supposed to Act?

Just eleven months after my parents' deaths, O.J. Simpson's low-speed car chase along the 405 freeway in Los Angeles would be broadcast live, with details of the high-profile double murder being endlessly debated in the media as the "trial of the century" transfixed the nation. Like most incidents of domestic violence and uxoricide (the little-known word for the murder of a wife by her husband), the Simpson case quickly devolved into an exhaustive examination of the perpetrator's identity and plight. The media blitz that surrounded the Simpson trial was never really about its victims, Nicole Brown and Ronald Goldman, but instead represented a lurid peep show that highlighted ugly truths about race, class, and the powerful role of the patriarchy in American culture.[305]

It has never been easy to share with others the fact of my parents' murder/suicide, and the case of O.J. Simpson did nothing to help flesh out my experience. During the first year or so of trying to reconcile myself with my orphaned reality, I felt compelled to disclose this information to just about everyone I met, imagining that I would find the sympathy of others to be of comfort. It wasn't. I also imagined that I would be allowed greater latitude in my behavior, given my fragile emotional condition. Again, I wasn't. While people are very quick to offer support during a crisis, the ongoing heavy lifting associated with dealing with an actual person in the depths of PTSD is something else altogether. In the beginning, nearly everyone tried to roll with my depressed and increasingly erratic moods, but most were on a highly unrealistic timetable, expecting I would show some improvement within a matter of months.

In actuality, I was getting worse. Oscar's act of murder/suicide psychologically infected those left behind with the emotional deadness he'd shouldered throughout his life. Absorbing this terrible teaching moment, my father contaminated my very soul with the experience of his childhood trauma and wartime PTSD. I suddenly felt like a member of the living dead buried under nine feet of ash, ash that continued to solidify into ever harder stone with each passing day. Within two years, I was quietly but decisively dropped by all but two of my friends. Each morning when I woke up, I was deeply, deeply (deeply) tired. I knew I would feel that way for the *entire* day because I'd been feeling the same way *every day* for *years* despite extensive therapy, an ever-evolving array of psych meds, and a move to San Francisco. Allowing myself the luxury of drifting back to sleep for another two or three or four or five hours every morning was the most reliable form of relief available. The sense of giving in to the sweet embrace of sleep provided a delicious release from my intolerable feelings of shame, loneliness, and self-loathing.

Taking a cue from the model set down by my mother and nana, my sole sense of feeling productive during that time became keeping my apartment clean and orderly. My rambling Victorian flat just off Dolores Park was a place I hoped others would admire and envy. On one occasion, my then boyfriend, Clark, invited another couple over to our place for dinner. This was an unusual occurrence given that he was a compulsive liar, alcoholic, and fellow depressive. (After all, how could I have attracted and maintained an emotionally healthy relationship given who I was at the time?) In the days leading up to the event, I constructed narratives of myself to perform for our guests that might somehow make my existence make sense to other people: "I'm a bon vivant who has retired after being given access to his inheritance upon the tragic death of his parents. Consider me an intelligent yet misunderstood world traveler who has begun a new chapter in San Francisco."

On the day of the dinner party, I remember knocking myself out all day to make our place spotlessly clean. Vacuuming, washing the hardwood floors by hand, scrubbing the bathroom and kitchen down —all the while high on Vicodin, stereo blasting away. I started drinking the moment the guests arrived. The combination of pills and alcohol left me so fatigued by the time we got to dessert that I went to bed and passed out without telling anyone. Months later, I suggested we invite the lucky couple over again. I was shocked when Clark told me that he didn't think they would want to repeat their visit. Incredulous, I asked what he had done to push them away. When I was informed it was *me* that the couple didn't like, I was so taken aback that I can still vividly remember the details all these years later.

Encased in stone, emotionally "numbed out" in the midst of PTSD, it's those kinds of revelations that teach a person not to trust themselves.

Starting Over in Name Only

It's true that I had inherited a bit of money when my parents died, but it wasn't a life-changing sum. I'd impulsively bought a small house (then, about the same price as a 2020 BMW 6-series), hoping the proximity to my mother's childhood home in Brookside (she regularly described her time there as the happiest of her life) would help fill some of the overpowering emptiness I felt inside. I managed to distract myself for about six months with painting and arranging the furniture, but I soon lost interest. A couple of my good friends were moving to the Bay Area during that same time, and my childhood friend, Denton, had been living in San Francisco for the past several years. Following in the footsteps of those who'd come to the city a generation before wearing "some flowers" in their hair, San Francisco seemed like a conspicuously fitting place to start over. With enough money to fund an apartment and not work for a few years, I sold the house in Brookside after just one year and left my nana and sister Barbara behind. (Barbara had married a man with five children less than a year after our mother's death. She had seemed to move on—or at least had her hands full, as did my sister Gail, whose two children were now on the cusp of starting families of their own.)

As we have seen, PTSD is most often triggered by an event where one's physical safety—or the safety of another person in close proximity—is violated, resulting in injury or death. On an experiential level, this powerful sensory input takes our generally abstract notions about death and transforms the naked facts of our mortality into a frightening reality. What's more, occurrences of PTSD almost always happen without warning and in the blink of an eye, adding even greater emotional intensity to these destabilizing events. It should really come as no surprise that many people who develop PTSD become absorbed with thoughts of death after being suddenly handed such life-altering insights. To further complicate this picture, many people suffering with PTSD become paralyzed with the anxiety that they will never recover from the deadness within and that they are fated to eventually die without ever having truly lived.[306]

During the first few years after my parents' deaths, it certainly must have appeared to others that I'd given up on the project of life. However, on the inside, I was doing daily battle with a terrible dread that I would never actually live. The gulf that existed between my imagined fulfilled existence and the living dead I'd come to embody would create an all-consuming preoccupation with my inadequacies that would prove highly self-defeating. To make matters worse, I didn't have the first clue about what constituted a fulfilling existence. I remember wanting a life that would impress others—a great home, an exciting, lucrative career, a coterie of fascinating and devoted friends, exotic travel experiences, etcetera. And—by the way—I needed these things *right now,* not ten years down the line! Saddled with such unrealistically high expectations and a frantic urgency to feel some measure of relief from my daily existence, everything I did was doomed to fall short of my expectations.

At that point, I was like one of those kids in Texas who seemed to be constantly falling down some forgotten backyard well during the 1980s. Ensconced in my cocoon at the bottom, I'd find myself peering up, groggy and dazed, as friends and family put in the occasional appearance from above. I was acutely aware of the fact that I needed to get my life together, but how could a person find a good job, take out a mortgage, or meet an emotionally healthy, loving partner under such circumstances? At the time, my emotional needs were so great and my sense of overwhelm so profound that I could only handle living day by day. Sometimes the best I could do was to cope minute by minute. Pooling my energy, I'd pop my head up for a few hours, consume three or four espressos, and do the absolute minimum needed to survive.

I'd taken over caring for my parents' dog, MacDuff, but being out on the street for his walks would trigger paralyzing feelings of paranoid self-consciousness. I felt transparent—like people could observe my psychological inner workings. I imagined strangers could see how bizarre and out of place I felt just by looking at me. I was dangerously overmedicated by a psychiatrist who prescribed Klonopin—a highly addictive benzodiazepine that leaves people at once high and vacant.[307] I would surreptitiously acquire codeine pills but they would leave me with an odd sort of elation, out of sync with normal day-to-day interactions. At the time, I saw these pills as a guilty pleasure because they helped me to relax around others, but I was seriously overcompensating—trying to reach too high—jumping right past feelings of normalcy and into socially off-putting, manic highs.

You Keep on Pushing Me Over the Borderline

Living with intense, unmanageable feelings, poor emotional support, and unrefined coping skills leads many sufferers of PTSD to behave in a manner that is frequently categorized as "borderline." Borderline Personality Disorder (BPD) is the experiential manifestation of unprocessed trauma and a particular style of communication that virtually guarantees the sufferer will be shunned, avoided, and blamed for their erratic and unhinged behaviors. BPD was first identified in 1978 and entered the third major revision of the DSM in 1980. Since its inception, BPD has been a controversial disorder with a reputation for being largely untreatable. Historically, clinicians and other mental health professionals have viewed BPD as an intractable personality flaw, stigmatizing sufferers as manipulative and self-indulgent.[308]

Childhood trauma has been found to be the single biggest risk factor for BPD, but it is by no means a precondition for the occurrence of the disorder. [309] The presence of childhood trauma necessarily implies there was a significant issue in the child's relationship with their key caregivers—in most cases, their biological parents. For children, a healthy attachment to their key caregivers is paramount. From the moment of birth, an infant must reliably sense that their inner states are well-intuited by their caregivers. This feat is accomplished first through eye contact, touch, facial expression, and the experience of having one's basic needs—food, shelter, and emotional comfort—dependably met. It is only then that the infant will have the confidence to explore their world without being overwhelmed with the fear that their key caregivers—their sole source of nurturance and protection—will simply disappear if they look away.[310] Occupying these protected zones of physical and interpersonal safety, the securely attached infant can comfortably interact with the wider world, spurring vital cognitive growth and emotional development. By contrast, BPD is often the result of an insecure childhood attachment pattern predicated on poor parenting, disrupted connections, and/or forced separation from key caregivers.[311]

Though BPD continues to be categorized as a personality disorder, many researchers now conceptualize this affliction as part of a larger spectrum of disorders associated with trauma. Recent studies have found the co-occurrence rate between PTSD and BPD to be incredibly high, exceeding 75%.[312] The biological and genetic markers of BPD are now well established, with the effects of these in-born traits being multiplied by detrimental environmental factors like childhood attachment disorders and PTSD. The shift to viewing BPD as a trauma-spectrum disorder rather than an enduring personality "defect"[313] has fostered a long overdue reduction in the overall stigma associated with this affliction. And over the past twenty-five years, Dialectical Behavioral Therapy (DBT) has, at long last, brought relief to people suffering with BPD.[314]

Those suffering with BPD experience their symptoms across four distinct dimensions:

1. Unstable Relationship Patterns

People with BPD live in terror of emotional abandonment by others. Whether a result of significant early childhood disruptions in attachment or PTSD, people with BPD regularly experience dramatic shifts in their views of others, alternating between over-involvement and dependence on others and complete social withdrawal. As a consequence, people with BPD are naturally hypersensitive to social threat, particularly real or perceived rejections. People with BPD often become overly dependent or clingy when they feel their needs for psychological safety are being met. When their emotional needs are not being met, abandonment trauma is triggered. During these retraumatizations, people with BPD are often seen by others as manipulative and demanding. Over time, these behaviors do push people away, creating a self-fulfilling prophecy that can snowball into lives of extreme social isolation.

2. Disturbances in Thinking and/or Identity

The trauma of early childhood attachment failures or PTSD often results in chronic feelings of emptiness and a highly unstable self-image. People with BPD are extremely self-critical. This self-contempt is a trigger for unstable mood patterns. Frequent, intense, inappropriate displays of anger, depression, anxiety, and irritability are not uncommon. Goals, aspirations, values, and career plans are inconsistent, frequently change, and are pursued without conviction.

3. Behavioral Dysregulation

Those suffering with BPD often involve themselves with self-harm behaviors including recurrent suicidal gestures, attempts, and threats.

4. Excessive Behaviors

People with BPD often engage in impulsive spending, indiscriminate sex, substance abuse, reckless driving, binge eating, and cutting.[315]

Reactive Attachment Disorder made its first appearance in the APA manual in 1980, the same year that BPD was introduced into the DSM-III. This diagnosis addresses symptoms specific to children under five years old who are responding to abnormal attachment patterns typically triggered by parental abuse and/or severe neglect.[316] Beginning in the late 1990s, Complex PTSD (aka Chronic PTSD) was first identified in the DSM. Complex PTSD came as a long-overdue recognition of the cumulative effects of multiple childhood traumas and as a nod to the fact that most people suffering with PTSD did not fully recover within the six-month time frame initially set down in the DSM. Complex PTSD has now been struck from the DSM, but remains in the ICD-10, the international usurper formulary of medical conditions utilized by insurers and behavioral health providers in the U.S.[317]

Even with years of training and experience, I can still find myself falling into the same old traps when a patient suffering from Complex Trauma whacks me over the head with their BPD abandonment fears by becoming extremely angry over some real or imagined misstep I might have made. During these episodes, there is only space in the room for one victim, and the person with BPD will go to great lengths to illustrate the harm I have inflicted. Most will attempt to leverage their sense of abandonment into a sort of force field that they believe immunizes them against considering *my* subjective experience. This mental device allows people with BPD to remain effectively blind to the extreme challenges others face with regard to their behaviors.

To accommodate the person with BPD, those without strong boundaries often deprioritize their own needs. Those prone to guilt (like my mother) may even feel they are deserving of their ill-treatment. However, most people come away from these intense exchanges feeling angry and confused, unable to let go of the mental instant replay that keeps looping in their head (I often find myself repeatedly imagining a patient finally "seeing the light" with my logical reasoning). But any explanation, no matter how objectively sound, is taken by the person with BPD as further evidence of your insensitivity. Your needs are perceived as both a betrayal and a trigger for their righteous anger. The problem is the person with BPD has long since stopped relating to *you*. Instead, you have been unknowingly cast in the role of the perpetrator of their initial trauma. Of course, the person suffering with BPD is only trying to protect themselves, but in these highly charged moments, trauma survivors often lose touch with the social norms that traditionally guide social interactions.[318]

Undoubtedly, BPD played a pivotal role in Oscar's life and death. Never having dealt with his childhood abuse and neglect, his wartime PTSD, his feelings of abandonment after his parent's deaths, and the narcissistic blow of the loss of his first wife and family, my father was left with deep insecurities and an abiding sense of shame. While BPD most often results in self-harm behaviors like mutilation and suicide attempts, there is ample evidence that some number of people with BPD direct their physical violence outward. Furthermore, people with BPD will often use their emotional outbursts as a sort of loyalty test. If the victim remains in the wake of the abuse, the perpetrator's abandonment anxieties are quelled for a period. This twisted (largely unconscious) logic holds that "if I can be this terrible and they still stay with me, then I must be safe." However, the emotional numbing and unstable self-image that plagues the abuser will inevitably return, leading to yet another cycle of testing their partner.[319] My parents' final argument over Father's Day is riddled with the stench of BPD abandonment paranoia. Like most abusive partners, Oscar sought to control every aspect of Judy's life because he was terrified that she would leave him.

I feel the crucial—and eventually deadly—gulf that developed between Oscar and his family involved a failure to communicate to one another that which was most vital. My father never realized his mask of hyper-competence and the corking up of his traumatic pain resulted in borderline behaviors that kept us from connecting with the full magnitude of his sacrifice, suffering, and achievement. What we saw was a one-dimensional tyrant who could be decent to others only when the time and place was of his choosing. As a result, our capacity for empathy decreased incrementally with each unhinged outburst. This feedback loop became a virtual guarantee that Oscar would feel more and more unloved as the years passed. My mother, sisters, and I could at least take emotional comfort in one another. My father had no one.

• • •

The emergence of my own "borderline personality" in the midst of Complex PTSD was not helped by the fact that I spent great chunks of my teens watching soap operas with my mother. I started out with *All My Children* over one summer vacation and quickly expanded into the full ABC afternoon line-up that included *One Life to Live* and *General Hospital*. This was the era when soaps went mainstream and "Luke and Laura" ruled the daytime airwaves. I became so addicted that I bought our very first VCR so I wouldn't miss a single episode. In many ways, the highly charged emotional atmosphere of these shows mirrored that of my childhood homelife, so it only made sense that I'd be drawn in by the melodramatic happenings in Pine Valley and Port Charles.

As a teen and young adult, I was the type of person who wasn't completely in on the joke that these over-the-top soap performances weren't necessarily a "how to" manual for conducting adult relationships. At the time, being highly emotional and dramatic felt grown up—even sophisticated. In soap opera land, these highly charged emotional displays were how characters stood up for themselves (i.e., set boundaries) and gained the grudging respect of others. While you may have loved to hate

Susan Lucci's character, supermodel and serial seductress Erica Kane, it was clear that you tangled with this vivacious vixen at your own risk.

The sense of catharsis that Erica experienced as a result of giving voice to her unvarnished emotions gave viewers like me a vicarious sense of wish fulfillment in the midst of our own, trampled-upon lives. To add fuel to the fire, my own overheated emotions often seemed to make everything more eventful and exciting—like I was living in a movie. I distinctly remember thinking others would find me complicated and interesting if I emulated the characters on daytime television. Perhaps I latched onto these ludicrous examples of interpersonal relations because I didn't have the first clue about how to cope with the pain of living in a society that, by and large, viewed my innate sexuality as a perversion— to say nothing of my experience of having been raised under the shadow of a father suffering with untreated PTSD and BPD. The melding of these characteristics made for a curious mix—a bright young man with a markedly boy-like demeanor who was at turns shy and aggressive; haughty, yet insecure. At my best, I was a warm-hearted kid who would give you the shirt off his back—but during my worst moments, I was, of course, emulating my father's borderline behavior.

Only in Miami

Being thus absorbed by my tumultuous inner world—not to mention my daily regimen of soap operas—I graduated near the bottom of my class at Barstow, achieving only slightly above average SAT scores. Washed ashore in the lifeboat of my safety school, the University of Miami, I landed in Coral Gables, Florida, in 1983, the same year the cocaine bloodbath movie and immigrant-makes-good allegory *Scarface* was released. In the first weeks of my freshman year, I was discovered by two very domineering individuals, one female, the other male. She, a first-generation Cuban immigrant studying at Miami-Dade Community College, and he, a fraternity brother from West Palm with flaming orange hair. I was a kid who basically didn't know how to say no—though I dropped many hints and avoided their advances as much as possible. It would take my first two years at U.M.—and an unnecessary amount of teenage drama—to extricate myself from these two ill-suited relationships.

The glamorous luster of the television's *Miami Vice* cast a sprinkling of pastel-colored fairy dust across South Florida as I raced about making up for lost time. My overriding preoccupation became finding true love. I wanted the right guy to love me, but more often than not, it was the wrong guys who actually pursued me (see Keats's "Ode on a Grecian Urn" for a more poetic rendering of this intrinsic human folly). On the two occasions when the right guy told me that he loved me, I was immediately catapulted into a state of transcendent bliss beyond anything I had ever known. But it never lasted. I was unceremoniously dumped—though I was too naive to realize it at the time—and then quickly shuffled onto a plane at the Cincinnati airport (don't ask) by my first love. Then, a little over two years later, it at long last dawned on me that Dennis, the man who had healed that first broken heart, was unconstitutionally incapable of remaining even a little bit faithful. In a move that would do Erica Kane proud, I rammed the bumper of my car into the vintage VW van Dennis was restoring in a desperate bid to exact my revenge. I would grieve deeply over the loss of these two relationships and spend years romanticizing the greatest hits of our shared pasts. To cope, I would lose myself in late-night drinking and searching, exalting in my power to control men—at least for a few hours—with my innocent looks and wafer-thin body.

During college, I developed a small circle of gay friends, picking up with the same type of boys who had fallen by the wayside during my disastrous transition to junior high. For my generation of gay men, no tragic Judy Garland, clutched at the lip of the stage, torching *The Boys in the Band* with her rendition of "The Man That Got Away." We'd cut our teeth watching "Liza with a Z," and now had our own Madonna to revere. I became preoccupied with attending *Dynasty* parties and acquiring yet another new wardrobe, this time inspired by Miami's fashion-conscious Cuban-American culture. My grades fell so low after declaring a Business major (Accounting? Economics? What was I thinking?)—that I was suspended for a semester.

Just to set the record straight, several of my good friends and acquaintances did not turn their backs on me after I became a full-fledged "borderline" in the wake of my parents' deaths. Rather, many had, or would very soon die of, AIDS. During the time when I was just becoming sexually active, staggering numbers of the generation of gay men just ahead of my cohort were being cut down by the disease. Yet for me, the stricken skeletons cloaked in Kaposi sarcoma would continue to exist solely on the evening news throughout much of the 1980s. We all blamed Ronnie for his calculated "obliviousness," and debated if ACT UP and Larry Kramer were "going too far" in their fierce confrontation of a largely homophobic nation that saw the "gay plague" as a just punishment for our wicked ways. Though AIDS was frequently discussed in my superficially minded circle of friends, and I vividly recall participating in a candlelight vigil on Christopher Street in NYC in 1988, I was never a member of the more savvy, well-connected contingents of gay people who were volunteering their free time to help support the afflicted, all the while channeling their growing rage into the popular refrain, "We're here. We're Queer. Get used to it!"

The Trauma of Living Though the AIDS Epidemic

Upon graduating from the University of Missouri, Denton relocated to Boston. As I was finishing my fifth and mercifully final year of college, I was planning to follow Denton to Boston. At long last, we would be roommates, ready to take on the world together. However, a few months before I was supposed to move, he became very deeply involved with a grown-up-seeming journalist and quickly moved in with him. After graduation, I went forward with my plan anyway, but soon found myself a very lonely and unnecessary third wheel, directionless, and living with random roommates in Somerville. It was around that time that AIDS settled into my friend group.

Denton and I had finally come out to one another in college. Since that time, we'd logged an impressive number of late-night hours hitting the Kansas City gay club scene together on our school breaks. We were close friends who had been a part of one another's lives since we met in third grade. As teens, a spark of sexual energy fortunately never developed between the two of us—we functioned more like brothers. While Denton and I could have a lot of fun hanging out together, there were times when we didn't like each other very much. Nevertheless, throughout the years, like family, the two of us were confident that we would always remain in one another's orbit.

Denton had what I can only describe as a rhythm for being in the world. Even in elementary school, other kids were drawn in by his charm and charisma. There was just something about his blend of intelligence and sense of fun that felt contagious to everyone he met. Like many gay men, he had amazing taste—a fusion of the low brow and the high concept. He collected modernist furniture when you couldn't give it away and graced these minimalist trophies with campy tchotchkes like coasters adorned with pictures of mariachi bands. One minute he would be listening to Sarah Vaughan, the next, Malcolm McLaren. He loved making himself tea in his iconic Japanese iron teapot and was one of the coolest dancers I've ever seen. Even his name was quirkily memorable.

While Denton was clever in his banter, he was never one to swim deeply in his emotions. His parents didn't abide by complainers, and the apple didn't fall far from the tree. One Friday evening about a year after I'd moved to Boston, Denton invited me to meet him at Club Cafe, hours before the arrival of the late-night crush of South End bar hoppers. I can still see his matter-of-fact expression as he shared with me the news that he had tested positive for HIV, the volume of his voice artificially elevated to make himself heard over Paula Abdul's "Straight Up" playing in the background. Like some dopey guy who's been caught off guard by his girlfriend's unexpected disclosure that she is pregnant, I responded with something along the lines of, "What are you going to do?" Then, even worse, "Do you think you got it from the journalist?"

While I was shocked by this revelation, I was more astonished that I wasn't already showing signs of the virus myself. Of the two of us, I was, without a doubt, the more promiscuous. Though I practiced safe sex, there were many times when I'd been drunk and careless in the heat of the moment. At that point in my life, I was unsurprisingly a pessimist through and through. On a gut level, I'd assumed that most gay men would eventually die of AIDS. In fact, I'd largely fashioned my life, like many of my peers, to live for the here and now, not wasting my days planning for a future that would never come. At the time, there were no truly effective treatments for HIV, making it much easier to hold this nihilistic approach. Foolish as it may seem today, it would still be another three years before I was finally tested.

After two years of living in this unfulfilling limbo-land, not cultivating any significant ties to Boston, I'd saved up enough money to take advantage of my extreme flexibility and desire to live for the day. I arrived in Amsterdam at the same moment Europe was flying on an edgy high over the fall of the Berlin Wall. My wanderings by Eurail, though interesting, eventually took on an air of aimlessness after several months. I became increasingly isolated and lonely. So lonely, in fact, that I decided to try and make a go of it with my former love, Dennis, who was then living in an RV parked next to his parents' house in San Diego. As fate would have it, after several months of being unable to find work in California, I felt I had no other choice but to move back to Boston where my old restaurant job was still waiting for me. The plan had been for Dennis to eventually join me there; however, during yet more lonely months back in New England (Denton and the journalist had moved to San Francisco in the interim), Dennis had landed a plum job managing a club back on Miami's South Beach. The plan was revised yet again. I was now to follow him to Miami. I quit my job, gave up the room I was renting, and scheduled a long overdue visit with my family before finally making my way back to South Florida. The night before I was to leave Boston for good, Dennis broke up with me over the phone. I had reached the end of a road.

For me, the first AIDS deaths came while I was living back on Blue Ridge Boulevard, during the two years that would culminate in my parents' deaths. When I visited Denton in 1992, his journalist partner was a walking cadaver. During that same visit, I put in a call to Michael, a photographer friend from college. He hadn't been returning my messages, and I was becoming increasingly concerned about his welfare. He had been on an accelerated downward spiral, having first given up his jobs in NYC due to HIV-related illnesses, then fully spinning out in New Orleans among friends whom he'd hoped would support him as his physical and emotional health continued to deteriorate. He'd finally landed back in Florida, living with his mother—his doomsday scenario—sharing unnerving stories of taking his motorcycle on 100 mph jaunts along traffic-congested I-95.

The person who picked up my call that day informed me that Michael was in the hospital. Filled with dread, I immediately dialed the number I was given. Within seconds of being connected to Michael's room, his mother thrust the receiver to his ear. He was on his deathbed. Hoarsely, he choked out the words, "Tim, I'm really afraid." Frightened and devastated, I could only manage something like "It's going to be okay." It was a brief call. I had no idea how to respond.

Denton, who had been sitting nearby, was empathetic, but didn't have much to say when I related to him what had just happened. Only the day before, he'd disclosed, in his nonchalant way, that every time he went to work, he was worried that he might return to find that the journalist had died. Following on the heels of these deaths, Dennis informed me that he, too, had tested positive. His tone, unlike Denton's, was grave and tinged with fear as one might expect of a person who had been handed, in the overused parlance of the day, "a death sentence." My mother had been nervously aware of what had been transpiring in the lives of my friends, but when I shared the news of Dennis's HIV status, she was rightly terrified, insisting I be tested right away. After an excruciating week waiting for my test results—which happened to coincide with a drunken, surrealistic trip escorting my elderly (still teetotaling) nana around Honolulu—I was stunned to learn that I was still HIV-negative.

Denton and I moved into that rambling flat near Dolores Park for a couple of years. However, the exciting prospect of being roommates I'd eagerly anticipated just a few years earlier in Boston was a different story at this stage of the game. Denton was already beginning to show signs of a severely compromised immune system, despite being treated at San Francisco General's renowned Ward 86.[320] My fraternity brother, the persistent boy with the flaming orange hair, was now living in the Bay Area. Soon after my move to San Francisco, we'd arranged to catch up over lunch. I still remember the feeling of lurching despair that passed through me as my eye picked out his emaciated frame from the crowd of parishioners emerging from Sunday morning services at Grace Cathedral. During our meal, he was distracted, barely touching his food. He spent most of our visit in the men's room, throwing up. A few months later, I would enter the cathedral's cavernous sanctuary for the first time, joining with the small group of mourners assembled for his funeral mass. These were my worst years. The years of sleeping the day away. Unemployed. Unemployable. Self-medicating with pills and alcohol against Complex PTSD and the devastating traumas that continued to unfold.

A combination of life-saving HIV medications first known as "the AIDS cocktail" arrived with well-deserved fanfare in the mid-nineties, but it was too late for Denton. By the end, he'd lost his sight and was riddled with painful neuropathy. Remarkably, he adapted to each new setback without complaint. Though I very much wanted to provide my oldest friend in the world with emotional support, he rarely took me up on my bids to discuss his plight. Deep down, I can only imagine he must have found the reality of his ever-expanding needs and commensurate levels of emotional vulnerability to be deeply shameful. Denton was sharp up until the end and I'm certain that my unhinged behaviors must have also been a factor in his turning away from greater intimacies as this spirited young man transformed into a thirty-year-old invalid. Looking back, I imagine it must have been unbearable for Denton to watch from the sidelines, fighting off attacks from life-threatening opportunistic infections, as I needlessly abused my healthy body. Yet, while others distanced themselves or sat in silent judgment of the wretched wasteland my life had become, he said nothing.

I'd urged Denton to move in with me when I first arrived in San Francisco. At that point, he was no longer able to work and was living off disability benefits. But after three years, I had become totally overwhelmed by the realities of living at the side of a loved one in the middle of a death spiral. The setbacks, appointments, medication regimens (with twice daily IV treatments) combined with the parade of health care workers, and Denton's loud-mouthed boyfriend (who would cruise by every day for about an hour) would prove too much. I made two suicidal gestures that landed me in San Francisco General, choking down charcoal fiber in the emergency room to soak up the toxins in my belly. I'd reached a breaking point. I eventually asked Denton to leave.

At the time, I rationalized this decision by telling myself that I needed to be able to breathe in my own home. While that was true, I now see I was trying to release myself from the noose that had been constricting ever-more tightly around my neck since my parents' deaths four years earlier. Denton, a wonder of organization, had already sorted through his hospice options and had a preferred facility lined up. For this decision, I was demonized by the boyfriend, who'd made no offer to allow Denton to move into his own home (I later learned that he'd made a point of telling each of my neighbors that I had kicked Denton out). The day Denton moved to hospice, the brat smugly smiled as he silently packed up my friend's collection of mid-century furniture and other prized belongings to take to his house. Denton sat nearby, literally blind to the proceedings.

Denton's parents made a single trip to San Francisco during one of his many hospitalizations, but no other family members or college friends tried to visit during his prolonged illness. When someone is critically ill, no one knows just how long they will live or in what state they will continue to survive before finally passing. Sometimes it's two years, sometimes six months. Denton died less than a month after moving to hospice care—much sooner than I'd imagined. Finding release in his absence, I had neglected my friend, only maintaining sporadic contact in the weeks after his move. His two remaining supporters, angry over my "abandonment," didn't inform me when he was rushed to the hospital, unable to breathe. They didn't call when the decision was being made to intubate. Didn't let me know that he had not regained consciousness and that life support was being removed. I received a terse call after the fact, informing me that he was dead.

Denton was cremated and his funeral was held back in Kansas City a few months later. No one in my family offered to accompany me to his service so they might offer their respects and support. Denton's college roommate, his wife in tow, was invited to give the eulogy. Introduced that morning with the honorarium "Doctor" by the funeral director, a patina of academic and heterosexual legitimacy was bestowed on mourners no doubt made uncomfortable with the gory details of the deceased's death (and life) as the more palatable college glory days were unpacked for public consumption. Denton's ashes were wedged next to his father's grave, the tiny marker inches from the cemetery driveway. Afterward, Denton's college friends had their own get-together. I was pointedly not invited. At a potluck held at his mother's house—a house that had been something of a second home to me as a boy—I was briefly acknowledged but not engaged. After about a half hour of trying unsuccessfully to chat with his family members, I left. I had known his mother and three older siblings since I was seven years old. I was then thirty-two, and I never heard from any of them again.

It Takes a Village

Interdependence is not only the key factor in our success as a species, it is also a necessary precondition to our collective and individual survival. On a physiological level, we see evidence of this truth reflected in the neurological structure of our brains. We are quite literally wired to connect with other people to meet our myriad physical and emotional needs. In essence, our minds do not distinguish between physical and social survival. Seen in this light, it should come as no surprise that we have come to associate social exclusion with death and annihilation.[321] Is it any wonder that people attempting to manage occurrences of PTSD and Complex Trauma—at times when their worlds have been turned upside down, often by their nearest and dearest—might develop an acute sensitivity to their fears of social abandonment? By expressing their overpowering needs to be made psychologically safe (i.e., to be *reliably* cared for and attended to) through the language of BPD, those most in need of steadfast support instead end up pushing others away.

While trauma is frequently triggered by an event like my parents' murder/suicide, it is just as often the result of a series of tragic events that snowball out of control. For me, the sense of being a member of the living dead was compounded by existing for many years in close proximity to death; stalked by a virus that wiped away the lives of many of my closest friends, rejected by others who could not handle my erratic behaviors, my BPD abandonment fears were well-earned. All the while, the powerful blamed the victims of the contagion, using disease as a political weapon to amplify damaging oppressions, sow dissension, and shore up their position in the chaos that ensued.

How one chooses to respond to one's experience of trauma and PTSD can, as we have seen, mean the difference between life and death. Luckily, none of us need end up like Oscar, rendered mute and psychotic, living out the defining years of his life at a time when no reliable structure existed to identify, much less provide effective treatment for, his suffering. Today, most of us are like Judy, born in the middle of a bridge; behind us, my father's era of shame, concealment, and ego-driven violence; ahead, we recognize a place of safety—abundant in reserves of self-compassion and respectful recognition for our experiences of trauma and oppression. Although Judy was able to glimpse that place of peace and personal fulfillment on the other side, the forces of oppression proved so powerful in her lifetime that she was unable to complete her journey there. I, too, nearly died in the middle of that bridge. However, with the right combination of luck, timing, and informed choices, I was able to make it to the other side.

Chapter 14

Satori

For over a decade now, my husband, Steve, and I have spent every Labor Day weekend celebrating our wedding anniversary at a tiny cabin in the foothills of the Sierra Mountains. Secluded on forty forested acres, our cabin—christened "Satori" by its owners—sits on a bluff overlooking a small tributary of the American River. The smell of pine lingers in the air and the sound of water rushing over granite boulders is never completely out of earshot as we spend our days reading books, playing cards, and soaking in the hot tub. *Satori* is a Japanese Buddhist term for awakening, comprehension, or understanding. In the Zen Buddhist tradition, satori refers to the experience of *kenshō*, or "seeing into one's true nature."[322] A short hike down a steep, twisting path from the cabin's perch is a picture-perfect swimming hole fed from above by an exuberant cascade of water. Our daughter, Gemma, has been splashing around in these waters since joining our family just a few weeks after her second birthday. While these scenes might appear similar to any other *typical* family vacation, none of this was a given for me. From my former place of despair, I couldn't have magically wished my days at Satori into existence no matter how much I wanted them.

Like most truly meaningful experiences, this picture of domestic tranquility arose out of a painstaking focus on my physical and psychological self-care. Like other survivors of trauma, I had no other option than to be patient, measuring my progress in small increments over the years—not in one fell swoop like winning the lottery. While I have found many of my deepest moments of peace within myself—and with the world—at Satori, for me, the real victory is not about having these experiences reserved for special occasions. Instead, my return to the "land of the living" via various types of therapy, meditation, education, medication, and self-care practices is based on my relatively newfound ability to bask in moments of personal fulfillment throughout my day-to-day life.

Warts and All

Throughout the course of my training and clinical work, I've come to appreciate that the stigma associated with therapy usually boils down to some combination of prideful independence and the perception that psychological suffering is a shameful personal failing meant to be concealed at all costs. Short of these obstacles, those who decide to seek treatment must, in some measure, come to understand that they are both a victim of circumstance *and* an essential catalyst in the perpetuation of their own difficulties. If a prospective therapy patient is ever to improve their lot, they must recognize that their level of participation in the treatment process tracks directly with the benefits to be gained from this highly emotional, labor-intensive project. Unfortunately, many, like my father, spend their lives blaming those around them for their miseries—constantly challenging others to meet their unquenchable needs with their angry words and aggressive deeds.

Most people think seeking treatment is the end of the road, tantamount to an admission of failure. Some wrongly believe their inability to manage their problems on their own is a sign of mental weakness or worse yet, gross incompetence. Adding to these challenges, those who have been tested only by the normal range of setbacks in life often stand in judgment of those who cannot "get their act together." When you think about it, there are many more obstacles than enticements to seeking treatment—and I haven't even mentioned the cost, hassles of confusing insurance plans, time commitment, and legwork involved in finding a skilled therapist who is a good fit. Sadly, most people overlook the fact that seeking treatment signals a leap of faith and a courageous admission that no matter the extent of our psychological damage, we can be empowered to improve our situations. For this reason, I maintain that seeking treatment represents an act of optimism, not a sign of defeat.

Strange as this may sound, the initial building block in addressing the effects of traumatic experience began about two miles up the road from my childhood home. In the decade before I was born, Oscar had constructed and managed what we referred to as The Building. Beginning at age eleven, I was required, by both my parents, to pick up trash, sweep sidewalks, and cut weeds outside The Building every Sunday afternoon in return for a cool ten bucks. While I readily chose to spend much of my free time as an adolescent tending to my neighbors' lawns, I found these tasks to be particularly dirty and demeaning. Left alone at The Building, I would, like any kid, become distracted over the course of the two or three hours it normally took to complete these loathsome chores. Taking a break inside my father's office, I often found myself perusing a thick, hardbound dictionary that, for some reason, included overviews of different types of occupations listed in a glossary at the back of the book. It was here that I first became acquainted with the term "psychologist."

I remember being so taken with the idea that there were actual scientists who studied human behavior and doctors who helped others with their mental health problems, that I flagged this profession for the "number two" position on my "potential careers" checklist—just below architect. Today, it seems obvious why I was affected in the way that I was by this new piece of wisdom. You will recall that as a young child, I secretly envied (and even imitated) the tragic heroes depicted in disaster movies. These characters always seemed to have a ready audience to empathize with their pain—no matter what improbable situation they found themselves in. By comparison, my father's rages left me feeling trapped, alone, and frozen. In the process of coming to better understand the role of psychologists, I recognized that I might find my own "audience"—knowledgeable people who would help make sense of my unfathomable depths, and people who would empathize with my plight and help me escape my painful inner world. The idea that I might someday put an end to my family's emotional abuse by learning about what makes people like my father "tick" also presented an attractive vision for the future. Furthermore, the appeal of helping other families escape needless psychological suffering only made sense in light of my desire to rescue my own family from our emotional torment.

By the time I was in high school, I'd developed the understanding— mainly through Woody Allen movies—that therapy was a luxury afforded only to wealthy Manhattanites who made "mountains out of molehills" with their comically neurotic problems. Luckily, I never viewed treatment with the same stigma that continues to plague many today, largely because I secretly aspired to be one those privileged few.

During my senior year of high school, I took a couple of classes in drafting at the local community college, but my math skills turned out to be relatively weak, and I had no portfolio. The path to becoming an architect was effectively ruled out. After I washed out of the business school at the University of Miami, I switched to become an English major at the urging of a kindly dean who saw that I was able to pull off at least Bs in those courses. Nevertheless, psychology remained in the background, becoming my undergraduate minor. Regrettably, the handful of psych courses I took concerned themselves with the broadest of strokes, requiring the memorization of endless lists of terms, historical figures, and intricacies of foundational experiments like Albert Bandura's "bobo" dolls and Harry Harlow's "wire monkey" mothers.[323] I distinctly remember feeling let down because it all seemed so scattershot, like the greatest hits of an unfamiliar and inscrutable musical genre. These courses did nothing to help me better understand the actual people and emotional problems I encountered in my own life. What's more, it never actually occurred to me to find out if the university had a counseling center, even though I was facing the challenges of coming out, drug and alcohol abuse, and endless relationship issues.

I finally started therapy in my mid-twenties as the AIDS crisis came crashing down around me. These initial sessions seemed helpful in the sense that an empathic person was focused on me and my problems, but I can't say that I was deeply changed as a result. Like many people who enter treatment, this issue was, to a considerable degree, a matter of expectations. Much as we would prefer otherwise, we are not built with on/off switches for our "problems," and a lifetime of emotional scarring (and a life-threatening viral plague) cannot be overcome with a few pithy insights by a well-trained therapist.

Like most, I was not a well-educated consumer. At the time, I didn't even realize there were different treatment approaches. I'd simply asked for recommendations from my physician and soon found myself in analytically inspired "psychodynamic" treatment. I remember thinking at the time that my therapist didn't offer much reflection about what she might be thinking, but I'd imagined that she must know what she's doing since she had such a nice office. After moving to San Francisco, I increased my sessions with my new psychodynamic therapist to twice a week, but it was pretty much the same story. I clearly remember latching on to one highly out-of-character statement this second therapist once made ("I think you might be angry") because it had felt like manna from heaven to my starving psyche.

Psychodynamic therapists are highly selective about sharing what they think—much of their goal is to carefully lay the groundwork for you to "happen" onto these "discoveries" on your own. As such, the patient is often unable to recognize their therapist to be the powerful agent in the alleviation of their symptoms that they actually represent. This traditional treatment method has received many hard knocks because the work is highly subtle, with countless variables that make it comparatively difficult for academic researchers to study next to insurance company darlings like Cognitive Behavioral Therapy (CBT). None of this is to say that a psychodynamic approach is unsound. Far from it. Those carefully timed "aha" moments can be extremely powerful, but sometimes years in the making.[324] Clearly, time is not on the side of suicidal people living with

Complex PTSD and drug addiction. As you will recall, during those first years in San Francisco, I was so out of it that I am probably not the best judge of what exactly did or did not transpire in those sessions. However, with the benefit of more effective treatment, education, training, and my own clinical work with trauma survivors, I now recognize that I would have been helped immeasurably by a far broader range of interventions.

What Trauma Recovery Actually Feels Like

The waters of Satori's swimming hole eventually spill over onto a large field of flat stone that is often baked to a toasty temperature by the afternoon sun. Here, the ground's elevation shifts downward, and the water gains an impressive momentum as it is funneled into a single channel carved deep into the rock. I sometimes linger here, warming my bones after a dip, considering the water's hastening path. Researchers tell us that our brains function in much the same way as this field of stone, but instead of the carving out of rock by rapidly moving water, rivers of experience give shape to select neural pathways in our brains.[325] Like well-worn channels of rushing water, these neural networks become ever more powerful by virtue of the frequency of their use, creating a type of feedback loop that can leave other areas relatively untouched. Unlike Satori's field of stone, our minds encompass great numbers of these highly developed neural networks and are the points by which we come to orient our understanding of ourselves and our world.

We consciously recognize these orientation points as "memory" (or the stories we tell ourselves about our lives) and the "facts" that help us navigate our shared reality.[326] Today, many psychologists refer to these orientation points as "schemas."[327] It's helpful to think of the concept of schemas as something akin to celestial navigation wherein one determines one's boat's location by taking measurements based on the positions of the stars above. For example, as an adolescent, my schemas about relationships were sculpted by the "guiding stars" of my parents' marriage and soap operas. On a neurological level, these channels of interpretation were sculpted by my powerful emotional reactions to my parents' behavior and my avid viewership of television shows whose depictions of intense interpersonal conflicts reflected (and reinforced) my firsthand experience at home.

Up until about thirty years ago, most researchers believed these dominant neural networks become more or less "fixed" for a lifetime by the time we reach adulthood. However, advances in the concept of neuroplasticity—the ability to "grow" new neural connections throughout the lifespan—has demonstrated that you indeed can teach an old dog new tricks.[328]

In reality, there are infinitely more stars in the sky than can be viewed with the naked eye. In much the same way, our schemas can be as self-limiting as navigating by the stars because these orientation points compel us to make decisions based on the "visible" or the "tried and true." While schemas are essential to the processing and interpretation of information, they should not necessarily be mistaken with objective facts. And over-reliance on these guiding stars can leave other, more pertinent data unseen, ignored, or minimized.

The truth is, we must each wake up to the fact that we possess more potential schemas than we usually acknowledge. I often explain this to my patients by having them look at a small design on the carpet in my office. I tell them to imagine that everything they have ever known about a particular trauma is contained in that one small design. I then share that successful treatment is something like looking up from that small design and noticing there is an entire room around them filled with books, furniture, plants, and windows.

What the resolution of a traumatic experience *feels* like is the act of directing your attention outward and developing new orientation points rather than the same old stars. These new points represent new ways of relating to the world, new habits, and new strategies to care for yourself. Importantly, the small design on the carpet—your old traumas—will never go away. Rather, that area of the carpet that had been your entire world will begin to appear much smaller in comparison to the rest of the room, whereas before it was all you could see. By learning to recognize opportunities to direct your attention outward, your connections to the rest of the room are strengthened. New neural connections are created, and more useful schemas are enhanced.

Most people now come to treatment asking me for tools and strategies to use when they find themselves stuck in old patterns of thinking, feeling, and behaving. In the forty years since the reframing of psychological suffering into a cookbook of maladies and therapeutic treatments by the DSM-III revolution, the public (and behavioral healthcare administrators) have been led to believe that this is what one should demand of therapy. As a result, the spread of "evidence-based" treatments like Cognitive Behavioral Therapy (with their easy to understand, hands-on interventions) have proliferated. CBT has much to offer in helping each of us talk ourselves down from our personal ledges by fostering the development of a type of internal dialogue that can help defuse self-sabotaging behavior. No doubt, I could have been helped much sooner if I'd been educated about strategies that have proven beneficial to others in similar situations. Nevertheless, the evidenced-based toolkit perspective also illustrates a serious lack of appreciation for the complex nature of human beings.

Many interventions like CBT don't go far enough to address our proclivity—in reality, a compulsion—to prioritize feelings over logic. To illustrate, just take a moment to reflect on some of the questionable choices you make on a daily basis. As for myself, I think about all the missed opportunities to stretch my body or take a short walk between sessions. Usually, I will scroll dead-eyed through something on the internet for ten minutes instead of taking part in an activity that would refresh my body and clear my mind. Undoubtedly, we are aware of many of these decisions before we make them, but when it comes down to it, it is likely that we will act in our own best interest only part of the time. When we later reflect on these choices, many of us are prone to heaping on extra servings of self-criticism, erroneously believing we are either too weak or stupid to make other choices. Even with a great deal of practice, the logic and insight deployed from the CBT toolkit can often fail to sway our impulsive, feeling-based decision-making at the moment of truth. What's more, these evidence-based interventions, if utilized as a one-stop solution, offer little to those "zombie captains" who, in their dissociative state, blindly comply with the pirate takeover of their vessel. CBT and its ilk are great at training captains to be better captains, but they offer little in the way of curing zombiism for good.

What Worked for Me

An important piece of the puzzle obscured by academic researchers and medical practitioners (and not well-articulated by the collective voice of clinicians) is the fact that therapy has the potential to offer much more than tips and tricks. Human beings grow and develop through education and insight to be sure. But they *transform* through experiences with other human beings—especially a good therapist. The problem is, this fundamental truth of the human experience is somewhat subjective in nature and does not lend itself well to quantification and statistical analysis—the key ingredients to peer-reviewed studies and scientific legitimization. What's more, these transformative experiences are not typically recognized by the patient because they occur incrementally and are sometimes perceived as overpowering, difficult, or highly negative emotions. Strangely enough, what at first glance might appear to be a treatment setback often coalesces into a significant leap forward given sufficient patience. For instance, if you're a generally meek person, getting angry at your therapist for charging a cancellation fee is a therapeutic opportunity to address and improve your conflict resolution skills.

During my first year of graduate school, I found myself confounded by the sheer number of psychological theories that seek to capture the essence of these transformative relational experiences. Traditionally, the theoretical orientations that have best elucidated this type of dynamic interpersonal interaction have stemmed from Freud's analytic tradition. These theories tend to be highly refined, but are often couched in jargon-filled, paragraph-long sentences diabolically designed to winnow out the intellectually faint of heart.

I can't tell you how relieved I felt after coming across a book with the refreshingly straightforward title *How Psychotherapy Works*. With a direct approach and clarity of language, psychoanalyst and researcher Dr. Joseph Weiss lays out (in this comparatively slim volume) the framework of his influential Control Mastery Theory (CMT). While the title 'Control Mastery' has the unfortunate tendency to evoke associations with sado-masochism, the name actually refers to the theory's premise that people have *control* over the content of their minds and the belief that people seek out treatment in the hopes that they can *master* their lives. CMT teaches that we develop beliefs about ourselves and the world through early childhood experiences that can be thought of as akin to schemas. Identified in the language of CMT as pathogenic beliefs, these schemas become something like an operating manual for life and many of us do very little (to no) updating of these systems as we grow and develop. As adults, these presumptions can come to dominate our lives—even when we have lived for many years outside paradigms like those that existed in our childhood homes. As a result, a person will often react in ways that have little to do with the reality of the present situation.[329] This undermining dynamic can create self-fulfilling prophecies, as others do not respond well, when, for example, your abandonment trauma from the murder/suicide of your parents or the deaths of your friends from AIDS is activated in full when they do not check in with you for a week.

In most mental health settings, these enactments—patronizingly referred to as "acting out"—are viewed as a setback, a sign that the patient is resistant to treatment because they are not adhering to some theory-driven set of rules. By contrast, CMT asserts that people come to treatment to "test out" their pathogenic beliefs by re-creating situations during sessions that have the same emotional flavor as their initial wounding. The patient's hope is the therapist will have a healthy, adaptive response to their reactions—that they will not be punished (or traumatized) in the same manner as their initial wounding. As these tests are passed, the patient frequently experiences a newfound sense of emotional safety, is relieved to let their guard down, and begins to build trust with the therapist. With time, the patient will try out these new tactics with others, eventually developing ever-greater levels of resilience against the inevitable setbacks in life. CMT contends that people come to therapy to get better, reinforcing the idea that seeking treatment is an act of optimism rather than an admission of defeat.[330]

For many people, there is a clearly defined incident they refer to as their "rock bottom." The thing is: you don't know you've hit rock bottom until well after the fact. For some, a corner is turned, old ways are exchanged for a new, healthier life. Yet for most, life's trajectories are not so clean. What I have found in my own life and in the lives of many of my patients is that recovery comes in fits and starts. Healthier coping strategies deployed on January 1st come to be ignored by February. Even in the most perfect of lives, there will be setbacks and poor choices. The most important piece of the puzzle is to pick yourself up and keep trying. As Dory from *Finding Nemo* wisely advises, "Just keep swimming."

Therapy Alone Is Not Enough

If a single incident stands out as my personal rock bottom, it would be the pain that immediately surrounded Denton's death. I had lost my oldest friend in the world. Most of my other friends had abandoned me and I was living with a boyfriend I couldn't trust. I hadn't worked in four years, and my self-esteem was in the gutter. I was worried that I wasn't smart enough or strong enough to figure things out. I luckily made a choice to keep swimming.

Soon after Denton's death, I found a part-time job working as a counselor at a halfway house. I wasn't much more than a glorified babysitter, but it got me out of the house. I was interacting with other people and being productive with my time. I reasoned that if I were to ever have a chance of being accepted into a graduate-level psychology program, it would help to have some relevant experience to offset my dismal college performance. Within a year, I had done well enough to turn this position into a full-time job with benefits. My work also acted as a stabilizing force, helping me to finally get Clark, the compulsive liar, out of my life.

I was in treatment with Control Mastery therapist Dr. Molly Sullivan for almost sixteen years. I'd ended my work with that first San Francisco therapist after a couple of years and had not bothered to seek out a new prescriber after my old psychiatrist stopped returning my calls. I later found a psychiatrist who put me on an antidepressant that finally helped. The pill-popping and hard liquor days were over, but most evenings were still passed chugging down tumblers of white wine.

At the time I went into treatment with Dr. Sullivan, I was terrified of my own shadow. I'd started graduate school a few months earlier and soon found myself unable to sleep for days at a time. I was incapable of controlling the frenzied, fearful thoughts that would pinball around my head as I tossed and turned, my body well past the point of exhaustion. It was unlike anything I'd ever experienced. I wasn't suicidal, but I was terrified that I would do something completely impulsive and dangerous.

Looking back, I now understand the realities of grad school had forced me to face the fact that I could no longer stay in my shell and rely on the same old self-sabotaging strategies. Loss, abandonment, and betrayal had become my guiding stars. Within the narrow confines of these schemas, there was a perverted logic to my modes of self-protection and my continued numbing out with alcohol, but the stranglehold of these strategies was now unsustainable given the growing demands of graduate school. There were many times during those first six months when I almost quit. I think what kept me going was the storm of self-recrimination I would subject myself to if I abandoned this ambitious project; after years of hopeful planning, I would find myself imprisoned with nothing more than the deafening roar of my self-destructive thoughts.

In the absence of these life-saving ambitions, I knew the center could no longer hold. The final doorway to the type of life I'd want to live would be closed for good. The flame of life I had kept buried deep in my soul, and had so doggedly protected since I was a child would finally be extinguished. I would end up like my father: convinced that I was irredeemable and unlovable; shutting out everyone and everything that could have helped reduce my intolerable feelings; concluding that the pain of living eclipsed my fear of dying; and ultimately I would commit suicide.

Overshadowed by Trauma

Looking back over the pages of this story, I can't help but find my portrayal of my mother to be inadequate. People like my father always seem to be stealing the spotlight. Though we are forever seeking out harmonious relationships of the type I experienced with my mother, they don't always make for particularly compelling storytelling. In any event, these competing narrative interests have led to the nagging feeling that I've downplayed the importance of my relationship with my mother. My mother was, by a long shot, the most significant relationship in my life at the time of her death. No doubt my father, grandmother, and sister would have said the same. While we were all severely impacted by my father's behaviors, Judy was the emotional nexus of our family. Truth be told, she bestowed on me what I consider to be my greatest gift in life: the capacity to love and be loved in return.

Having once held the capacity for a healthy, mutually loving relationship, I was in need of the right therapist (Dr. Sullivan) and the right situation (grad school) to join forces to help me overcome my most powerful self-limiting schema: the belief that I could not trust others. Like many abused and emotionally neglected children, I learned early on that I was to be seen and not heard. Observing the outcomes of Judy and my sister Barbara's confrontations of Oscar's rage only served to confirm that I should have no outward reaction to my father's outbursts. As a result, I never learned how to have a healthy give and take with another person. At the first sign of a problem, I would draw up like a turtle into my shell. Existing within the confines of these limited narratives, I became hyper-vigilant in protecting myself against betrayal and abandonment. Unsurprisingly, brain scans of trauma survivors reveal an unusually high level of activation of the amygdala, the area of the brain responsible for threat detection.

Not only was I unable to trust others, but I also didn't trust myself. In response, Dr. Sullivan offered acceptance and appreciation for my essential self. I "tested out" the authenticity of these sentiments with countless opportunities for her to judge or criticize my experience and choices. My ability to build trust in her never could have been accomplished with just a handful of validating statements. I would have immediately become suspicious if her approval ever reeked of knee-jerk platitudes. To demonstrate her sincerity, she had to share her rationale for her support over and over again. And each time, these rationales had to fit with a worldview she presented through scores of real-life anecdotes and examples she'd previously shared. Within the confines of this zone of psychological safety, I was able to transfer my experience of having been loved by (and given love to) my mother onto my relationship with my therapist, thereby nurturing long dormant, deeply protected emotional needs. By contrast to the withholding stance of most psychodynamic treatment, Dr. Sullivan's sharing of what she thought was paramount. Neither did she disclose these things willy-nilly. Each element was carefully selected to support my plan to build trust in others. I was also allowed helpful glimpses into her own challenges—without ever being made to feel responsible for solving these problems. Unlike CBT, none of this came out of a one-size-fits-all treatment manual. It was a bespoke relational experience that would allow me, over time, to gain control over my emotionally crippling self-loathing—empowering me to build healthy, new relationships outside of our sessions.

Trauma and other forms of severe psychological distress possess an underlying capacity for the development of stifling levels of self-absorption. In the beginning, my treatment with Dr. Sullivan allowed for a window on this hermetically sealed universe to crack open just enough to allow for a bit of breathing room. Personal growth came in fits and starts as I took on new projects and regularly interacted beyond my self-imposed safety zones. For three years I was a full-time student, writing endless papers and working part-time at various clinical postings. I ate a lot of In-and-Out Burger and gained thirty pounds. I chain-smoked as I downed my nightly bottle of wine. About halfway through graduate school, I was startled into action by the bulging outline of my potbelly in a snapshot taken from an unflattering angle. I started working out and I kept it up. I went on Match.com and seriously began looking for a life partner. I fell in love with Steve. I took a year off. We biked, hiked, and lounged around on the beach together. Most weekends we went to the theater or a concert. We prepared elaborate meals and indulged ourselves in the San Francisco restaurant scene. We planned our wedding and anxiously hosted family and friends over the scorching weekend when we were finally able to make it legal.

What Is Happiness Anyway?

My dear nana, after suffering for many years with dementia, passed away the week before our wedding ceremony at the age of ninety-four. Shortly after returning from our honeymoon, I learned that changes in the disbursement terms of my grandmother's trust had been initiated during the final years of her unwinding. My hopes to pay off my student loans and to put a down payment on a house were dashed. Nevertheless, life went on. Steve and I traveled regularly. I finally learned to ski. I spent many more years in internships, working on my dissertation, and studying for my licensing exams. I continue to carry a massive student loan debt that hangs heavily on our shoulders. Steve experienced long bouts of unemployment as he edged closer and closer to aging out of the youth-obsessed tech industry. Regardless, we are White men in America—clearly living at a great remove from poverty.

After passing my licensing exams, I started my own practice. Concurrently, after a lengthy and heart-wrenching foster and adoption process, we took in a medically fragile toddler. Gemma had been roughly the size and weight of a Coke can when she was born at twenty-two weeks. It would take another two years for her adoption to finally be secured, and for our little girl to be able to walk unassisted.

My practice was not turning out to be successful so I took a job at a public health clinic, commuting two hours every day. I stopped smoking and drinking altogether. We have dealt, as best we can, with Gemma's autism diagnosis, and have learned to love our daughter for the person she is. I relaunched my practice and have since made it into something of a success. I have spent two and a half years writing this book in my spare time. At the time of this writing, the three of us are quarantining against COVID-19. I fantasize about escape, but in the next moment acknowledge there is nowhere I want to go. This is the home I have carefully constructed on the ashes of everything that came before.

I list this most recent succession of events to illustrate the difference between the effects of Complex PTSD (and other severe and persistent mental health problems) and the everyday awful happenings of life. While the years since the rock bottom of Denton's death have brought many difficulties, they were also, in many ways, quite wonderful. As the veil of traumatic response was lifted, my burdens increasingly felt more in line with the typical challenges to be expected in life.

I am also fortunate to have survived far longer than many of my close friends and have now surpassed the age my mother was when she died. As previously discussed, the weight of how I might best spend those extra years paralyzed me with fear during the worst years of my crisis. I knew I had to make the most of my allotted time, but I was mired in unrealistic expectations and self-defeating idealizations about what my life should look like. Even when my hopes fell within the ballpark of the possible, I lacked the solid grounding and proper framework to meet these goals.

The pursuit of happiness enshrined in our founding document has, over the years, become inextricably bound to our notion of the American Dream. Consequently, the concept of happiness is often seen as nothing more than the inevitable by-product of financial prosperity, upward social mobility, and equal opportunity. The Bay Area, by virtue of its position as the global capital of the tech industry, acts as a magnet for many of the greatest beneficiaries of this proposition. Accordingly, many of these ostensibly successful people find their way to my door because I have built my practice around my drive to help others to lead more fulfilling lives. The overwhelming majority of these individuals have had the good fortune to be born on a track that meticulously nurtured their abilities, with their hard work yielding a coveted position at the latest hot start-up or a berth at "mothership" corporations like Apple, Google, and Facebook. Through this work, I've discovered that many of these highly driven individuals often find their impressive, well-paying jobs dissatisfying. While most are truly appreciative of their high degree of privilege, they find their days lacking. They see their work as challenging, but abstract and disconnected from "real life" accomplishments. Many of them struggle in their personal relationships. They become frustrated when their toys and exotic vacations no longer suffice to quell their restless minds. They *all* say that they want to be more directly helping other people.

Since adopting Gemma, I've gotten into the habit of carrying Kleenex with me everywhere we go because she has one of those noses that starts dripping the moment she becomes even just a little bit cold and the fog in San Francisco can blow in at any minute. The other day, I pulled out one of those pocket-sized containers of tissues and was struck by the stress-inducing slogan "seize this moment" mocking me from its cellophane package. This well-meaning and some would say *very* American ethos is everywhere these days. However, I have found that most people are uncertain about just what to seize, and when they do, they soon find their attention wandering elsewhere. Similarly, we are told to "find your passion"—the all-purpose remedy for our various dissatisfactions—as if those passions were immediately obvious and attainable to everyone. The problem is, these are very tall orders to be taken from a Kleenex package or the overheated language of bumper-sticker wisdom. What most people need is a detailed map leading from their stalemate of confusion to these lofty, idealized heights.

Almost everyone I've ever met has a sense that there are certain things they want to do before they die, and the "bucket list" has become a catch-all term for these types of aspirations. Depicted in books, movies, and songs, these "marquee" moments have become an organizing principle that provides a reassuring sense that we have not wasted the precious years we have been given. I remember the uplifting chorus from the Tim McGraw song "Live Like You Were Dying" that reflects this approach: "I went skydiving, Rocky Mountain climbing, I went 2.7 seconds on a bull named Fu Manchu." While there is much to be said for these pursuits, many of us have been misled into believing that stringing together enough of these types of experiences will result in a sustained sense of personal fulfillment, or what some might call the sensation of happiness. These bucket list experiences might be better defined as the simple pleasures in life—high points that primarily concern themselves with a sense of elation and states of high positive arousal. Unfortunately, if you are looking only to these types of pleasures for lasting contentment, you will find yourself living on a treadmill, always on the lookout for your next fix. Our pleasures are inherently fleeting, that's what makes your new car smell so special!

Throughout the first century of psychological inquiry, clinicians looked to what psychiatrist R.D. Laing once referred to as the "disease model" of mental health.[331] Under this paradigm, patients were defined by their pathology or what "ails" them. Psychological "disorders" were equated with a broken bone that needs mending or cancerous cells in need of eradication. By contrast, beginning in the 1990s, figures like psychologist Martin Seligman began to shift the focus from disorders like depression, schizophrenia, and PTSD to the components of psychological health and well-being. In a movement collectively known as Positive Psychology, rigorous study of positive psychological states like hope, optimism, gratitude, and love were undertaken for the first time, unlocking the psychodynamics of a well-lived life.[332]

Characteristic of the inventories of positive psychological traits that would emerge, Seligman and his colleague, psychologist Chris Peterson, identified twenty-four universal character strengths that drew from thousands of years of philosophical discourse across various cultures. Seligman maintains that we must continually engage with, and build upon, our character strengths to cultivate a meaningful, purpose-driven life or what he calls "authentic happiness." Ranging from creativity to self-control to humor and fairness, these positive psychological characteristics can be thought of as beacons that give much needed shape to ill-defined ideas like "finding your passion" and "seizing the day."[333]

Seen through this lens, my years of ups and downs since hitting rock bottom can be framed as a cultivation of my own authentic happiness through positive pursuits related to the areas of education, career, and family. My successful treatment with Dr. Sullivan allowed me to turn my focus toward nurturing underutilized character strengths like creativity, love of learning, kindness, and social intelligence. My graduate school career, which took the better part of ten years, yielded countless opportunities to develop greater strength of character in each of these domains. For example, by accessing my love of learning, I was able to establish a framework of human experience that gave context to my emotional suffering, providing the tragedies I'd witnessed with a greater sense of personal meaning. Through my clinical work, I discovered that in helping others I was released from my fixation with my own needs and preoccupations, placing me in a role where I was able to channel my anxious energies into empowering others to make critical modifications to their lives. Now well into my career, the daily practice of psychotherapy regularly calls upon my intellect, compassion, and empathy to develop productive, emotionally focused relationships.

In forging an intimate partnership with my husband, Steve, I've experienced the emotional safety to be found in a lifelong, loving commitment. The security provided by his ongoing acceptance and support has fostered ever-greater levels of self-confidence, allowing me to tackle difficult yet highly rewarding challenges. In becoming a father, I've come to recognize that empowering others by nurturing their abilities is the greatest gift I can give myself. When Gemma first came into our lives, Steve's cousin sent us a plaque that touchingly read "having a child means that your heart will forever reside outside your body."

While the levels of protection and nurturance called upon by parents is unique in their depth and scope, I believe these sentiments can be said of all reciprocally loving relationships. We cultivate value in one another

245

through healthy emotional intimacy, allowing our subjective, singular experience to be multiplied, expanding our lives beyond the confines of our own minds, empathically joining in the pain and triumphs of others. I take great joy in the teaching and mentoring aspects of this dynamic, helping others to cultivate their own character strengths, shepherding them to a day when they are no longer reliant on my support.

Unlike bucket list items, developing our character strengths does not have a beginning or end. We can access the fruits of these strengths at any moment by engaging with or reflecting on the expressions of these efforts. As long as we continue to cultivate our strengths, they don't wear out or fade away. Moving beyond the ephemeral nature of bucket list items and the finite nature of our minds, we can experience what I believe to be the key ingredient to happiness: a sense of transcendence.

Mindfulness Approaches to Managing PTSD and Trauma

Cultivating your character strengths takes clarity of intention and a sustained focus that is best accomplished without a lot of distractions, but our minds think and feel constantly—even when we're asleep. The internal racket can be deafening to the point that we come to mistake each of our passing thoughts and emotions for our essential selves. If an alien landed on my rooftop and asked me for a sample of what it's like to live inside a human mind, I would tell it to take a sixteen-hour flight to Sydney with a seatmate who won't stop talking. That's what it's like to just sit and think, sometimes. Then, I'd tell the alien to imagine that a sadistic flight attendant (let's call him Todd) allows us to change seats, but only at random and not at a time of our choosing. While we might relish sitting next to Betty White for a few hours, what happens when we're led down the aisle to be seated beside Donald Trump? In "Song of Myself," Walt Whitman famously wrote, "I contain multitudes." No doubt, we each contain multitudes and wrangling this motley crew of fellow passengers into some sort of productive working relationship is essential if we are to ever find happiness in life.

While I've just explored some of the tools I used in my recovery, there are many paths to dealing with mental illness and addiction that I didn't take. I didn't set out to write a how-to book, but of all the approaches I've learned about (and utilized on myself and my patients), I have found mindfulness meditation to be the single most impactful and accessible. I feel it would be a missed opportunity if I didn't add my own two cents to the conversation about mindfulness and to give some direct information about how a beginner can approach this intervention. I am also aware that many people do not have the luxury of time to ponder their character strengths or cannot afford things like therapy or a total job makeover. I'm including a short primer on mindfulness meditation because it is effective, free, and available to everyone on the planet.[334]

Personally, I have found that mindfulness meditation is an invaluable tool to help calm the mind and find greater equanimity with the diverse planeload of passengers we each carry inside. Familiar to most as a component of the vast and complex system of Buddhist and Hindu spiritual philosophy, mindfulness meditation has gained popularity in the West in recent decades as a stand-alone, non-secular approach to stress reduction. I had long avoided looking too deeply into mindfulness meditation, first popularized by the research of Jon Kabat-Zinn, Ph.D., because I felt it was unscientific and had negative associations with New Age charlatans and middle-aged men with ponytails. However, a few years ago, something finally clicked after I took some time to carefully examine the overwhelming empirical support for the benefits of meditation from study after study coming out of major universities. I finally had to ask myself a very rational question about something that appeared highly irrational: "If even a fraction of what researchers are claiming is true, then why aren't you giving this a fair chance?"

The most popular way to practice mindfulness meditation is to find a quiet spot where you won't be interrupted. Then, sit in a comfortable, upright position, with your eyes closed. Next, turn your attention to the process of the exchange of air as it passes in and out of your nostrils. Don't take deep "gulps" or try to control your breath in a forced manner. Just breathe naturally through your nose, not your mouth. When you notice that your mind has drifted off, gently guide your attention back to your breath in a non-judgmental fashion. Simply set a timer and try it for about ten minutes a day. That's it. That's the primer: sit down and shut up.[335]

This approach is often referred to as "anchored" meditation because we are using our breath as an anchor point for our attention. Inevitably, the first thing people notice when they attempt this type of meditation is just how often their focus wanders away from their anchor point. Even under the best of circumstances, you will notice that your mind will replay events from the past or delve into future concerns.[336] This mental "time travel" is typically layered with complicated feelings, judgments, and associations that our minds find highly stimulating. Consequently, when you sit down to meditate, you should fully expect your attention to be drawn to the voice of that talkative seatmate from your flight to Sydney. If you're anything like me, he'll probably start guffawing with Donald Trump from across the aisle. This does not mean it is a failed meditation: this is what meditation is. Over time, you will learn to *observe* your thoughts as they flit across your awareness rather than *identifying* with every single one.[337]

Unfortunately, those new to meditation are prone to regularly assessing their efforts, feeling frustrated they are not "better" at doing something that, on its face, seems so straightforward. Many people make the mistake of trying to measure the relative success or failure of a single meditation based on how long they were able to keep their minds focused on their breath and how relaxed they feel after finishing.[338]

In my work coaching patients through the ins and outs of developing a mindfulness practice, I've found these judgments can often be traced to a pop-culture misconception that achieving a Zen state (an empty mind, free of worldly concerns, absent of thought and feeling) is the goal of meditation. While these sentiments may be valid in some regards, it's important for beginners to approach this process with humility, and not to get ahead of themselves by imagining themselves to be on par with a Tibetan monk who has been practicing since childhood and has renounced all worldly obligations and belongings. This is akin to someone trying yoga for the first time after sitting at a desk for ten years and then proclaiming, "I can't do this, I'm not flexible." Going to yoga is doing yoga; there is no other goal.

Because mindfulness meditation and most self-care strategies *appear* quite simple and straightforward (it doesn't help that people who are meditating look like they are napping in an upright position), most novices approach these practices with unexamined hubris. Although we all sometimes wish for an off switch to the parade of thoughts and feelings that constantly vie for our attention, I'm sorry to tell you that there is simply no such thing: there are no grand tricks to be shared because the system cannot be gamed. What we do possess, however, are powerful self-care *practices* (meditation, exercise, healthy diet, psychotherapy, cultivating core strengths and positive psychological traits) that enhance overall health and well-being. Rather than an on/off switch, these practices can be thought of as analogous to a dimmer switch that adjusts our internal settings by incremental degrees over an extended period of time.

Building the Muscle of Present Focus

In many respects, the practice of meditation *should* be thought of as an activity like physical exercise. When we work out, we build our strength by engaging our muscles in repetitive movements against a force (weight + gravity). In meditation, the strength of our non-judgmental, present awareness (*not* an "empty" mind) is the muscle we are trying to build. The persistent, non-judgmental redirection of our wandering mind back to the breath might be thought of as the equivalent of doing a rep at the gym, building up the muscle of non-critical, present focus.

It's important for those new to meditation to understand that you may or may not feel more relaxed during or immediately following a sitting—but that's not really the point. Remember that you might feel nauseous, sore, and worn-out after a particularly intense workout. Then, after some time exercising in this way, you'll suddenly realize you can lift a couch all by yourself. What the practice of mindfulness meditation facilitates is a growing power to non-judgmentally observe each present moment without reflexively involving ourselves in the types of mental time travel to which we have become accustomed. Therefore, "mindfulness" refers to being as attentive as we can possibly be to each passing moment as they arise throughout our day-to-day life—not just during the times when we are "officially" meditating.

Most people scarcely recognize that they live much of their lives in a state of autopilot. While our bodies are moving through the present moment, our minds are constantly engrossed in a form of mental time travel, only partially attentive to what is happening around us. When we're on autopilot, we exist largely in a reactive state, our responses grounded in the well-defined, self-limiting schemas reflected in the select neural pathways of the brain. On autopilot, our awareness can be said to be psychologically fused with our reactive thoughts and emotions. People vary greatly in the degree to which they are fused with their thoughts and emotions, with our capacity to observe these passing phenomena fluctuating over the course of a day (or a lifetime) depending on the nature of the events and the demands at hand. Those at the extreme end of this continuum have no objective distance between their thoughts, feelings, and awareness. There is little sense of being a detached observer to one's inner experience. Like breathing, these reactive thoughts and emotions are viewed as an automatic part of the self—they occur without warning and require no mental effort. From someone fused with their reactive thoughts you will often hear statements like, "This is just who I am" or "I'd have no idea about how to go about things differently."

For those suffering with PTSD, Complex Trauma, and BPD, the sense of fusion with reactive thoughts and emotions is pervasive—much the same can be said of phobias, severe anxiety, and depressive disorders. Psychological material related to traumatic events becomes the locus of all automatic responses. This is our famed zombie captain, also known as dissociation. In the midst of my own dissociative states and traumatic responses, I treated my every feeling and thought as a fact. To understand just how problematic this approach can be, let's return to the example of our talkative seatmate on our flight to Sydney.

Let's say we hit some mild turbulence and he starts freaking out, racing up and down the aisle screaming, "We're all going to die!" Then, he starts demanding that you put on a parachute and jump out of the airplane. How would you react? If you are fused with your thoughts and feelings, it's very likely you'd start looking for an emergency exit to pry open and anxiously wait to be suited up. Clinically, this is the definition of "psychosis." While we all sometimes have thoughts and feelings that might otherwise be known as "batshit," fortunately, few of us take action on these thoughts because we recognize them as dangerous extremes. Nevertheless, these types of thoughts and feelings tend to persist, causing great mental anguish and leaving us puzzling over how to calm these irrational parts of ourselves. If you take the Cognitive Behavioral Therapy approach to managing these experiences, you would, in essence, ask your irrational seatmate to suddenly—some might say magically— become rational. You'd ask that he somehow break through his panic and logically consider the evidence that you are safe based on mathematical calculations involving atmospheric disturbances and g-force stresses on aluminum welds. Perhaps as a follow-up, you would tell him to write down the alternative scenarios where the plane won't go down, and then ask him to distract himself with the in-flight magazine. Or maybe you'd try the "power of positive thinking" approach and tell him to "believe really hard that the plane is not going to crash."

I don't know if you've ever tried to reason with someone who is being swept under by powerful emotions, but you're not likely to get very far if you start off by trying to deny their reality. Often, the frightened person will respond defensively and double down on their convictions. Although the CBT approach is not off target, you would first need to understand this passenger's motivations, misguided though they may be. For example, would it change your approach to know that your seatmate has survived a plane crash? That he'd been

251

trapped in the wreckage for days, watching his fellow passengers die one by one? Maybe he had the chance to parachute out of the plane and bring back help, but refused because he was too afraid? Would it help to understand that amid powerful emotions, our physiology is in a state of fight, flight, fawn, or freeze? There is adrenaline and other powerful hormones being released into the body, and blood being siphoned away from the prefrontal cortex (the seat of executive functioning) and into our limbs.

Considering the full context of our panicked seatmate, you can see that from his perspective, he is acting as a vigilant protector, sounding the alarm against danger. Leading with a dismissal of his powerful feelings, criticizing him, or telling him to white-knuckle it until our flight attendant comes along to reassign us to another seat is tantamount to a failure of empathy against ourselves (remember, he is part of us). Besides, what happens if Todd next seats us at the side of Trump, who proceeds to tell us that he's going to replace that "disappointing loser," the pilot, and fly the plane himself? This might be enough for some people to assume the crash position, living out what is left of their life in a state of hopelessness (a.k.a. the "living dead").

To add yet another layer of complexity to our action-packed trip, let's say Todd reappears with a cart full of goodies that includes bourbon, Twinkies, oxycodone, and sex? Maybe then we can settle in for a while, distracting ourselves with our smartphone (Reddit, Pornhub, Candy Crush...) or the five hundred channels of free programming embedded in the screen in front us. Sooner or later, these addictions and distractions will wear thin, and we awaken from our stupor to find our seatmate is buckling us into that parachute while Trump bangs his tiny fists on the door of the cockpit screaming, "You're fired!"

While experiencing particularly intense thoughts and feelings, our minds and bodies enter a state of panic that tells us, "This experience must end, right this second, no matter what." That is the moment when many of us unwittingly make decisions that compound and prolong the problem at hand. While most of us can non-judgmentally observe the personalities of many of our seatmates while the flight is smooth, building the "muscle" of non-critical focus allows us to access these observational powers more easily during times of turbulence, providing greater psychological ballast during moments when we are being swamped by thoughts and emotions.

Being practiced in mindfulness doesn't mean you won't experience powerful thoughts and emotions, in fact, once the cobwebs of your reflexive responses begin to be cleared away, you're likely to notice a richer complexity and greater nuance to your inner life. And in the observing space that opens up, you'll begin to see that all overpowering thoughts and emotions have a sequence. Like a wave on the ocean, they gather force until reaching a crescendo, crashing down on the shore only to melt away on the sand.

We don't just work out to have muscles while we're at the gym—we do so because we want our bodies to be fit *all* the time. In much the same way, meditation improves the conditioning of our awareness (some refer to this as "stabilizing" our awareness) and increases our capacity to sit with powerful emotions and self-soothe during times of crisis. If we don't put the time in to mentally "work out" with mindfulness meditation, how can we expect our overwhelmed seatmates to calm themselves during moments of panic? Practicing mindfulness allows us to step outside our reactive minds and take a clear look at the operating principles of our most problematic fellow passengers. While some might appear to be villains bent on destruction, once unmasked, you will come to recognize the traumatized plane crash survivor, or the terrified, unloved little boy seated next to you. Approaching your panicked seatmate with compassion also opens the space for the physiology to return to a state of equilibrium after the release of hormones triggered by the fight, flight, fawn, and freeze reactions. If you provide yourself with greater emotional space during times of turbulence, you're more likely to avoid fear-based, reactive decisions like jumping out of a plane in mid-flight before you're sure it's actually going down.

These days, when I'm feeling particularly low, I deploy a subtle, but powerful reframing of my emotional environment by recognizing that "I *feel* depressed," or "I *feel* angry," rather than the global statements "I *am* depressed," and "I *am* angry." In other words, I am a planeload full of different passengers, not solely the depressed guy in 14A. During the worst years of my crisis, Todd left me sitting with that depressed guy far more often (and far longer) than I could bear. I drank, popped pills, and slept my days away to try to numb myself to the pain. I would deny that there was anyone else on the plane to sit with and imagined most people lived their lives in first class. Whenever I happened to be briefly seated next to one of my positive emotions, I was suspicious of their motives. I'd say to myself, "This isn't real. Don't get too comfortable. Todd is going to come along any second and put me back with the depressed guy again."

While it can feel truly awful to be seated next to our most troublesome seatmates, according to the Buddha, a fundamental source of human suffering is attempting to cling to the things we love while attempting to evade the things we don't like. This evasion is, however, not actually possible. In fact, facing things that make you uncomfortable—such as change—is the only way to achieve wholeness. After all, the one certainty in life we can rely on is change. Mindfulness meditation helps us to accept with grace the fact that we have little control over what life (the ultimate sadistic flight attendant) hands us. And you know what? Sometimes, Todd *does* seat you next to Betty White!

Chapter 15

The Reckoning

I happened to call my father "Daddy" until the day he died. It was the name my older sisters always called him and it never occurred to me to update my own language to the more adult-sounding "Dad." Like a fractal illustration whose smallest part is a reflection of the whole, as I have moved through the interceding years and these preceding chapters, my daddy has transformed before my eyes into capital "D" Daddy; a small reflection of a whole system I hadn't totally understood until now.

Our culture is organized in such a way that it concentrates power and resources in the hands of the few. This is the seemingly unavoidable endpoint for the capitalistic economic model. Standing at the pinnacle of this system—somewhat globally but certainly in the U.S.—is what is referred to as the White supremacist patriarchy. That is, a system where, it's easiest for a White male—such as myself—to succeed unimpeded by unfair treatment or structural limitations such as segregation. Those who knowingly or unwittingly maintain this system are what I now see as "Daddy."

Unlike the cabal of men cutting deals in a smoke-filled back room you might be imagining; I don't see Daddy as some well-oiled Machiavellian conspiracy, but a sociopolitical force that has emerged in the clear light of day and includes numerous proliferating characteristics that are no doubt familiar to my readers.

Of course, daddy—my father—pulled the trigger, but Daddy—the sociopolitical force—was responsible for turning him into a zombie. Daddy sent my father to war and abandoned him on the battlefield, then returned him home and told him to get a job, start a family, and make a normal life for himself without any emotional support—yet another abandonment. In this way and many others, Daddy is the single best answer to the question of *why* Oscar shot my mother and himself. Daddy is the ultimate progenitor of human violence and the wellspring of most forms of trauma. Daddy will have you believe that he is the light and the way, and that there is nobody else on the plane you could reasonably consider sitting next to.

Daddy is not solely American, but the American brand of Daddy is certainly a poster child. Daddy commands men like my father to go to war to maintain or expand his powers at the expense of their lives. Daddy blames soldiers traumatized on the field of battle for their PTSD reactions, abandoning them when they no longer prove useful. Left to fend for themselves, traumatized veterans have historically lived out the remainder of their lives attempting to manage their misunderstood symptoms on their own. Dangerous levels of shame collect in the shadows and compel some number of these veterans, isolated and without treatment, to act out in fits of violence against economic or emotional dependents—like my mother and myself—who were unlikely or unable to retaliate.

As such, my mother struggled throughout her life with cultural norms related to the role of women that were defined by Daddy, thereby fostering her own state of oppression. She was raised to be an obedient people-pleaser preoccupied with the cleanliness of her home and her social standing in the community. This cultural dissonance was magnified by marrying a man of her parents' generation, locking her into an antiquated version of marriage at the very moment in history when women were beginning to successfully rebel against these practices. Under threat of violence by my father, she was forbidden from developing her talents beyond parenting and housekeeping as she fell deeper and deeper into a state of total dependence on her marriage. Even in the presumably "safe" microcosm of a domestic home, Daddy works to coalesce power in the hands of men.

Becoming a *Real* Man

I was raised in a home where my father regularly engaged in BPD behaviors brought on by childhood abuse, the early loss of his parents, and wartime PTSD. As I began to regularly mix with other children, I intuited that I was different from many boys my age. These differences, though multifaceted, would coalesce in the minds of others, as if by magic, around one characteristic: the sex to whom I was attracted. I soon gathered that this supposedly defining characteristic was regarded by most people as a shameful perversion. Other boys shunned me as they upheld the divisive strictures of Daddy, asserting their dominance through ritual bullying and exclusion. Daddy considers anything that might challenge it to be an existential threat. In a prime example of cultural gaslighting, discussions and expressions of homosexuality, socialism, racial justice, and even environmentalism are still often branded as unnatural, evil, illogical, and outlandish through and through. In response—and defense—I attempted to suppress all aspects of my personality that might be seen by others as feminine. I became a highly adept chameleon, virtually invisible to my peers, hopeful that others would accept me as a "full-fledged" member of my gender. Daddy wanted to make sure I fit in nicely—this was the boots on the ground experience for people being ordered into the social hierarchy Daddy needs. Those who make too much trouble or offer up too much resistance are quickly brought to the lower rungs until they learn how to act. Of course, this charade of mine was doomed to fail. Living a life centered around rigid role expectations can force people to behave in ways that conflict with how they feel on the inside, the result being intolerable feelings of cognitive dissonance. What's more, these oppressive attitudes can become internalized, creating dubious workarounds. Failing to achieve acceptance from the world (and from myself) for my supposed lack of natural machismo, I sought out what I believed was the next best thing—to attract sexual partners who personified stereotypically Daddy-like qualities.

• • •

In one way or another, the book on *being* a man—that is, a good foot soldier for Daddy—was written by the twin monoliths of monarchy and the church. However, after thousands of years of uncontested rule, the liberalizing forces unleashed by Renaissance humanism during the Age of Enlightenment finally presented viable challenges to their warped power system. In conjunction with the advancements in psychology, these sociopolitical and scientific currents have slowly but surely empowered historically oppressed groups. Perhaps it was only in the clear light of day of these hard-won freedoms that the true scope of the damages inflicted by the forces of Daddy could be brought fully into our collective awareness.

The experience of oppression and the enactment of violence changes a person forever. Throughout my life, I have deliberately hidden from view many of the autobiographical details shared in these pages out of a wholly unnecessary sense of shame. Thankfully, I have come to appreciate that testimonies such as mine hold the potential to decrease the isolation of other trauma survivors. I have at the very least managed to fit the traumatic fragments of my life into a cohesive narrative that is at last intelligible to myself. By giving voice to the key figures and events of the first half of my life, I have finally integrated crucial pieces of my history— long abandoned to a haze of humiliation and regret—to become a man in full; a man who no longer quietly accepts a legacy of societal and internalized oppression as an inescapable precondition to my otherwise privileged American life.

What's to Be Done?
As individuals and as a nation, what actions can we take to address the myriad manifestations of societal manic defense and internalized

oppression? How do we hold others accountable for oppressive actions rooted in trauma-based dissociation or the dictates of corrupt, faith-based reasoning? Leo Eitinger, a psychiatrist who spent his life studying survivors of Nazi concentration camps, speaks eloquently to the forces that act to silence survivors of oppression. He sheds light on the role each of us play in combating the forces of Daddy. Spoken nearly thirty years ago, his words[339] offer a prescient message that bears repeating in the midst of our own issues of declining freedoms and rising inequities. For our purposes, I have taken some liberties by substituting Eitinger's term "perpetrator" for "Daddy."

"In order to escape accountability for his crimes, Daddy does everything in his power to promote forgetting. Secrecy and silence are Daddy's first line of defense. If secrecy fails, Daddy attacks the credibility of his victim. If he cannot silence her absolutely, he tries to make sure that no one listens. To this end, he marshals an impressive array of arguments, from the most blatant denial to the most sophisticated and elegant rationalization. After every atrocity one can expect to hear the same predictable apologies: it never happened; the victim lies; the victim exaggerates; the victim brought it upon herself; and in any case it is time to forget the past and move on. The more powerful the perpetrator, the greater is his prerogative to name and define reality, and the more completely his arguments prevail.

Daddy's arguments prove irresistible when the bystander faces them in isolation. Without a supportive social environment, the bystander usually succumbs to the temptation to look the other way. This is true even when the victim is an idealized and valued member of society. Soldiers in every war, even those who have been regarded as heroes, complain bitterly that no one wants to know the real truth about war. When the victim is already devalued (a woman, a child), she may find that the most traumatic events of her life take place outside the realm of socially validated reality. Her experience becomes unspeakable.

The study of psychological trauma must constantly contend with this tendency to discredit the victim or to render her invisible. Throughout the history of the field, dispute has raged over whether patients with posttraumatic conditions are entitled to care and respect or deserving of contempt, whether they are genuinely suffering or malingering, whether their histories are true or false and, if false, whether imagined or maliciously fabricated. In spite of a vast literature documenting the phenomena of psychological trauma, debate still centers on the basic question of whether these phenomena are credible and real. To hold traumatic reality in consciousness requires a social context that affirms and protects the victim and that joins victim and witness in a common alliance. For the individual victim, this social context is created by relationships with friends, lovers, and family. For the larger society, the social context is created by political movements that give voice to the disempowered.

The systematic study of psychological trauma therefore depends on the support of a political movement. Indeed, whether such study can be pursued or discussed in public is itself a political question. The study of war trauma becomes legitimate only in a context that challenges the sacrifice of young men in war. The study of trauma in sexual and domestic life becomes legitimate only in a context that challenges the subordination of women and children. Advances in the field occur only when they are supported by a political movement powerful enough to legitimate an alliance between investigators and patients and to counteract the ordinary social processes of silencing and denial. In the absence of strong political movements for human rights, the active process of bearing witness inevitably gives way to the active process of forgetting. Repression, dissociation, and denial are phenomena of social as well as individual consciousness."

As suggested by Eitinger, I believe we must, above all, help decrease the silencing of trauma survivors by speaking out against oppression whenever and wherever we see it. Through political activism, we must confront the enforcement of rigid hierarchies and block policies that seek to divide and/or roll back the rights of the traumatically oppressed. Furthermore, our leaders must clearly define the disruptive role of the false dichotomy regarding God's primacy over man with simple, consistent, uniform "dog whistle" messaging of the type utilized by White supremacists and religious conservatives. This messaging should be grounded in the language and rationales of the vast body of research on positive psychological traits that reveals, at heart, we share *nearly all the same values.*[340]

As a child, I was carefully taught to embrace racist beliefs and openly invited by my father to become yet another toxic male. Upon reflection, I now recognize that a few key factors helped to defuse this eventuality. More than anything, I happened to benefit from a great deal of luck in the timing in which I was born. I came into social consciousness in the choppy cultural wake created by the baby boomers, embracing the politics and social freedoms forged by this generation as my birthright. I was also lucky enough to be born into a solidly middle-class family that valued higher education. As a result, I had the opportunity to learn more about the wider world and to develop essential critical thinking skills.

While my grandparents harbored racist beliefs, they were also defenders of labor rights and Rooseveltian-style progressivism. They nurtured my early understanding of the vital connection between my personal well-being and the greater good of our society. In being categorized as a pariah by our culture for my sexual preference, my position outside the circle of men and the presumptive forces of Daddy was cemented. Thanks to Norman Lear and CBS, I was six when *All in the Family* first came on the air, seven when *Maude* and *Sanford and Son* first appeared, and ten when the Jeffersons took up residence in their Upper East Side condo. The Korean War dramedy *M*A*S*H** demonstrated that straight men (albeit sexist straight men) can also be emotionally complex, thoughtful individuals. I grew up watching strong, independent women (Mary, Rhoda, Alice, and the women of *One Day at* *a Time*) make their way in the world on our old black-and-white portable TV (sitting beside my mother and sister) as my father watched football alone in the family room. Although I didn't realize it at the time, these programs helped to foster a sense of empathy toward others.[341] These television programs (and movies like *Airplane!*) taught me to laugh and cry at the absurdity of men like Archie Bunker and the hollow authority claimed by Daddy's foot soldiers, helping me find common cause with women and people who looked different from me.

These lessons become necessary in an atmosphere where false narratives about power and survival are taken in as freely as oxygen; where Daddy tries with all his might to convince us that we live our lives in a zero-sum game. Consequently, whenever an oppressed group is given more power, we are taught to believe that this *automatically* diminishes our own power. For many people, this is a replay of a dynamic set up in childhood, where one must vie with siblings for the limited attentions of overworked and distracted parents. We each need to keep in mind that in the history of humanity, the well-worn trope of the "survival of the fittest" is just a sidebar; it's not an inescapable fate that compels us, like automatons, to pit ourselves against one another in the game of life.

Today, the overplayed hand of Social Darwinism exhorts us to disregard the humanity of particular individuals and groups because this misunderstood concept would have you believe this is precisely what the "other side" is doing. In response, I feel we must always do our best to embrace others as fully realized individuals—people, like ourselves, who will one day lose everything they have worked for and everyone they have ever loved. We must honor the fact that interdependence and meaningful cooperation are the true superpowers of our species and, it turns out, the "fittest" survival strategy. By learning to look beyond our fears and disowned aspects of ourselves to the level of compassionate understanding, we can reveal the beauty and comfort of the refuge of our shared humanity.

Arrested Development

Psychologist Erik Erikson's Stages of Psychosocial Development outlines the stages of psychosocial development, which tracks our path from infancy to old age, toward ever-greater levels of emotional maturity. Erikson's theory highlights eight key conflicts between our psychological needs and the demands of the social environment. Successful resolution of these conflicts leads to the development of universal virtues like hope, competence, and intimacy. During middle age, Erikson holds that our primary task is a resolution of the conflict between stagnation and a concept he refers to as "generativity." Generativity might be thought of as our drive to leave a positive mark on the world. It is characterized by productivity, nurturance, and the guidance of future generations. The central question we ask of ourselves during this stage of development is "Can I make my life count?" Successful resolution of this conflict results in a sense of accomplishment and the development of the ability to care deeply about the welfare of others. Those who are unable to move beyond this conflict often stagnate, feeling disconnected from others and disillusioned with their lives.[342] Unfortunately, far too many of us experience the ability to profoundly care for others only within certain narrowly defined parameters. After being "carefully taught" by Daddy to disregard the plight of groups ostensibly different from their own, their development is arrested.

To help bridge this gap in responsibility, I feel we each have a duty to examine the ways in which we might be blind to our privileges. Naturally, we should take pride in our accomplishments, but we must also learn to practice humility. Think, for a moment, about whose shoulders *you* stand upon. What sacrifices did they make in their lives? How might they have been privileged—or not? Ultimately, we must look to the realities of our *common disenfranchisement* by the forces of Daddy to find common purpose with one another. We must all make it a priority to recognize that power and resources continue to tilt dangerously toward a pernicious elite that exists to keep the playing field gamed to their advantage. Have you been hurt by that process? Have you been helped by that process? If you're anything like me, the answer to both of these questions is likely "yes."

Ultimately, I don't want more little boys to set leaf fires or to run around exposing themselves. I don't want more children to grow up in fear, with emotionally unfulfilled parents living in a state of arrested psychological development. I don't want more women to spend their days being exploited by Daddy. I don't want more people to be forced to fight wars that further consolidate Daddy's power. I don't want the circumstances or location of a person's birth to dictate their chances of a safe life. And I certainly don't want the amount of melanin in a person's skin to foretell a life of prejudice and other hardships. Above all, I don't want my daughter to live in a theocratic or fascist state, her every action controlled by Daddy.

I imagine most Americans *think* that they want these same things. But it is time for each of us, no matter how sterling we view our intentions, to carefully take stock of ourselves. The well-being of humanity and the preservation of our fragile ecosystem hangs in the balance.

The Last Fight

After that last fight with Oscar about Father's Day, my mother went to my grandmother's house for a few hours to calm down. According to my nana, Judy was upset, but she hadn't gone into the details of the argument. I'm convinced that if there had been anything groundbreaking said—like she threatened to leave him for good—she certainly would have relayed it to my grandmother. Naturally, I've often wondered if some minor detail of that morning was rearranged (if I had gotten up earlier, if Judy had stayed longer with my grandmother...), if things would have turned out differently. Perhaps, but not really. From my current vantage point, it feels like rearranging any one of those elements might have served, at best, to postpone the inevitable. As I now see it, the crux of my family's problem was that we were each invested, with the important exception of my father, in the preservation of our family. At the time, what we couldn't have known was that the cost of that preservation would come at the price of my parents' lives.

If I could roll back the years, I wouldn't have let myself become a bystander to my mother's trauma. It turns out I had been living in what has been identified by trauma theorists as a state of "knowing and not knowing."[343] This mental sleight of hand leaves survivors toggling between opposing states of awareness and unawareness of their traumatic circumstances. Knowing and not knowing is sometimes the result of the self-protective dissociative processes of PTSD wherein our subconscious mind cordons off psychologically threatening material from our day-to-day awareness. Knowing and not knowing also plays out against a societal backdrop wherein Daddy deploys a series of powerful strategies to draw attention away from his role in the perpetration of traumatic oppression. For bystanders to trauma, this "in-between" state can be deployed to provide a much-needed sense of normalcy to our everyday lives. On the surface, we pretend like everything is okay and vigorously ignore associations to intractable problems.[344]

Knowing and not knowing allowed me to occasionally offer my mother an ear, but as a young adult, my actions made it pretty clear that I was not interested in being pulled too deeply into her marital problems. And though I *thought* I understood the effects of my father's need for control over every aspect of her life, I now recognize that I didn't take into account the profound influence of gender bias on the way she saw herself and the decisions she made. Like those who turned their backs on me in the aftermath of my parents' deaths, my help was provisional—I'd only tolerate so much. If she wasn't going to do something bold and definitive about her situation—like leaving him—then I would continue to passively communicate that this was *her own* shortcoming, not a byproduct of the larger system of oppression of women. I now understand that if our intention is to truly stand with someone trapped by traumatic circumstances, we must *not* make our acts of compassion and empathy contingent on changes we would like to see them make. This response takes their state of knowing, where they are aware of their abuser, and forces them into a state of unknowing. They are looking for another soul to reflect that their circumstances are working against them, and when that other soul says, "Nope, you've got to just act different," it amounts to telling them that the pirates taking over their ship have their best intentions in mind.

This state of knowing and not knowing also played a pivotal role in my family's ongoing assessment of the threat posed by my father's guns (e.g., the dread we associated with his gun use on New Year's Eve and checking to see if the Luger was loaded in the weeks before he acted vs. the outward reality of our inaction and silence). In our private cost/benefit analyses, we each *entertained* the idea of the threat of violence as a *possibility*, but that contingency appeared to have a low probability because Oscar hadn't ever (to our knowledge) become physically violent with Judy. Before he pulled the trigger, we could have imagined a lot of different scenarios, as well as a vast array of rationalizations for our choices. And what if we had somehow managed to take away his guns? I've no doubt that he would have only bought another and kept it hidden in a bank safe deposit box until he decided to use it. As a result, we resigned ourselves to biding our time—knowing and not knowing about the threat of violence posed by my father—assuming his health would continue to deteriorate and that he would eventually die of natural causes. That was a mistake.

As implausible as this may sound, I believe a far better approach would have been to attempt to forge an authentic connection with my father during his final years. Although we are regularly reminded by the voices of pop psychology that to improve our relationships, we need to become "better communicators," I think most people miss the mark on how to go about improving these skills. Outwardly, my family's disputes probably looked like most—we would heatedly present our evidence like lawyers in a courtroom, trying to sway the opposing side.

I might have started out "communicating better" with my father by routinely exploring what his life *felt like* to him as opposed to simply asking how he was doing or silently judging him. I could have given him space to express himself and validated how hard things were for him *from his perspective*. Doing so *might have* provided an opportunity for the

268

rejected and vengeful little boy inside Oscar to feel truly "seen" for the first time. As previously discussed, many people feel as though they can't help themselves from responding defensively, lashing out with emotional and/or physical aggression as a primitive means to quell internal tensions. In the case of BPD, individuals are attempting to cope with their fears of abandonment. In the case of trauma, the culprit is dissociation. However, I believe the issue often may simply be that the person has never learned to be a mindful observer to their passing thoughts and emotions. They are automatically acting on the impulses of their panicked seatmates.

Radical Acceptance

As recipients of these ill-conceived strategies and outbursts, we are prone to mistaking someone's limited skill set in managing intense thoughts and emotions for characterologically based maliciousness. Of course, those who are victimized by an abuser rightly resent bearing the weight of compassionate understanding on top of an already compromised situation. However, this approach is not about establishing who is at fault or other scorekeeping measures, but rather an act known as "radical acceptance." The concept of radical acceptance was first developed by psychologist Marsha Linehan as part of Dialectical Behavioral Therapy for people suffering with BPD. [345] Radical acceptance challenges us to recognize reality as it is—not as we would like it to be. Although we cannot avoid the psychological pain caused by others, resisting the reality of a given situation by actively or passively demanding a desired resolution only yields additional layers of emotional suffering on top of our initial pain. It can also delay our ability to heal from these injuries and prevent us from decisively moving on with our lives. Instead of being freed up to enjoy life, we become fixated on the problem at hand, replaying emotionally charged incidents, imagining in minute detail both good and bad outcomes. Regrettably, many people spend a lifetime waiting in vain for an apology that they imagine will make everything better. Unfortunately, no amount of apologizing on the abuser's part—if that ever were to come—would actually make someone feel better for long, especially if the abuse continues.[346]

Many people reject the basic premise of radical acceptance because they mistake it for passivity or condoning the behavior. They become preoccupied with the idea that they will be overcome with a sense of defeat if they fully accept a given situation by "giving in." However, accepting a situation is not the same thing as agreeing with the other person's convictions. In the case of my father, I could have improved our communications by accepting his subjective experience (e.g., "I can see that how you feel makes sense from your perspective"). This approach differs markedly from Battered Woman Syndrome because the injured party does not buy into their perpetrator's narrative or inadvertently invite him to continue his abusive behavior. This is not to say that such actions will necessarily disarm the dangerous pent-up energy of every emotionally isolated and psychologically damaged abuser, but I have found that leading with empathy and compassion gives me a much better chance to defuse the defenses of many of these aggressors.

Why Did Judy Stay?

In the final years of her life, I remember pushing my mother on the question of why she didn't leave Oscar. She told me, "He could have left me when I got pregnant with you—I can't leave him now that he's in the final stages of his life." So, it appears, she may have remained committed to my father out of a sense of loyalty. Some years earlier, when I'd posed the same question, she'd disclosed how she had witnessed Oscar cheat his first wife out of a fair settlement by hiding the family's assets. That, in fact, makes a compelling reason to stay. In abandoning relationships with spouses and other family members, economic stability also plays an outsized role. There is a well-documented financial hit most women take after leaving their male partners.[347]

If you find yourself living in an abusive situation and have read this far, your level of understanding of the factors impacting your circumstances and ideas for a path out are light-years ahead of where my family stood in the years leading up to my parents' deaths. Unfortunately, knowledge alone is not always enough to make a difference. I only wish I could offer a clear-cut, foolproof strategy to remedy the circumstances of *every* person who finds themselves being held hostage to spouses and parents like Oscar. The truth is, even if we'd mobilized to compel Judy to separate from my father, statistically, the dangers of lethal violence would have been compounded. It is an article of faith (and a statistical reality) within domestic violence treatment circles that taking action (or making threats) to leave an abusive partner routinely multiples the likelihood of bloodshed.[348]

So, what should be said to the multitudes of financially dependent, oppressed people who have an overabundance of compelling reasons for not leaving their abusive partners or family members? Take your children and go to a shelter? Ideally, yes. It could save your life. But then what? Start a new life? Easier said than done. After careful consideration, I've determined that an all-purpose strategy eludes me because our Daddy-focused society is not set up to accommodate these transitions. Police are not set up to surveil every dangerous perpetrator, our judicial and mental health systems are not set up to mandate treatment for every abuser, and shelters are notoriously underfunded and do not offer a long-term solution. But that is not the same as saying there is a total absence of resources, allies, and safe harbors to be found. Unlike many places in the world, no matter where you are in this country, some degree of services are available to victims of abuse. Even if it's a hotline or a chat room, it's a start.

Redemption

I still remember the mixture of awe and incredulity I felt as congregants and family members of those killed at Mother Emanuel African Methodist Episcopal Church in Charleston, South Carolina, offered forgiveness to Dylann Roof in the days following his pitiless shooting rampage in 2015.[349] While these sentiments represent a superlative act of empathy, I would like to point out that this granting of forgiveness was also an act of radical acceptance. Accepting reality *as it is* allows us to access one of the natural healing balms to emotional suffering—the experience of compassion. In this light, we can view radical acceptance as a logical and necessary survival strategy in overcoming the experience of trauma.

That said, many people question if there are limits to what we should radically accept in another person. It can be confusing to know how to cope with those who have hurt us. Some may sacrifice their own peace of mind to support a mentally unstable parent. Those with a grown child suffering with mental health or addiction issues can find setting healthy boundaries even more confounding.

The Alcoholics Anonymous "Serenity Prayer" is a useful jumping-off point in assessing how far radical acceptance should be extended to those who actively damage our lives—"God, grant me the serenity to accept the things I cannot change, the courage to change the things I can, and the wisdom to know the difference." The ability to recognize the difference between the things you can change and those you cannot is an extremely useful life skill regardless of the type of problem you're dealing with. Obsessing over matters over which you have little (or no) influence is a recipe for anxiety and heartache. But where, exactly, should you begin if you are looking for the *wisdom* to know the difference between these two contingencies?

Coming to grips with the limits of your control over others is an important first step. Even in healthy relationships, we must do our best to radically accept the limits of our ability to change other people no matter how close our relationship to them. At many points during his life, my father was told in no uncertain terms that he must go to therapy—or else. He never sought out a therapist and no one ever made an appointment for him. If I were to guess the probability that his behavior was going to change and the degree of control I might have had over his actions, I'd probably say zero and zero. But what should we consider when a person makes incremental progress, but then takes a huge step backward? Gray areas like these are common and make the assessment of your degree of control exponentially more difficult. It can feel like you're getting tugged around or that your only role is emotional punching bag. In these situations, it can help to list the factors involved in the individual's successes and setbacks. Then, assess how instrumental you are to their achieving and maintaining these milestones. Other relevant questions to ask yourself include: Are they responding to some physiologically based issue that impedes their ability to control their actions? Do they seek (and consistently follow through with) treatments that are recognized to be effective in managing their symptoms? Are they able to respond to constructive feedback and apply these ideas?

After making a realistic assessment of your degree of control and ability to effect change in this relationship, the central question you must ask yourself is *just how responsible you want to be for this individual.* If the person in question demonstrates little regard for your welfare or appears to have limited awareness of the impact of their behavior on you and other people, your choice may be made easier. Often, as discussed in the incidence of Battered Woman Syndrome, the challenging individual might initially be apologetic, but resume their damaging behaviors after a little time has passed.

Sometimes it's necessary to radically accept that no more can be done—by you at least—and the cost of continuing the relationship is much too high. But only you—not a therapist, priest, guru, spouse, or trusted friend—can decide if you should sever an important relationship. That's because you are the one who will have to live with the consequences of this decision. Canceling an important relationship can be a merciful option if you've reached the conclusion that the sacrifice of your own stability and peace of mind has little impact over creating positive change in the other person's life or there is little regard for your boundaries and needs.

As difficult as it might seem, it is crucial to be deliberate in your decision-making process. The most common mistake people make is to approach these situations in an ad hoc fashion, reacting to the latest crisis, hoping things will get better with time. Unfortunately, wishing things were different or trying to avoid the hard facts, as we did with my parents, will only prolong the agony and allow the situation to worsen.

If you have the strength, it is best to be direct with the other person about stepping away from the relationship. It is possible the other person will refuse to accept the severing of the relationship. However, if you've reached the point of ending the relationship, there is nothing left to discuss. Keep it brief. Many people find putting their thoughts and intentions into a letter (or phone call) more palatable (and safer) than a face-to-face meeting. If you have even the slightest concern about your physical safety, do not meet in person. If you do feel that you must meet in person, it would be best to have one or more friends there to help provide support. You must take care to be consistent in your follow-up. Mixed messages can confuse the situation and prolong a definitive resolution.

Although some might initially feel relief at the severing of ties, it's natural to suffer with feelings of guilt, sadness, and a sense of loss. It's common to experience grief and mourn the loss of a person you've left behind. If you have been pushed to the point of severing a relationship, it is important to remember that you were well beyond the point where there were any options that would have left you feeling good about *any* decision left on the table. Under these circumstances, radical acceptance is all about trying to accept this complicated emotional landscape. You may need to accept that you will continue to second-guess your decision, possibly even feeling guilt and shame for your choice—especially if the person self-destructs or harms others. You might also need to accept that sometimes you might regret your decision or (unfairly) hold yourself responsible if something goes terribly wrong.[350]

If you decide to keep the problematic person in your life, always remember that you were an active, intentional participant in this decision. Don't forget that this decision led you to a conscious choice that regularly calls for a sacrifice of your own well-being. You must also be reasonably sure that you are *not* making this decision because you think you will change the other person. Otherwise, you will forever be reassessing your decision based on the actions of someone over whom you have limited control. When things are going well, you'll probably think you made the right decision. When things are going badly, you'll likely resent the person, maybe even hate them—then blame yourself for keeping them in your life. It will be worthwhile to regularly remind yourself that you made a conscious decision to remain connected knowing full well the hardship this relationship places on you. During hard times, this awareness can provide emotional comfort in the knowledge that you have prioritized the value of self-sacrifice, allowing you to find meaning and sense of purpose in your efforts. Without that step, caring for anyone, even under the best of circumstances, can become just another painful chore.

By exhaustively detailing and contextualizing the life of the unhealthy and violent person who played a pivotal role in my own life, I've come to unequivocally *accept* my father's actions. These measures have allowed me to generate the experience of compassion to soothe the pain of my anger and hurt. I cannot say that I feel love for my father nor that I forgive him, but I *have* developed a deeper understanding of the hardships he faced, and I find his plight to be truly compelling. I do not, however, believe that his victimization by the forces of Daddy absolves him of his final acts. I will never hear him take responsibility for his actions or issue a heartfelt apology—this account will never be settled and I've learned to be okay with that. Despite everything that's happened, I've been able to create a meaningful, purpose-driven life.

Afterword

My father and I made very different choices in life, but we remain connected by one important thread: we both lost crucial relationships that should have endured many decades longer. Separated by death from those like his parents who were best positioned to provide emotional support and a sense of community, our sense of continuity was lost, leading to lives that were lonelier and more fractured than they could or should have been. In response to these circumstances, my father once attempted to bring the disparate members of his family together at Mount Moriah Cemetery as part of his unspoken wish to finally experience his family as a unified whole. Within these pages, I now recognize that I have been responding to my own needs to gather my loved ones close around me once more; all the old ghosts have been exhumed and I've conducted a thorough sociopsychological autopsy. I've examined the wounds and put these events into their proper context once and for all. No longer a zombie captain assisting pirates in the traumatic occupation of my ship, I am satisfied that I've created something useful from the many terrible (and wonderful) things that have happened in my life. I hope that as a reader, you will come away with a better understanding of the universal nature of these stories and a recognition of the nobility that can be found in *each of our lives*.

And so, we've reached the end of our murder mystery. Never again will I dance with my old ghosts as intimately as I have over the years I've spent writing this book. I notice a familiar emptiness creeping in around the edges as I consider the process of reinterring my loved ones—leaving their memories to fade from my day-to-day awareness once again. But it is time. If I have learned anything, it is that the living cannot long endure sharing such tight quarters with the dead.

Goodbye, Mom.
Goodbye, Nana.
Goodbye, Grandpa.
Goodbye, Denton.
Goodbye, Michael.
Thank you.
I love you all. I miss you terribly.
–Tim

Resources

If you are having suicidal thoughts or are worried about someone who might be suicidal, call or text 988 for confidential help. For chat, contact 988lifeline.org.

If you know someone who has committed suicide or are concerned for a person who might be suicidal,
I recommend *Why People Die by Suicide* by Thomas Joiner

If you are in an abusive relationship, contact the National Domestic Violence Hotline at thehotline.org or call 800-799-HELP. Text "start" to 88788.

If you are struggling with alcohol or substance abuse, go to: https://www.samhsa.gov/find-help/national-helpline or call 1-800-662-HELP

For evidence-based, non-religious addiction recovery,
check out SMART Recovery: https://www.smartrecovery.org/

For more information about Happiness and Well-being:
https://www.authentichappiness.sas.upenn.edu/

For help understanding violence:
https://www.penguinrandomhouse.com/books/60198/violence-by-james-gilligan-m-d/

If someone you know might be dealing with borderline personality disorder:
https://www.newharbinger.com/9781684036899/stop-walking-on-eggshells/

To learn more about Dialectical Behavioral Therapy:
https://dialecticalbehaviortherapy.com/

For a complete guide to establishing a mindfulness practice:
https://www.penguinrandomhouse.com/books/89149/full-catastrophe-living-revised-edition-by-jon-kabat-zinn-preface-by-thich-nhat-hanh-foreword-by-joan-borysenko/

Endnotes

1   Dell, P.F., & O'Neil, J.A., eds. (2010). *Dissociation and the Dissociative Disorders: DSM-V and Beyond.* New York: Routledge.

2   Williams, M.B., & Poijula, S. (2010). *The PTSD Workbook: Simple, Effective Techniques for Overcoming Traumatic Stress Symptoms, 3rd edition.* Oakland, CA: New Harbinger Publications.

3   Ovuga, E. (2012). *Post Traumatic Stress Disorders in a Global Context.* Rijeka, Croatia: Books on Demand.

4   Kelly, R. (2011). *Soula Coaster: The Diary of Me.* New York: Smiley Books.

5   Miller, B. (2022). *Reducing Secondary Traumatic Stress: Skills for Sustaining a Career in the Helping Professions.* New York: Routledge.

6   Goodman, R.D., & Gorski, P.C., eds. (2015). *Decolonizing "Multicultural" Counseling through Social Justice.* New York: Springer.

7   Fisher, J. (2017). *Healing the Fragmented Selves of Trauma Survivors: Overcoming Internal Self-alienation.* New York: Routledge.

8   Li, Y. (2022). *Becoming Guanyin: Artistic Devotion of Buddhist Women in Late Imperial China.* New York: Columbia University Press.

9   SantaCaliGon Festival. https://www.santacaligon.com/history

10 Wareing, J. (2016). *Indentured Migration and the Servant Trade from London to America, 1618-1718: "There Is Great Want of Servants."* https://doi.org/10.1093/acprof:oso/9780198788904.003.0003

11 Louis, W.R., & Canny, N., eds. (1988). *The Oxford History of the British Empire: The Origins of Empire.* New York: Oxford University Press.

12 Bradford, W. (2002). *Of Plymouth Plantation, 1620-1647.* New York: Knopf.

13 Louis, W.R., & Canny, N., eds. (1988). *The Oxford History of the British Empire: The Origins of Empire.* New York: Oxford University Press.

14 Rountree, H.C. (2005). *Pocahontas, Powhatan, Opechancanough: Three Indian Lives Changed by Jamestown.* Charlottesville, VA: University of Virginia Press.

15 Peberdy, R., & Waller, P. (2021). *A Dictionary of British and Irish History.* Hoboken, NJ: Wiley.

16 Gaskill, M. (2014). *Between Two Worlds: How the English Became Americans.* New York: Basic Books.

17 Miller, J.L., & Garran, A.M. (2017). *Racism in the United States: Implications for the Helping Professions.* New York: Springer.

18 Wickham, C. (2005). *Framing the Early Middle Ages: Europe and the Mediterranean: 400-800*. New York: Oxford University Press.

19 The Statute of Labourers. (1351). https://avalon.law.yale.edu/medieval/statlab.asp

20 https://encyclopediavirginia.org/entries/indentured-servants-in-colonial-virginia/

21 https://thenapministry.com/

22 Statute of Artificers. http://www.ditext.com/morris/1563.html

23 http://explorehistory.ou.edu/wp-content/uploads/2019/08/An-act-concerning-Servants-and-Slaves.pdf

24 Fort Osage National Historic Landmark. (n.d.). "Fort Osage History." https://fortosagenhs.com/history/T

25 Ibid.

26 O'Brien, W.P. (2014). *Merchants of Independence: International Trade on the Santa Fe Trail, 1827-1860*. Kirksville, MO: Truman State University Press.

27 Ibid.

28 American Psychiatric Association. (2013). *Diagnostic and Statistical Manual of Mental Disorders (5th ed.)*. Arlington, VA: American Psychiatric Association.

29 Kosminsky, P., & Lewin, D. (2009). Counseling approaches for bereaved adolescents. In *Adolescent Encounters with Death, Bereavement, and Coping*. C.A. Corr & D.E. Balk, eds. New York: Springer.

30 Persico, J.E. (2008). *Franklin and Lucy: President Roosevelt, Mrs. Rutherfurd, and the Other Remarkable Women in His Life*. New York: Random House.

31 Darwin, C. (1872). *The Expression of the Emotions in Man and Animals*. New York: D. Appleton & Company.

32 https://www.britannica.com/topic/Akedah

33 Brown, L.S. (2013). Treating the effects of psychological trauma. In *Psychologists' Desk Reference* (pp. 289-293), G.P. Koocher, J.C. Norcross, & B.A. Greene, eds. New York: Oxford University Press.

34 National Archives. (n.d.). "Vietnam War U.S. Military Fatal Casualty Statistics." https://www.archives.gov/research/military/vietnam-war/casualty-statistics#page-header

35 Brittanica. (n.d.). Vietnam War. https://www.britannica.com/event/Vietnam-War

36 Friedman, M.J., Resick, P.A., & Keane, T.M., eds. (2007). *Handbook of PTSD, First Edition: Science and Practice*. New York: Guilford Press.

37 Ibid.

38 Samelson, F. (1977). World War I intelligence testing and the development of psychology. *Journal of the History of the Behavioral Sciences, 13*(3), 274-282.

39 Friedman, M.J., Resick, P.A., & Keane, T.M., eds. (2007). *Handbook of PTSD, First Edition: Science and Practice*. New York: Guilford Press.

40 Mendes Da Costa, J. (1867). *Observation on the diseases of the heart noticed among soldiers, particularly the organic diseases.* https://collections.nlm.nih.gov/catalog/nlm:nlmuid-65540560R-bk

41 Friedman, M.J., Resick, P.A., & Keane, T.M., eds. (2007). *Handbook of PTSD, First Edition: Science and Practice.* New York: Guilford Press.

42 Mendes Da Costa, J. (1867). *Observation on the diseases of the heart noticed among soldiers, particularly the organic diseases.* https://collections.nlm.nih.gov/catalog/nlm:nlmuid-65540560R-bk

43 National Museum of Civil War Medicine (2016). Irritable heart and coping with the trauma of war. https://www.civilwarmed.org/irritableheartptsd

44 Ibid.

45 https://journals.sagepub.com/doi/pdf/10.1177/003591571600902313

46 Wooley, C.F. (1986). "From irritable heart to mitral valve prolapse: World War I, the British Experience, and Thomas Lewis." *The American Journal of Cardiology, 58*(9), 844-849.

47 Vacario, V., Goldberg, J., Rooks, C., Shah, A.J., Veledar, E., Faber, T.L., Votaw, J.R., Forsberg, C.W., & Bremner, J.D. (2013). Post-traumatic stress disorder and incidence of coronary heart disease: A twin study. *Journal of the American College of Cardiology, 62*(11), 970-978.

48 Dercum, F.X. (1889). *Remarks on Spinal Injuries, More Especially Railway Spine, with Hints on Expert Testimony: Addressed to the Medical Jurisprudence Society of Philadelphia.* FB&C Limited.

49 Erichsen, J.E. (1866). *On Railway and Other Injuries of the Nervous System.* London: Walton and Maberly.

50 Ibid.

51 Ibid.

52 IIbid., 28-29.

53 Ibid., 29.

54 https://www.etymonline.com/search?q=trauma

55 Bistoen, G. (2016). *Trauma, Ethics, and the Political beyond PTSD: The Dislocations of the Real.* New York: Palgrave MacMillan.

56 Denzin, N.K., & Lincoln, Y.S. (2013). *Strategies of Qualitative Inquiry.* Thousand Oaks, CA: SAGE Publications.

57 Barrett, M.J., & Stone Fish, L. (2014). *Treating Complex Trauma: A Relational Blueprint for Collaboration and Chance.* New York: Routledge.

58 Geroulanos, S., & Meyers, T. (2018). *The Human Body in the Age of Catastrophe: Brittleness, Science, Integration, and the Great War.* Chicago: The University of Chicago Press.

59 Eghigian, G. (2010). *From Madness to Mental Health: Psychiatric Disorder and Its Treatment in Western Civilization.* New Brunswick, NJ: Rutgers University Press.

60 Goetz, C.G., Bonduelle, M., & Gelfand, T. (1995). *Charcot: Constructing Neurology*. New York: Oxford University Press.

61 Zukas, J.A., & Walters, W. (1998). *Explosive Effects and Applications*. New York: Springer.

62 Rule, J.C. (1970). *Louis XIV and the Craft of Kingship*. Columbus, OH: The Ohio State University Press.

63 Collins, J.B. (1989). The economic role of women in seventeenth century France. *French Historical Studies, 16*(2), 436-470.

64 Risse, G.B. (1999). *Mending Bodies, Saving Souls: A History of Hospitals*. New York: Oxford University Press.

65 Bynum, W. (2008). *The History of Medicine: A Very Short Introduction*. New York: Oxford University Press.

66 Fink, P.J., & Tasman, A. (1992). *Stigma and Mental Illness*. Washington, D.C.: American Psychiatric Press.

67 Hough, M., & Tassoni, P. (2021). *Counselling Skills and Theory, 5th edition*. New York: Hachette.

68 Simon-Kerr, J.A. (2012). "Moral Turpitude." *Utah Law Review, 1001*.

69 Foucault, M. (1988). *Madness and Civilization: A History of Insanity in the Age of Reason*. New York: Vintage Books.

70 https://www.biblegateway.com/passage/?search=Matthew%20 8&version=NIV

71 Foucault, M. (1988). *Madness and Civilization: A History of Insanity in the Age of Reason*. New York: Vintage Books.

72 Ibid.

73 Young, A. (1997). *The Harmony of Illusions: Inventing Post-Traumatic Stress Disorder*. Princeton, NJ: Princeton University Press.

74 Foucault, M. (1988). *Madness and Civilization: A History of Insanity in the Age of Reason*. New York: Vintage Books.

75 Mathews, H.F., & Manago, A.M. (2019). *The Psychology of Women under Patriarchy*. Albuquerque, NM: University of New Mexico Press.

76 Hinton, E. (2016). *From the War on Poverty to the War on Crime: The Making of Mass Incarceration in America*. Cambridge, MA: Harvard University Press.

77 Prison Policy Initiative. (2020). "What percent of the U.S. is incarcerated?" and other ways to measure mass incarceration. https://www.prisonpolicy.org/blog/2020/01/16/percent-incarcerated

78 Southern Coalition for Social Justice. (2021). "Mass Incarceration and People of Color." https://southerncoalition.org/mass-incarceration-people-color

79 Prison Policy Initiative (2021). Race and ethnicity. https://www.prisonpolicy.org/research/race_and_ethnicity

80 Brown, C., & MacDonald, J.E. (2020). *Critical Clinical Social Work: Counterstorying for Social Justice*. Toronto: Canadian Scholars.

81 Neukrug, E.S. (2017). *A Brief Orientation to Counseling: Professional Identity, History, and Standards*. Boston: Cengage Learning.

82 Young, A. (1995). *The Harmony of Illusions: Inventing Post-Traumatic Stress Disorder*. Princeton, NJ: Princeton University Press.

83 https://www.etymonline.com/search?q=hysteria

84 Cleghorn, E. (2021). *Unwell Women: Misdiagnosis and Myth in a Man-made World*. New York: Dutton.

85 https://www.mcgill.ca/oss/article/history-quackery/history-hysteria

86 Micale, M.S. (1989). Hysteria and Its Historiography: A Review of Past and Present Writings. *History of Science, 27*(4), 319-351.

87 Brian, K.M., & Trent, J.W. (2017). *Phallacies: Historical Intersections of Disability and Masculinity*. New York: Oxford University Press.

88 Lewis Herman, J. (1992). *Trauma and Recovery: The Aftermath of Violence—from Domestic Abuse to Political Terror*. New York: Basic Books.

89 American Psychiatric Association. (2022). *Diagnostic and Statistical Manual of Mental Disorders*. Washington, D.C.: American Psychiatric Association Publishing.

90 Goetz, C.G., Bonduelle, M., Gelfand, T. (1995). *Charcot: Constructing Neurology*. New York: Oxford University Press.

91 Oppenheim, H. (1911). *Textbook of Nervous Diseases*. (Vol. 1). Darien Press.

92 Ibid.

93 Muñoz, P., & Correira, S. (2021). The Great War and the Fifth International Psychoanalytic Congress in Budapest: Psychoanalysis in the 1910s. *Historica Crítica, 84*, 3-125.

94 Rosen, G. (2004). *Posttraumatic Stress Disorder: Issues and Controversies*. West Sussex, England: John Wiley & Sons.

95 Lewis Herman, J. (1992). *Trauma and Recovery: The Aftermath of Violence—from Domestic Abuse to Political Terror*, New York: Basic Books.

96 Coined by one Breuer's best known patients, Anna O. (aka Bertha Pappenheim), who would go on to become a significant force in her own right, blazing a trail in the area of Jewish women's rights up until the rise of Germany's Nazi party. From Akhtar, S. (2013). *Psychoanalytic Listening: Methods, Limits, and Innovations*. New York: Routledge.

97 Van der Kolk, B.A., McFarlane, A.C., & Weisaeth, L. (1996). *Traumatic Stress: The Effects of Overwhelming Experience on Mind, Body, and Society*. New York: Guilford Press.

98 Ibid.

99 Ribot, T.A. (1882). *Diseases of Memory: An Essay in the Positive Psychology*. New York: D. Appleton & Company.

100 Leys, R. (2010). *Trauma: A Genealogy*. Chicago: The University of Chicago Press.

101 Ibid.

102 Ibid.

103 Ibid.

104 As Pierre Janet described it over a century ago. Ibid.

105 Michelson, L.K., & Ray, W.J. (1996). *Handbook of Dissociation: Theoretical, Empirical, and Clinical Perspectives*. New York: Springer.

106 If all of this sounds familiar, it should. Our current understanding of dissociative states finds its spiritual antecedents in the mysteries of Charcot's hypnotic trance discussed on page 58.

107 Leys, R. (2010). *Trauma: A Genealogy.* Chicago: The University of Chicago Press.

108 Ibid.

109 Neu, J. (1991). *The Cambridge Companion to Freud.* New York: Cambridge University Press.

110 Eagle, M.N. (2018). *Core Concepts in Classical Psychoanalysis: Clinical, Research Evidence and Conceptual Critiques.* New York: Routledge.

111 Freud, S. (1896). The aetiology of hysteria. The Standard Edition of the Complete Psychological Works of Sigmund Freud 3. London: Hogarth.

112 Storr, A. (1989). *Freud: A Very Short Introduction.* New York: Oxford University Press.

113 TK Footnote about difference between Psychiatry and Psychology

114 Lewis Herman, J. (1992). *Trauma and Recovery: The Aftermath of Abuse—From Domestic Violence to Political Terror.* New York: Basic Books.

115 Holdorff, B. (2011). The fight for 'traumatic neurosis,' 1889-1916: Hermann Oppenheim and his opponents in Berlin. *History of Psychiatry, 22,* 465-76. https://doi.org/10.1177/0957154X10390495

116 Stewart, R.W. (2009). *American Military History, Volume II, The United States Army in a Global Era, 1917-2008.* Washington, D.C.: Center of Military History.

117 Alexander, C. (2015, February). The invisible war on the brain. *National Geographic.* https://www.nationalgeographic.com/healing-soldiers/blast-force.html

118 https://archive.org/details/warneurosesshell00mottuoft/page/24

119 https://sites.google.com/a/golosal.net/ptsd-mr-hart-row-1/shellshock

120 Webster Brown, M. (1918). *Neuropsychiatry and the War: A Bibliography with Abstracts.* New York: War Work Committee of the National Committee for Mental Hygiene. https://archive.org/stream/neuropsychiatryw00brow_1/neuropsychiatryw00brow_1_djvu.txt

121 Young, A. (1995). *The Harmony of Illusions: Inventing Post-Traumatic Stress Disorder.* Princeton, NJ: Princeton University Press.

122 Ibid.

123 Webster Brown, M. (1918). *Neuropsychiatry and the War: A Bibliography with Abstracts.* New York: War Work Committee of the National Association for Mental Hygiene. https://archive.org/stream/neuropsychiatryw00brow_1/neuropsychiatryw00brow_1_djvu.txt

124 Young, A. (1995). *The Harmony of Illusions: Inventing Post-Traumatic Stress Disorder.* Princeton, NJ: Princeton University Press.

125 Alexander, C. (2015, February). Blast force. *National Geographic.* https://www.nationalgeographic.com/healing-soldiers/blast-force.html

126 Ibid.

127 Ibid.

128 Alexander, C. (2016, June 9). Shell shock: The 100-year mystery may now be solved. *National Geographic*. https://www. nationalgeographic.com/science/ article/blast-shock-tbi-ptsd-ied- shell-shock-world-war-one

129 Baughman Shively, S., et al. (2016). Characterisation of interface astroglial scarring in the human brain after blast exposure: A post-mortem case series. *The Lancet, 15*(9), 944-953.

130 Ibid.

131 Dursa, E.K., Reinhard, M.J., Barth, S.K.,& Schneiderman, A.I. (2014). Prevalence of a positive screen for PTSD among OEF/OIF and OEF/ OIF-era veterans in a large population-based cohort. *Journal of Traumatic Stress, 27*, 542-549. https://www.pbs.org/wgbh/pages/ frontline/shows/heart/themes/ shellshock.html

132 Imperial War Museums. (n.d.). What was the Battle of the Somme? https://www.iwm.org.uk/history/ what-was-the-battle-of-the-somme

133 van Bergen, L. (2014). Medicine and medical service. *International Encyclopedia of the First World War*. https://encyclopedia.1914-1918- online.net/article/medicine_and_ medical_service

134 NHS Foundation Trust. (n.d.). World War I: A pre-history of the Tavistock Clinic. https://100years. tavistockandportman.nhs.uk/ world-war-1a-prehistory-of-the- tavistock-clinic

135 Ibid.

136 Young, A. (1995). *The Harmony of Illusions: Inventing Post-Traumatic Stress Disorder*. Princeton, N.J.: Princeton University Press.

137 Ibid.

138 Ibid.

139 Wilson, J.P., & Brwynn Thomas, R. (2004). *Empathy in the Treatment of Trauma and PTSD*. New York: Brunner-Routledge.

140 For a concise and cogent distinc- tion between animal behaviorists and behaviorists, check out note 8 on p. 257 of *What Animals Want: Expertise and Advocacy in Laboratory Animal Welfare Policy*, which can be accessed here: https://books.google.com.mx/ books?id=Iheg3hkj99AC&p- g=PA257&dq=%22animal+behavior- ists%22+%22shock%22&hl=en&sa=X- &ved=2ahUKEwioiN2Fgrb6AhXkH0Q- IHTroDJgQ6AF6BAgDEAI#v=onep- age&q=%22animal%20 behaviorists%22%20 %22shock%22&f=false

141 Southard, E.E. (2020). *Shell Shock and Other Neuropsychiatric Problems*. Frankfurt: Outlook Verlag.

142 https://openlibrary.org/books/ OL14014046M/Hysterical_disorders_ of_warfare

143 Yealland, L.R. (1918). *Hysterical* London: MacMillan and Co.

144 Young, A. (1995). *The Harmony of Illusions: Inventing Post-Traumatic Stress Disorder*. Princeton, N.J.: Princeton University Press.

145 Imperial War Museums. (n.d.). Cylindrical stick grenade (stielhandgranate). https://www.iwm.org. uk/collections/item/object/30020454

146 Appel. J.W., & Beebe, G.W. (1946). Preventive psychiatry: An epidemiologic approach. *Journal of the American Medical Association, 131*, 1469-1475.

147 https://minds.wisconsin.edu/handle/1793/8516 https://gulflink.health.mil/library/randrep/marlowe_paper/mr1018_11_ch7.html

148 United States Army Medical Service. (1966). *Medical Department US Army in World War II*. Washington, D.C.: Office of the Surgeon General.

149 https://www.ncbi.nlm.nih.gov/pmc/articles/PMC2089086

150 Pols, H., & Oak, S. (2007). War and military mental health: The U.S. psychiatric response in the 20th century. *American Journal of Public Health, 97*(12), 2132-2142.

151 Steeling book

152 Special Commission of Civilian Psychiatrists (1945). *Report of U.S. Special Commission of Civilian Psychiatrists Covering Psychiatric Policy and Practice in the U.S. Army Medical Corps, European Theater, 20 April to 8 July 1945*. https://collections.nlm.nih.gov/bookviewer?PID=nlm:nlmuid-14321200R-bk

153 Ibid.

154 Van Ells, M.D. (2001). *To Hear Only Thunder Again: America's World War II Veterans Come Home*. New York: Lexington Books.

155 McManus, J.C. (2014). *The Dead and Those About to Die: D-Day: The Big Red One at Omaha Beach*. New York: Dutton Caliber.

156 Ibid.

157 Tom Lea Institute. https://www.tomlea.com/4-World War Ii?lightbox=dataItem-ka7mvjoc1

158 Gayle, G.D. (1996). *Bloody Beaches: The Marines at Peleliu*. Washington, D.C.: Marine Corps Historical Center.

159 (11 June 1945). Peleliu: Tom Lea paints island invasion. *LIFE Magazine*.

160 Menninger, K.A., Mayman, M., & Pruyser, P. (1963). *The Vital Balance: The Life Process in Mental Health and Illness*. New York: Viking Press.

161 Appel, J., & Beebe, G. (1946). Preventive psychiatry. *JAMA, 131*(18), 1469-1475. https://www.deepdyve.com/lp/american-medical-association/preventive-psychiatry-hK9zMNzXla

162 Caruth, C. (2014). *Listening to Trauma: Conversations with Leaders in the Theory and Treatment of Traumatic Experience*. Baltimore, MD: Johns Hopkins University Press.

163 https://www.imdb.com/title/tt0082766

164 Grant, N. (2018). *The Luger*. New York: Bloomsbury.

165 https://ammo.com/articles/georg-luger-pistol-9mm-ammo-9×19mm-ammunition-designer-history

166 Walter, J. (2018). *Luger: The Story of the World's Most Famous Handgun*. New York: Skyhorse Publishing.

167 https://www.kansasmemory.org/item/316295

168 https://biblehub.com/genesis/3-16.htm

169 Yes, her high school was already channeling its students into the Greek system. Judy was the treasurer—a position that allowed her to regularly cut out of school to make bank deposits of a supposedly time-sensitive nature. This cover story was just a silly ruse so she could grab a cheeseburger and cherry limeade at Winstead's drive-in.

170 https://worldpopulationreview.com/state-rankings/divorce-rate-by-state

171 U.S. Public Health Service. (1965). *Vital Statistics of the United States 1965, Volume III—Marriage and Divorce*. Washington, D.C.: U.S. Public Health Service.

172 Rees, A. (2004). *The Great Plains Region: The Greenwood Encyclopedia of American Regional Cultures*. Westport, CT: Greenwood Publishers.

173 Wishart, D.J. (2004). *Encyclopedia of the Great Plains*. Lincoln, NE: University of Nebraska Press.

174 https://www.okhistory.org/publications/enc/entry?entry=DO007

175 https://www.legendsofamerica.com/we-dalton

176 Gould, L.R. (2001). *America in the Progressive Era: 1890-1914*. New York: Routledge.

177 The American Presidency Project. (1892). https://www.presidency.ucsb.edu/statistics/elections/1892

178 Ibid.

179 Ford, A.G. (1956). Argentina and the Baring Crisis of 1890. *Oxford Economic Papers, 8*(2), 127-150.

180 Steeples, D.O., & Whitten, D.O. (1998). *Democracy in Desperation: The Depression of 1893*. Westport, CT: Greenwood Press.

181 https://www.thirteen.org/wnetjimcrow/stories_org_populist.htmlhttps://encyclopediaofarkansas.net/entries/panic-of-1893-4292

182 https://www.history.com/this-day-in-history/dalton-gang-commits-its-first-train-robbery

183 Ibid.

184 https://www.usmarshals.gov/who-we-are/about-us/history/historical-reading-room/deputies-versus-wild-bunch

185 Stratton, W.K. (2019). *The Wild Bunch: Sam Peckinpah, a Revolution in Hollywood, and the Making of a Legendary Film*. New York: Bloomsbury Publishing.

186 https://www.usmarshals.gov/who-we-are/about-us/history/historical-reading-room/deputies-versus-wild-bunch

187 https://truewestmagazine.com/article/who-is-rose-of-cimarron

188 https://darkheartedwomen.wordpress.com/2017/02/13/the-rose-of-cimarron

189 http://sites.rootsweb.com/~okmurray/stories/dalton.htm

190 https://www.okhistory.org/publications/enc/entry?entry=DA006

191 Dacus, J.A. (2017). *The James and Younger Brothers: The Story of One of the Most Notorious and Legendary Outlaw Gangs of the American West*. London: Leonaur.

192 Fadness, A.K. (2022). *Capturing the Younger Brothers Gang in the Northern Plains*. Charleston, SC: The History Press.

193 https://avalon.law.yale.edu/ancient/hamframe.asp

194 https://www.biblegateway.com/passage/?search=Exodus%2021%3A24-26&version=NLT

195 Nichols, B. (2014). *Guerrilla Warfare in Civil War Missouri*. Jefferson, NC: McFarland and Company.

196 Ibid.

197 Castel, A.E. (1962). *William Clarke Quantrill: His Life and Times*. Tulsa, OK: Oklahoma University Press.

198 Rosen, F. (2005). *The Historical Atlas of American Crime*. New York: Facts on File, Inc.

199 https://www.sandiegouniontribune.com/news/150-years/sd-me-150-years-october-6-htmlstory.html

200 Dalton, E. (1918). *Beyond the Law*. Gretna, LA: Pelican Publishing Company.

201 https://www.imdb.com/title/tt0182787

202 Bushman, B.J. & Thomas, S. (2011). When narcissistic ego deflates, narcissistic aggression inflates. In *The Handbook of Narcissism and Narcissistic Personality Disorder: Theoretical Approaches, Empirical Findings, and Treatments*. New York: Wiley & Sons.

203 Ibid.

204 Ibid.

205 Hofer, P. (1989). The role of manipulation in the antisocial personality. *International Journal of Offender Therapy and Comparative Criminology, 33*(2), https://doi.org/10.1177/0306624X890330020

206 Like the Dalton Gang, there is no evidence that the James Gang ever shared their spoils with anyone beyond immediate family. https://www.pbs.org/wgbh/americanexperience/features/james-newspapers

207 https://www.pbs.org/wgbh/americanexperience/features/james-newspapers

208 Russell, B. (1945). *History of Western Philosophy*. New York: Simon & Schuster.

209 Robertson, J. (2015). *The Enlightenment: A Very Short Introduction*. New York: Oxford University Press.

210 Ibid.

211 Pinn, A. (2021). *The Oxford Handbook of Humanism*. New York: Oxford University Press.

212 Pichersky, E. (2021). *Plants and Human Conflict*. Boca Raton, FL: CRC Press.

213 Horton, J.O., & Horton, L.E. (2006). *Slavery and Public History: The Tough Stuff of American Memory*. New York: The New Press.

214 Ellman, P.L., & Goodman, N.R. (2017). *Finding Unconscious Fantasy in Narrative, Trauma, and Body Pain: A Clinical Guide*. New York: Routledge.

215 Conlan, R. (1999). *States of Mind: New Discoveries about How Our Brains Make Us Who We Are*. New York: Wiley & Sons.

216 Wilson, J.P., & Raphael, B. (1993). *International Handbook of Traumatic Stress Syndromes, Volume II*. New York: Springer.

217 Charles, D.M. (2012). *The FBI's Obscene File: J. Edgar Hoover and the Bureau's Crusade Against Smut*. Lawrence, KS: University of Kansas.

218 Erikson, E. (1993). *Childhood and Society.* New York: W.W. Norton.

219 "You've Got to Be Carefully Taught." https://rodgersandhammerstein.com/song/south-pacific/youve-got-to-be-carefully-taught

220 Goldman Rubin, S. (2016). *Brown v. Board of Education: A Fight for Simple Justice.* New York: Holiday House.

221 Bolton, C.C. (2005). *The Hardest Deal of All: The Battle over School Integration in Mississippi, 1870-1980.* Jackson, MS: University of Mississippi Press.

222 Goldman Rubin, S. (2016). *Brown v. Board of Education: A Fight for Simple Justice.* New York: Holiday House.

223 Brown Nagin, T. (2022). *Civil Rights Queen: Constance Baker Motley and the Struggle for Equality.* New York: Knopf Doubleday.

224 Smith, D., & Winn Tutwiler, S. (2010). *The Contradicitions of the Legacy of Brown v. Board of Education, Topeka.* New York: Routledge.

225 Harasymiw, T. (2020). *Justice for All: Landmark Civil Rights Cases.* New York: Lucent Press.

226 Huh, J. (2015). *The Arresting Eye: Race and the Anxiety of Detection.* Charlottesville, VA: University of Virginia Press.

227 Luxenberg, S. (2019). *Separate: The Story of Plessy v. Ferguson, and America's Journey from Slavery to Segregation.* New York: W.W. Norton.

228 https://www.archives.gov/milestone-documents/plessy-v-ferguson#transcript

229 Ibid.

230 Ibid.

231 Ibid.

232 Wimeth, D.B., & Bigsby, C. (1998). *The Cambridge History of American Theatre, Volume I, Beginnings to 1870.* New York: Cambridge University Press.

233 Berrey, S.A. (2015). *The Jim Crow Routine: Everyday Performances of Race, Civil Rights, and Segregation in Mississippi.* Chapel Hill, NC: UNC Press.

234 Masur, K. (2021). *Until Justice Be Done: America's First Civil Rights Movement, from the Revolution to Reconstruction.* New York: W.W. Norton.

235 https://www.archives.gov/founding-docs/declaration-transcript

236 https://www.monticello.org/thomas-jefferson/jefferson-slavery/thomas-jefferson-and-sally-hemings-a-brief-account

237 https://www.monticello.org/slavery/slavery-faqs/property

238 https://quod.lib.umich.edu/cgi/t/text/pageviewer-idx?c-c=evans;c=evans;idno=n33967.0001.001;node=N33967.0001.001.3;se-q=7;page=root;view=text

239 Little, L.A., & Olinskey, J.M. (2013). *Early Kansas City, Missouri.* Charleston, SC: Aroadia Publishing.

240 Rothstein, R. (2017). *The Color of Law: A Forgotten History of How Our Government Segregated America.* New York: W.W. Norton.

241 Coulter, C.E. (2006). *Take Up the Black Man's Burden: Kansas City's African American Communities.* Columbia, MO: University of Missouri Press.

242 United States Department of Commerce, Bureau of the Census. (1970). *Census Tracts: Kansas City, MO-Kans. Standard Metropolitan Statistical Area*. Washington, D.C.: United States Department of Commerce.

243 Brown Nagin, T. (2022). *Civil Rights Queen: Constance Baker Motley and the Struggle for Equality*. New York: Knopf.

244 https://constitutioncenter.org/the-constitution/supreme-court-case-library/brown-v-board-of-education

245 Lamb Schirmer, S. (2002). *A City Divided: The Racial Landscape of Kansas City, 1900-1960*. Columbia, MO: University of Columbia Press.

246 Caro, R.A. (1974). *The Power Broker: Robert Moses and the Fall of New York* New York: Knopf.

247 Gotham, K. F. (2001). A city without slums: Urban renewal, public housing, and downtown revitalization in Kansas City, Missouri. *American Journal of Economics and Sociology, 60*(1), 285-316.

248 Panaitiu, I.G. (2019). Apes and anticitizens: Simianization and U.S. national identity discourse. *Social Identities; Journal for the Study of Race, Nation and Culture, 26*(1), 109-127.

249 Hobofil, S.E., & de Vries, M.W. (1995). *Extreme Stress and Communities: Impact and Intervention*. New York: Springer.

250 van der Hart, O., & Horst, R. (1989). The dissociation theory of Pierre Janet. *Journal of Traumatic Stress, 2*(4), 397-412.

251 Spatz Widom, C. (1989). The cycle of violence. *Science, 244*(4901), 160-166.

252 https://addhealth.cpc.unc.edu

253 Spatz Widom, C. (1989). The cycle of violence. *Science, 244*(4901), 160-166.

254 Livings, M.S., Hsiao, V., & Withers, M. (2022). Breaking the cycle of family violence; A critique of family violence interventions. *Trauma, Violence, and Abus*. Advance online publication. https://doi.org/10.1177/152483802210980

255 Spatz Widom, C., & Wilson, H.W. (2014). Intergenerational tranmission of violence. In *Violence and Mental Health*, Jutta Lindert & Itzhak Levav, New York: Springer.

256 Currie, J., & Tekin, E. (2012). Understanding the cycle: Childhood maltreatment and future crime. *Journal of Human Resources, 47*(2), 509-549.

257 Retz, W., Ginsberg, Y., Turner, D., Barra, S., et al. (2021). Attention-Deficit/Hyperactivity Disorder (ADHD), antisociality, and delinquent behavior over the lifespan. *Neuroscience and Behavioral Reviews, 120*, 236-248.

258 Janagan Johnson, E., & James, C. (2015). Effects of child abuse and neglect on adult survivors. *Early Child Development and Care, 186*(11), 1836-1845.

259 Wiehe, V.R (1989). *Understanding Family Violence: Treating and Preventing Partner, Child, Sibling, and Elder Abuse*. Thousand Oaks, CA: SAGE.

260 Young, A. (1995). *The Harmony of Illusions: Inventing Post-Traumatic Stress Disorder.* Princeton, NJ: Princeton University Press.

261 Ibid.

262 Ibid.

263 Ibid.

264 Ibid., 109.

265 Ibid., 113.

266 Ibid.

267 Ibid.

268 American Psychiatric Association. (2022). *Diagnostic and Statistical Manual of Mental Disorders: DSM-5-TR.* Washington, D.C.: American Psychiatric Association.

269 DeYoung, A., & Landolt, M.A. (2018). PTSD in children below the age of six years. *Current Psychiatry Reports, 20*(97). https://doi.org/10.1007/s11920-018-0966-z

270 Toobin, J. (2016). *American Heiress: The Kidnapping, Crimes, and Trial of Patty Hearst.* New York: Doubleday.

271 Schreiber, B. (2016). *Revolution's End: The Patty Hearst Kidnapping, Mind Control, and the Secret History of Donald DeFreeze and the SLA.* New York: Skyhorse Publishing.

272 Ibid.

273 Ibid.

274 https://www.pbs.org/wgbh/americanexperience/features/guerrilla-rise-and-fall-symbionese-liberation-army

275 Ibid.

276 https://www.pbs.org/wgbh/americanexperience/features/guerrilla-rise-and-fall-symbionese-liberation-army

277 Toobin, J. (2016). *American Heiress: The Kidnapping, Crimes and Trial of Patty Hearst.* New York: Doubleday.

278 Ibid.

279 Schreiber, B. (2016). *Revolution's End: The Patty Hearst Kidnapping, Mind Control, and the Secret History of Donald DeFreeze and the SLA.* New York: Skyhorse Publishing. During her year in hiding, an innocent mother of four was shot in the stomach and died during a bank robbery committed by one of the remaining SLA abductors in suburban Sacramento, California.

280 Toobin, J. (2016). *American Heiress: The Kidnapping, Crimes and Trial of Patty Hearst.* New York: Doubleday.

281 Charles, D.M., & Stockham, A.J. (2022). *The Federal Bureau of Investigation: History, Powers, and Controversies of the FBI.* Santa Barbara, CA: ABC-CLIO.

282 King, D. (2020). *Six Days in August: The Story of Stockholm Syndrome.* New York: W.W. Norton.

283 Toobin, J. (2016). *American Heiress: The Kidnapping, Crimes and Trial of Patty Hearst.* New York: Doubleday.

284 Thompson, E.G. (2020). *Cults Uncovered: True Stories of Mind Control and Murder.* New York: Penguin.

285 Fergusson, A., & Gutiérrez-Peláez, M. (2022). *Sándor Ferenczi: A Contemporary Introduction.* New York: Taylor & Francis.

286 Dupont, J. (1998). *The Concept of Trauma According to Ferenczi and its Effects on Subsequent Psychoanalytical Research.* https://ur.booksc.me/book/35711441/1fd8e4

287 http://library.allanschore.com/docs/FerencziTraumaDupont.pdf

288 Ibid.

289 Ibid.

290 Frankel, J. (2008). Exploring Ferenczi's concept of identification with the aggressor: Its role in trauma, everyday life, and the therapeutic relationship. *Psychoanalytic Dialogues, 12*(1), 101-139.

291 Herman, J. (1992). *Trauma and Recovery: The Aftermath of Violence —from Domestic Abuse to Political Terror.* New York: Basic Books.

292 Stark, E. (2007). *Coercive Control: The Entrapment of Women in Personal Life.* New York: Oxford University Press.

293 Wiesel, E. (2013). *Night.* New York: Farrar, Straus & Giroux.

294 Ibid.

295 Interagency Floodplain Management Review Committee. (1994). *Sharing the Challenge: Floodplain Management into the 21st Century.* Washington, D.C.: Interagency Floodplain Management Review Committee.

296 Waddell, M. (2002). The psychodynamics of bullying. *Free Association, 9,* 189-210.

297 Ibid.

298 https://www.barstowschool.org/about-us#discover-barstow

299 My grandmother, Mildred, was in one of those cars out on the road. She happened to be riding by with her friends on their way to some Sunday outing. I don't know that then. They don't come in. Maybe they weren't allowed to. They go directly to the hospital.

300 http://pompeiisites.org/en/pompeii-map/analysis/the-casts

301 Ibid.

302 Gilligan, J. (1997). *Violence: Reflections on a National Epidemic.* New York: Vintage Books.

303 Ibid.

304 Ibid

305 Hunt, D.M. (2016). (Re)affirming race: Reality, negotiation, and the Trial of the Century. *The Sociological Quarterly, 38*(3), 399-422.

306 Preston Wilson, J., & Martin, T. (2004). *Assessing Psychological Trauma and PTSD.* New York: The Guilford Press.

307 https://www.webmd.com/drugs/2/drug-920-6006/klonopin-oral/clonazepam-oral/details

308 Gunderson, J.G. (2009). Borderline personality disorder: Ontogeny of a diagnosis. *The American Journal of Psychiatry.* https://ajp.psychiatryonline.org/doi/full/10.1176/appi.ajp.2009.08121825

309 Laporte, L., & Guttman, H. (1996). Traumatic childhood experiences as risk factors for borderline and other personality disorders. *Journal of Personality Disorders, 10*(3), 247-259.

310 Holmes, P., & Farnfield, S. (2014). *The Routledge Handbook of Attachment Theory.* New York: Routledge.

311 Ibid.

312 Westphal, M., et al. (2014). Borderline personality disorder, exposure to interpersonal trauma, and psychiatric comorbidity in urban primary care patients. *Psychiatry, 76*(4), 365-380.

313 Lewis, K.L., & Grenyer, B.F.S. (2009). Borderline personality or complex posttraumatic stress disorder? An update on the controversy. *Harvard Review of Psychiatry, 17*(5), 322-328.

314 Gillespie, C., Murphy, M., & Joyce, M. (2022). Dialectical behavior therapy for individuals with borderline personality disorder: A systematic review of outcomes after one year of follow-up. *Journal of Personality Disorders, 36*(4), https://doi.org/10.1521/pedi.2022.36.4.431

315 Fox, D.J. (2019). *The Borderline Personality Workbook.* Oakland, CA: New Harbinger Publications.

316 Shreeve, D.F. (2012). *Reactive Attachment Disorder: A Case-based Approach.* New York: Springer.

317 Chu, J. (2011). *Rebuilding Shattered Lives: Complex PTSD and Dissociative Disorders.* New York: Wiley. The field of trauma has seen a similar splintering into various subtypes over the past twenty years, making for an often confounding array of flavors and interpretations well beyond the scope of our current discussion. And so, the "beat goes on"—our quilting bee continues...

318 Kreger, R. (2008). *The Essential Family Guide to Borderline Personality Disorder.* Center City, MN: Hazelden.

319 Ibid.

320 Luce, J.M. (2012). A strange new disease in San Francisco. A brief history of the city and its response to the HIV/AIDS epidemic. *Annals of the American Thoracic Society, 10*(2). https://www.atsjournals.org/doi/full/10.1513/AnnalsATS.201208-039PS

321 Bechtel, R.B., & Churchman, A. (2002). *Handbook of Environmental Psychology.* New York: John Wiley & Sons.

322 McLelland, N. (2021). *Zen Koans: Paradoxical Awakening.* Denver: Outskirts Publishing.

323 Crosby Bergin, C., et al. (2018). *Child and Adolescent Development for Educators.* South Melbourne, Australia: Cengage.

324 Abrahams, D., & Rohleder, P. (2021). *A Clinical Guide to Psychodynamic Psychotherapy.* New York: Routledge.

325 Decety, J. (2015). The neural pathways, development, and functions of empathy. *Current Opinion in Behavioral Sciences, 3,* 1-6.

326 It is interesting to note that the physiological reality of these neural networks appears to support the structuralist perspective previously discussed—harkening back to Plato's concept of "essences."

327 Bordens, K.S., & Horowitz, I.A. (2002). *Social Psychology.* Mahwah, NJ: Lawrence Erlbaum Associates.

328 Costandi, M. (2016). *Neuroplasticity.* Cambridge, MA: MIT Press.

329 Weiss, J. (1993). *How Psychotherapy Works: Process and Technique.* New York: Guilford Press.

330 Ibid.

331 Costello, S.J. (2022). *A Tri-Dimensional Model of Mental Health: The Wellness Wheel.* London: Cambridge Scholars Press.

332 Seligman, M. (2003). *Authentic Happiness: Using the New Positive Psychology to Realize Your Potential for Lasting Fulfillment.* Boston: Nicholas Brealey Publishing.

333 Ibid.

334 See the Resources section for free mindfulness tools and education that is more in-depth than what I present here. Most meditation groups are free or ask only for a small donation based on what you can afford. People suffering with PTSD and traumatic pasts sometimes find the experience of meditation makes symptoms worse, leading to destabilizing flashbacks or other types of retraumatizing experiences. If you are dealing with PTSD or Complex Trauma, it would be best to speak to a mental health professional first. Starting meditation without the oversight of a qualified mental health professional is definitely not a good idea if you are dealing with issues like schizophrenia, delusional disorder, some forms of depression, or you are feeling suicidal. But as a general tool for the average person, it can't be beat. Like any tool, it's best to dip your toe in the water first and *not* launch into a ten-day silent retreat.

335 Kabat-Zinn, J. (2018). *The Healing Power of Mindfulness: A New Way of Being*. New York: Little, Brown Book Group.

336 Mindfulness meditation has been shown to decrease activity in the "default-mode network," an area of the prefrontal cortex responsible for threat detection. These findings suggest that mediation "throttles back" our mind's overactive scanning processes, providing relief from excessive ruminations.

337 Ibid.

338 Ibid.

339 Herman, J. (1992). *Trauma and Recovery: The Aftermath of Violence —From Domestic Abuse to Political Terror*. New York: Hachette.

340 Seligman, M. (2002). *Authentic Happiness: Using the New Positive Psychology to Realize Your Potential for Lasting Fulfillment*. New York: Atria Books.

341 I have found that many people continue to confuse the concepts of sympathy and empathy. Sympathy can be characterized as feelings of pity or sorrow for someone else's misfortune. On the other hand, empathy involves the ability to understand and share the feelings of another; to be able, as they say, to "walk a mile in another person's shoes."

342 Erikson, E. (1993). *Childhood and Society*. New York: W.W. Norton.

343 Laub, D., & Auerhahn, N. (1993). Knowing and not knowing massive psychic trauma: Forms of traumatic memory. *The International Journal of Psychoanalysis, 74*, 287-302.

344 Ibid.

345 Linehan, M. (2015). *DBT Skills Training Manual, Second Edition*. New York: The Guilford Press.

346 Ibid.

347 Sbarra, D.A., & Whisman, M.A. (2022). Divorce, health, and socioeconomic status: An agenda for psychological science. *Current Opinion in Psychology, 43*, 75-78.

348 http://www.ncdsv.org/images/dv_faqs.pdf

349 https://www.npr.org/2019/06/10/731250367/forgiveness-after-a-massacre-in-charleston

350 These are the perfect types of situations in which to apply the mindfulness tools discussed in the previous chapter. Keep in mind that a good therapist and/or support group (see Resources Section) is always a good idea.

Milton Keynes UK
Ingram Content Group UK Ltd.
UKHW041241281223
434991UK00001B/1/J

9 798986 026022